Heroes
and Rogues
of the Civil War

VOLUME 3

Wayne L. Wolf
South Suburban College

Jack Simmerling
Heritage Gallery

Patrick J. O'Connell
South Suburban College

The McGraw-Hill Companies, Inc.
Primis Custom Publishing

New York St. Louis San Francisco Auckland Bogotá Caracas Lisbon London
Madrid Mexico Milan Montreal New Delhi Paris San Juan Singapore Sydney Tokyo Toronto

McGraw·Hill

A Division of The McGraw·Hill Companies

Heroes and Rougues of the Civil War
Volume 3

McGraw-Hill's Primis Custom Publishing consists of products that are produced from camera-ready copy. Peer review, class testing, and accuracy are primarily the responsibility of the author(s).

1 2 3 4 5 6 7 8 9 0 GDP/GDP 9 0 9 8 7

ISBN 0-07-072153-x
Editor: Reaney Dorsey
Illustration: Jack Simmerling
Cover Designer: Maggie Lytle
Printer/Binder: Greyden Press

DEDICATION

No book is ever written without the assistance or inspiration of others. If it was not for the patient assistance of my wife Lynn, the start of my parents, Joseph and Vivian Wolf, the encouragement of my sister Cheryl, and the stalwart company of Smiley and Doodle this book may never have become a reality. To all of them my sincere thanks and love.

—Wayne L. Wolf

TABLE OF CONTENTS

PASSING DREAMS

The hooped ladies stared as columns passed by
With bare heads bowed ready to cry
For four grueling years they gave their all
To answer Jeff Davis' urgent call

Now as they marched their last miles
Thoughts brought them back to smiles
As plantations and crops of cotton
No longer appeared burned and rotten

In their dreams the past was then
When chivalry and honor belonged to men
Defending the principles their fathers bore
As badges of honor within a Southern core

They slogged on in the mud and mire
Leaving behind only widows and mothers to admire
The fading gray trousers and coats eaten by shot
All that remained of dreams come to naught.

—Wayne L. Wolf

PREFACE

From 1861 to 1865, the nation was exposed to a fratricidal war that shaped the essential character of America from that day forward. The union had been dissolved by eleven states that felt they were preserving the concepts that defined them as a people. In opposition, the North held the bindings of nationhood to be indissoluble. Thus, the "Rebs or Secesh" and the "Yanks or Unionists" fought a war not based on despotic whim, land acquisition, or religious convictions. Rather, they each defended their homeland as they interpreted it and their lifestyle as they believed defined it. To each, more was at stake than a hill, field or valley. What was to be won was a victory of principles, values and beliefs—principles that defined the essence of the inhabitants and the guiding beacons of their concept of what America meant.

America survived this brutal family struggle, went on to become one of the greatest industrial and technologically superior nations of the Twentieth Century, and created a better standard of living for its citizens than most of the modern world. Yet, it still grappled in its political institutions, social undertakings, and cultural arrangements with the issues that gave rise to this original rending of America. The Civil War solved many of these underlying intellectual and moral differences in a military sense but not in the minds and hearts of millions of Americans who never surrendered their ideals as defined by the geography of the Mason-Dixon barrier.

Authors have struggled with this dichotomy since the end of Reconstruction. They have interpreted these issues, reinterpreted them, revised them and reconstructed them. Yet today they remain the enigma that spawned the War Between the States or perhaps more appropriately the War of Divergent Values. Historians can thus posit their theories, add the factual data, and draw reasoned conclusions. But they seem powerless to inject the emotions expressed by the great heroes of the war—the ordinary soldiers, wives, and manufacturers who endured the hardships of five years of hell.

More books have been written about the Civil War than any other period of American history, precisely because this half decade presents such an horrific clash of ideas. For the American interested in trying to gain an understanding of why this conflict occurred, primary source material provides a unique window into the past. The words of the participants can be read unaltered by the historian's interpretation. Analysis and conclusion can be sought by the individual reader without historical bias. And, emotions can be drawn from the included incidents reported to loved ones at home. All of the material thus presented in this book has never appeared in print before. Except for the loving care of relatives and historians who have preserved these windows of the past from destruction, they would have been lost to the ravages or disinterest intervening years. To this end the authors wish to extend their appreciation to Pat McCready of Chicago, who preserved the wonderful diary of her ancestor Capt. W.S. McCready. For the insightful letters of Jerome B. Satterlee of the 44th New York Regiment sincere thanks to Mr. Len Karczewski of Chicago. And to Dan Weinberg of the Abraham Lincoln Bookstore in Chicago, our thanks for many of the letters of the general officers on both sides of lines. And finally to Mr. Rafferty of Chicago who preserved many of the rescued arrest warrants and commitment orders from Washington D.C. that reveal the intimate "darker side" of the Reconstruction Era in American history.

The authors have transcribed the letters and documents exactly as they appear in the original with grammatical errors, improperly spelled words, and slang expressions all exactly as they were uttered by the original writers. To have done otherwise would have violated the primary source value of the material. It furthermore allows the individual reader to see into the thoughts and soul of the writers and draw their own interpretations from the newly discovered material. We trust your historical journey will be rewarding.

Wayne L. Wolf
Jack Simmerling
Patrick J. O'Connell

PART I

GENERALS OF THE
CIVIL WAR:
THEIR PERSONAL CORRESPONDENCE

*"We have enjoyed ourselves pretty well
generally & have never flinched in the hour of danger or duty."*

—*J.B. Setterlee*

INTRODUCTION

   A man's writings are a window unto his soul. The correspondence of the generals of the North and South contained in this section, all of which have never before been published, provide that window into the lives and emotions of those fighting the Civil War. The reader can hear in their words the bursting of shells, the falling of tears, and the mundane tasks of daily camp life. It is their emotions, hopes, fears and even business transactions in later life that tell their story—the story of the men who wore the stars in the bloodiest war America ever fought. These labors of penmanship transport the reader back to the era of the Civil War and Reconstruction for a personal glimpse of this defining moment of American history. The letters by Gens. Fitz John Porter, Robert Patterson, Julius Stahel and John Dix will add a small bit of new information to historians' grasp of the nature of the men and the intricacies of the events that have fascinated Americans since the Civil War. They additionally provide a rich source of primary source material for the lovers of history and the writers that make it come alive.

DEMAND FOR GLORY

Sheridan, Patterson, Dix and Mott
Each a regiment was their lot
To train and in maneuvers marched
With feet swollen and throats parched

Many barefoot and chafed by stone
Others exhausted and by a roadside left alone
Those unwell their commanders soon alone send
To field hospitals for quinine to mend

Then back to duty the soldiers must go
Still coughing and on crutches ever so slow
To sate the general's demand for glory
And provide cherished tales for a future story

Struck by mini balls and fragments of shell
The weary volunteers endured fires of hell
While from rear positions the generals silently waited
Only fearing their reputations would be greatly abated.

—Wayne L. Wolf

GEORGE ARCHIBALD McCALL
BRIGADIER GENERAL, U.S. VOLUNTEERS

Gen. McCall was born in Philadelphia on March 16, 1802. He graduated from West Point in 1822 and began his career in the 1st Cavalry. Until 1842 he spent his career in Florida fighting the Seminoles. During the Mexican War he was a Captain of the 4th Infantry was brevetted major and lieutenant colonel for bravery at Palo Alto and Resaca del la Palma. In 1850 he was given the rank of Colonel and became an army inspector general. In 1861 Gen. McCall came out of retirement and was commissioned Major General of Pennsylvania Volunteers by Gov. Curtin. On May 17, 1861 President Lincoln appointed McCall Brigadier General of Volunteers. He then assumed command of the Pennsylvania Reserves as a division of the Army of the Potomac, planned operations against Dranesville and Mechanicsville and formed the advance of Porter's V Corps at Chickahominy. On June 30, 1862 he was taken prisoner at the Battle of Glendale and was confined to Libby Prison until August 18, 1862 when he was exchanged for Confederate General Simon Bolivar Buckner. From his release until his resignation on March 31, 1863 he was on sick leave. Gen. McCall died on February 26, 1868.

Camp Pierpont, Va.
February 20, 1862

My young friend,

  Altho' I received your polite note many days since, a press of business has prevented my offering, at an earlier moment, my thanks, which now please accept, & Believe me very truly yours,

       Geo. A. McCall
       B.G. Comg. Divs.

Wm. Welsh Jr.
Philadelphia

Camp Pierpont, Va.
February 20. 1862

My Young friend,

Altho' I received your polite note many days since, a press of business has prevented my offering, at an earlier moment, my thanks, which now please accept, &

Believe me very truly Yours,
Geo. A. McCall
B.Gy. comg. Divn

Wm. Welsh Jr.
Philadelphia

BENJAMIN F. BUTLER
MAJOR GENERAL, U.S.V.

Gen. Butler was born on November 5, 1818 in Deerfield, New Hampshire. After graduating from Colby College in 1838 he taught school until 1840 when he passed the bar and entered law practice. He was elected as a Democrat to the Massachusetts House in 1853 and its Senate in 1859. At the 1860 Democratic Convention he supported Jefferson Davis for President but later became one of the nation's foremost Radical Republicans. He began his military career as a Brigadier General of the Massachusetts militia and was Lincoln's first appointment of a Major General on May 16, 1861. During the war he commanded the attack on Hatteras Inlet and in May 1862 occupied New Orleans. During the occupation he was declared an outlaw by President Davis and earned the reputation of governing effectively but enriching himself and his friends at the expense of the city. He was removed of his New Orleans command in December 1862 but given command of the Army of the James in 1863. After his army's debacle at Bermuda Hundred, and brief service in New York, General Grant ordered Butler to return home and await orders. Instead, Butler, on November 30, 1864 resigned his commission. He was subsequently elected to Congress as a Republican in 1866, serving until 1875. In 1882 he was elected Governor of Massachusetts. In 1884 General Butler was the Presidential candidate of the Greenback Party. On January 11, 1893 he died and was buried in Lowell, Massachusetts.

Boston Dec. 29 1883

My Dear Barrett

    Nothing is to be done, so far as I can judge, but to repair the ceiling, that is if there is any danger of any more falling down. If not let it remain until I come.

    I don't think it was the result of a leak, but think it was the result of an overflow heretofore permitted by the persons who occupied the bath-room above.

    You cannot have pigs in a house and not have it used as a stye.

Yours Very Truly
Benj. F. Butler

O.D. Barrett Esq.
Washington D.C.

Boston, Dec 29-1883

My dear Barrett:—

Nothing is to be done, so far as I can judge, but to repair the ceiling, that is. if there is any danger of any more falling done. If not let it remain untill I come.

I don't think it was the result of a leak, but think it was the result of an overflow heretofore permitted by the persons who occupied the bath-room above.

You cannot have pigs in a house and not have it used as a stye.

Yours Very truly,

Benj. F. Butler

O. D. Barrett Esq
Washington D.C.

SIMON BOLIVAR BUCKNER
LIEUTENANT GENERAL, C.S.A.

Gen. Buckner was born on April 1, 1823 in Hart County, Kentucky. He was a graduate in the Class of 1844 from West Point, won two brevets for service in the Mexican War, was a Chicago businessman, and, upon the start of the Civil War was serving as Kentucky's adjutant general. On September 14, 1861 President Davis appointed Buckner a Brigadier General. He was the unhappy general assigned by default to surrender Fort Donelson, was later exchanged in a prisoner-of-war swap, and assumed command of a division of Bragg's Army fighting at Perryville, fortifying Mobile, and directing a Corps at Chickamauga. Gen. Buckner then served in the trans-Mississippi where he was promoted to Lieutenant General and Chief of Staff to Kirby Smith. After the war, Buckner lived in New Orleans for three years and then returned to Kentucky to edit the *Louisville Courier*. In 1887 he was elected Governor of Kentucky and was the Vice-Presidential nominee of the Gold Democrats in 1896. Gen. Buckner died on January 8, 1914, the last survivor of the three highest grades in the Confederate Army.

Rio P.O. Hart Co. Ky.
Sept. 13, 1902.

Dear John,

I have just received your letter, relating to a $1000.- Bond of the Southern Railway of St. Louis. I will take the bond if still obtainable. On hearing from you affirmatively I will come up and pay for it.

Very truly,
S.B. Buckner.

J. W. Green

P.S. I expect to go to Franklin on the 18th and can settle then if desirable.

S.B.B.

Rio P.O. Hart Co. Ky
Sept. 13, 1902.

Dear John,
        I have just
received your letter, relating
to a $1000. Bond of the
Louisburn Railway of N. Sonis.
I will take the bond if
still obtainable. On hearing
from you affirmatively I will
come up and pay for it.

        Very truly,
        S.B. Buckner.

J. W. Green.
        P.S. I expect to go to Franklin
on the 18th and can settle there
if desirable   SBB

EDWIN DENISON MORGAN
MAJOR GENERAL OF VOLUNTEERS, U.S.A.

Gen. Morgan was born February 8, 1811 in Washington, Massachusetts. He was a merchant, banker, philanthropist and politician of high regard. After a series of local offices he was elected to the New York state senate in 1850, was the first chairman of the Republican National Committee and was elected Governor of New York in 1858. He was reelected in 1860 and assisted Lincoln by enrolling, arming and equipping over 223,000 men for the Union army. Lincoln made Morgan a Major General of Volunteers on September 28, 1861 and gave him command of the Department of New York. On March 4, 1863 he was elected to the U.S. Senate having resigned his military commission on January 1, 1863. He was twice offered the job of Secretary of the Treasury by Presidents Johnson and Arthur but declined preferring instead to concentrate on his philanthropic activities. He died on February 14, 1883.

54 & 56 EXCHANGE PLACE.
NEW YORK,   JAN. 30. 1873

Revd. Edwin F. Hatfield

My Dear Sir:

I enclose herewith my check on the National Bank of Commerce for one thousand dollars, being the amount of my donation made through you in 1871. to the Union Theological Seminary. Please hand it to the Treasurer of the Seminary and forward his receipt to me for the same.

Yours very truly,
E.D. Morgan

54 & 56 Exchange Place,

New York, Jun 30 1873

Rev. Edwin F. Hatfield

My Dear Sir.

I enclose herewith my check on the National Bank of Commerce for One thousand dollars. being the amount of my donation made through you in 187. to the Union Theological Seminary. Please hand it to the Treasurer of the Seminary. and forward his receipt to me for the same. Yours very truly

G. D. Morgan

ROBERT PATTERSON
MAJOR GENERAL,
PENNSYLVANIA VOLUNTEERS

Gen. Patterson was born on Jan. 12, 1792 in County Tyrone, Ireland. Immigrating to Pennsylvania in 1798 he began in a banking career, fought in the War of 1812, won successive promotions to the rank of Colonel in the Pennsylvania militia and to Captain of the 32d U.S. Infantry. Over the next three decades he became an active Jacksonian Democrat, traveled to the Iowa frontier, stretched his business interests to both the West and the South, and rose steadily to the power broker status in Pennsylvania politics. He became a Major General of Volunteers during the Mexican War fighting gallantly at Cerro Gordo and Jalapa. He spent the next two years as a member of Gen. Winfield Scott's staff. Prior to the Civil War he managed a Louisiana sugar plantation and 30 Pennsylvania cotton mills. At the outbreak of the Civil War, Gen. Scott made Patterson a Major General of Pennsylvania Volunteers, charged with mustering troops and directing the Department of Pennsylvania. At age 69 however, he badly disappointed Gen. Scott when he was ordered to march and seize Harper's Ferry on May 24, 1861. Patterson did not move however until June 14, 1861, too late to capture Gen. Joe Johnston's retreating troops. Patterson was thus relieved of command on July 19, 1861 and received an honorable discharge on July 27, 1861. After the War Patterson authored *A Narrative of the Campaign in the Valley of the Shenandoah in 1861* which defended his actions. Gen. Patterson died on Aug. 7, 1881.

Head Quarters 1st. Div. Penn. Vol.
Phila. 28th Dec. 1854

Sir.

Enclosed I send you the decision of the Board of Officers convened for the trial of the contested election of Brigadier General and Brigade Inspector of the 2d. Brigade.

You will observe that the election has been set aside and a new one ordered.

I respectfully and earnestly recommend that an order be issued from General Head quarters directing that a rigid inspection of the companies according to law be held in this Brigade before an election takes place—other wise we will in all probability have the same scenes over again—and this I am not willing to submit to. The order asked for is in some degree rendered necessary as prior to the late election his Excellency the Governor issued a special order dispensing with or rather postponing the usual annual inspection—with a condition that the inspection should be made within sixty days—which has not been complied with.

I have the honor to be & &
Very respectfully your Srt.
R. Patterson
Maj. Genl.

Honl. C.A. Black
Sec. of the Commonwealth

Docketed on the verso:
Gen. R. Patterson
To Hon. C.A. Black

Robt. Patterson

Head Quarters 1st Div Penn Vol
Phila 28th Dec 1854

Sir,

Enclosed I send you the decision of the
Board of Officers convened for the trial of
the Contested Election of Brigadier General and
Brigade Inspector of the 2d Brigade –
You will observe that the Election
has been set aside and a New One ordered
I respectfully and earnestly recommend that an order be issued from General
Head Quarters directing that a rigid inspection
of the Companies according to law be held in the
Brigade before an election takes place – otherwise we will in all probability have the same
scenes over again and this I am not willing
to submit to – The order asked for is in
some degree rendered necessary as Prior to the
late Election his Excellency the Governor issued
a special order dispensing with or rather postpone-
ing the usual annual inspections – with a condition
that the inspection should be made within Six
days – which has not been complied with –
I have the honor to be &c &c
very respectfully yours &c
R Patterson
Major Genl

Honl C A Black
Secy of the Commonwealth

JOHN GRAY FOSTER
MAJOR GENERAL U.S.A.

Gen. Foster was born on May 27, 1823 in Whitefield, New Hampshire. After graduating from West Point in the Class of 1846 he was commissioned in the Corps of Engineers and became part of the company of sappers, miners and pontoniers organized to accompany Gen. Winfield Scott to Mexico. Brevetted twice for gallantry he was severely wounded at Molino del Rey. At the outbreak of the Civil War, Gen. Foster acted as chief engineer of the fortifications of Charleston Harbor and was a leading participant in its bombardment. In October, 1861 he was promoted from captain of engineers to brigadier general of volunteers, taking an active part in Burnside's North Carolina expedition. In July, 1862 he was given command of the Department of North Carolina, relieving Burnside at Knoxville. In December 1863 he took command of the Department of the Ohio until February 1864 when he was injured during a horse fall. He was promoted to Major General on July 18, 1862 and was brevetted to the same rank in the regular service in March, 1865. After the war he served as a Colonel of the Corps of Engineers doing routine survey and construction work. In 1869 he published a definitive work on underwater demolition. Gen. Foster died on September 2, 1874.

Boston Mass.
June 18.67

Genl. H. Ware
A.D.C.

Dear Sir:

Your polite note conveying the invitation of His Excellency, the Governor, to join him in the procession to Arlington, did not, from some cause, reach me until this morning. This will explain my delay in joining the Governors party.

Very Truly
Your obt. servt.
J.G. Foster
Brvt. M.G. U.S.A.

Boston Mass.
June 18. 67

Genl H. Ware.
A.D.C.

Dear Sir.

Your polite
note conveying the
invitation of His Excel=
lency, the Governor, to
join him in the proces=
sion to Arlington, did
not, from some cause,
reach me until this
morning -; This will
explain my delay

in joining the Govern-
ments party.

Very Truly

Yours obt servt

J.G. Foster.

Bvt M.G. USA.

LUCIUS FAIRCHILD
BRIGADIER GENERAL, U.S.V.

Gen. Fairchild was born on December 27, 1831 in Portage County, Ohio. After attending Carroll College and travelling the country, he returned to Wisconsin (where his father was the first Mayor of Madison) and ran for Clerk of the Dane County Circuit Court to which he was elected in 1858. At the outbreak of the Civil War, Fairchild switched parties to the Republicans, enlisted five days after Fort Sumter as a private in the 1st Wisconsin, was elected its Captain in May, and took part in the Battle at Falling Waters, Md. in July. In August 1861 he became Colonel of the 2nd Wisconsin, which won fame as a unit of the "Iron Brigade." He then mustered into service as a Captain of the 16th U.S. Cavalry to which he took leave to act in his volunteer capacity. He fought bravely at Second Manassas, South Mountain and Sharpsburg, was promoted to Colonel on September 1, 1862, and was present at Fredericksburg and Chancellorsville. At Gettysburg his left arm was shattered and amputated and he was captured by Confederate troops. Fairchild saw no more service although he was promoted to Brigadier General of Volunteers on October 19, 1863 and resigned in November. In 1866 Fairchild was elected Governor of the State of Wisconsin and later served in several diplomatic posts abroad. He died on May 23, 1896.

STATE OF
WISCONSIN   EXECUTIVE OFFICE

Madison   Nov. 7 1869

Proprietors
    Sherman House

    Gentlemen

    Please reserve rooms for Mr. Stevens & wife, & myself & wife — we leave here tomorrow at 8 A.M.
    Also please secure two seats for the Opera, and two for "Jeffersons" tomorrow Eve.

                Yours & c.
                Lucius Fairchild

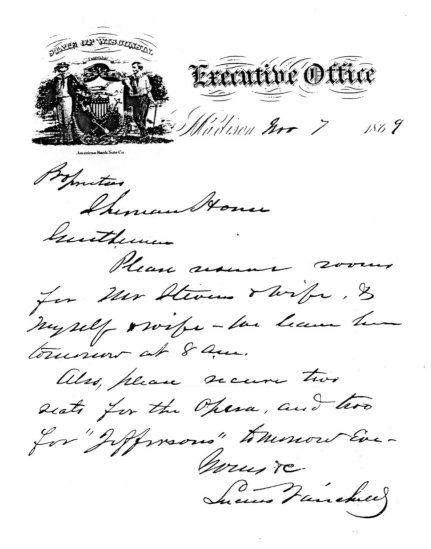

State of Wisconsin

Executive Office

Madison Nov 7 1869

American Bank Note Co.

Proprietors
        Sherman House
Gentlemen
            Please reserve rooms
for Mr Stevens & wife, &
myself & wife — we leave here
tomorrow at 8 am.
            Also, please secure two
seats for the Opera, and two
for "Jeffersons" tomorrow Eve —
                    Yours &c
                    Lucius Fairchild

WILLIAM HENRY POWELL
BREVET MAJOR GENERAL, U.S.V.

Gen. Powell was born on May 10, 1825 in Pontypool, Monmouthshire, South Wales. He came to the United States at age 5 and was educated in Nashville. Prior to the Civil War, Gen. Powell was an engineer in various ironworks. At the war's outbreak, he recruited a company of cavalry in southern Ohio and became its colonel (the 2nd West Virginia Cavalry). On July 18, 1863 he was wounded and captured at Wytheville, Virginia and not exchanged until February, 1864. Upon release, Powell was attached to Sheridan's cavalry in the Shenandoah and commanded the 2nd Div. Cavalry at Cedar Creek. As a result of his efforts, he was promoted to brigadier general of volunteers and later Major General at the end of the war. His resignation from the army was accepted by the War Department on January 5, 1865. After the war he founded the Western Nail Company in Belleville, Ill., which he managed until 1891. Gen. Powell was elected Department Commander of the G.A.R. in 1895 and was appointed Collector of Internal Revenue by President McKinley in 1898. Gen. Powell died on December 26, 1904.

Belleville Ills.   June 1st 1891

Ben. W. Austin Secy.
Trinity Historical Society

        Dallas Texas.

          Dear Sir

     I have the honor to acknowledge the receipt of your favor of 28th ult. Notifying me of the action of your Society in placing my name upon the roll of its honorary membership.

     Please accept thanks and best wishes for the success of your highly commendable organization and its purposes.

     Having complied to your request in sending my photograph in same mail.

              Remain yours very resply.
                W.H. Powell

Belleville Ills. June 1st 1891.

Ben. M. Austin Secy
Trinity Historical Society
        Dallas Texas.

                Dear Sir

I have the honor to acknowledge the receipt of
your favor of 28th ult. Notifying me of the
action of your Society in placing my name upon
the roll of its honorary membership.
Please accept thanks and best wishes for the success
of your highly Commendable Organization and
its purposes.

        Having Complied to your request in
Sending my photograph in same mail.
        Remain Yours Very Respfy
                W. H. Powell

PHILIP HENRY SHERIDAN
GENERAL OF THE ARMY, U.S.A.

Gen. Sheridan was born on March 6, 1831 in Albany, New York. He graduated from West Point in 1853 and spent the next eight years on the frontier not moving past his rank of 2nd Lt. until the start of the Civil War. On May 25, 1862 he was promoted to Colonel of the 2nd Michigan Cavalry. This began his meteoric rise in rank as he was promoted to Brigadier General of Volunteers on September 13, 1862. He then fought a succession of battles at Perryville, Murfreesboro and Chickamauga. He was promoted to Major General on March 16, 1863. Sheridan immediately distinguished himself at the Battle of Chattanooga capturing the Confederate stronghold and gaining the attention of U.S. Grant. He was then assigned command of all cavalry in the Army of the Potomac. In July 1864 Sheridan was placed in command of the VI and XIX Corps and ordered to clear out the Shenandoah Valley. He successfully drove the Confederates back at Winchester and Fisher's Hill and rallied his army to forstall defeat by Jubal Early. For this service he was granted the rank of Major General in the regular army on November 14, 1864. He then led the operations at Petersburg, Five Forks and Sayler's Creek. In 1867 Sheridan was appointed Commander of the Fifth Military District, a post he was removed from after only six months due to his harsh policies. In 1869 President Grant promoted Sheridan to lieutenant general. In 1884 he became commanding general of the army and full general as of June 1, 1888. He died on August 5, 1888.

Fifth Avenue Hotel
Nov. 5, (18)67

My Dear Fagnani

    Please send my over coat by the bearer. I will arrange to find you a good suiting tomorrow.

               Yours truly
               Phil. H. Sheridan
               Maj. Genl.

Fifth Avenue Hotel
Nov. 5. 67

My Dear Lyman

Please send
my Over Coat by the
bearer. I will arrange
to give you a
good suiting to
a Moment.

Yours truly,
Phil. H. Sheridan

Per.

DANIEL HENRY RUCKER
MAJOR GENERAL, U.S.A.

Gen. Rucker was born on April 28, 1812 in Belleville, New Jersey. He was commissioned directly into the army on October 13, 1837 as a second lieutenant. Over the next ten years he rose to the rank of Captain and was brevetted as a Major for gallantry at Buena Vista during the Mexican war. He was promoted to Major in August 1861 in the Quartermaster Department. During the Civil War, Rucker was promoted (brevetted) to the rank of Major General in both the volunteers and regular army. His duties included the procurement of wagons, horses, forage, etc., and he performed these "unglorious" activities with "diligence and faithful service." In July 1866, Gen. Rucker was promoted to assistant quartermaster general with the rank of colonel. On February 13, 1882, he was promoted to Quartermaster General with the rank of Brigadier General. Ten days later he retired from the army after 45 years of service. Gen. Rucker died at his home in Washington D.C. on January 6, 1910.

Washington D.C.
June 17, 1887

Mr. O.H. Peck
Denver, Colo.

Dear Sir

    Yours of the 8th inst. has been recd. I am unable to give you any information regarding the lineal descendants of Genl. Geo. H. Custer. My acquaintance with him was very slight.

                    I am Sir
                    Very truly yours &c.
                    D.H. Rucker

JACOB DOLSON COX
MAJOR GENERAL U.S.V.

Gen. Cox was born on October 27, 1828 in Montreal, Canada. He graduated from Oberlin College in 1851 and commenced his law practice in Ohio in 1853. A strong abolitionist he was elected as a Republican State Senator in 1858. Upon the outbreak of the Civil War, Cox entered the army on April 23, 1861 as a Brigadier General of Volunteers. His earliest war service was in western Virginia under McClellan and then with Pope's Army in Virginia. At South Mountain and Sharpsburg he commanded a division of the IX Corps. He was promoted to Major General of Volunteers on October 6, 1862. During most of 1863 he commanded the District of Ohio and in 1864 left to command a division in the Siege of Atlanta. He likewise fought at Franklin, Nashville, Kinston and with Schofield's command in North Carolina. Immediately after the war he was elected Governor of Ohio and served a two year term. He later served as Secretary of the Interior under Grant, President of the Wabash Railway, and Congressman from Ohio. From 1881 to 1897 he was Dean of the Cincinnati Law School and President of the University of Cincinnati. Gen. Cox died on August 4, 1900.

LAW SCHOOL
of the
CINCINNATI COLLEGE

JACOB D. COX
Dean of the Faculty.

Cincinnati, 12 October 1893.

Dear Mr. Ropes:

I assure you that I should exceedingly like to meet the Mass. Military Historical Soc'y, but it is practically impossible for me to leave home except during my summer vacation. My work is not so hard as it is continuous, for as Dean of the Law School I have the laboring oar, and very rarely get off even for a day.

I have spent several summers from 1 July to 1 Sept. on the Mass. coast at Magnolia, but as this is the time when everybody is also away from home, it has been an inopportune time for meeting my Eastern friends. I wish it were otherwise, but see no present help for it.

I read with both pleasure & profit whatever you write on military history, whether home history or foreign. Your Waterloo is a magnificent piece of work. By the way, if you have a copy (published separately) of your Atlantic Monthly paper on Sherman, I would like to have it for my file. Assuring you that to meet you personally would be a very great pleasure,

I remain,
Faithfully yours,
J.D. Cox

John C. Ropes Esq.

Cincinnati, 12 October 1893.

Dear Mr Ropes:

I assure you that I should exceedingly like to meet the Mass. Military Historical Soc'y, but it is practically impossible for me to leave home except during my summer vacation. My work is not so hard as it is continuous, for as Dean of the Law School I have the laboring oar, and very rarely get off even for a day.

I have spent several summers from 1 July to 1 Sept on the Mass. coast at Magnolia, but as this is the time when Everybody is also away from home, it has been an inopportune time for meeting my Eastern friends. I wish it were otherwise, but see no present help for it.

I read with both pleasure & profit whatever you write on military history, whether home history or foreign. Your Waterloo is a magnificent piece of work. By the way, if you have a copy (published separately) of your Atlantic Monthly paper on Sherman, I would like to have it for my file. Assuring you that to meet you personally would be a very great pleasure, I remain,

Faithfully Yours
J.D. Cox.

John C. Ropes Esq.

FITZ JOHN PORTER
MAJOR GENERAL. U.S.V.

Gen. Porter was born on August 31, 1822 in Portsmouth, New Hampshire. He graduated from West Point in the Class of 1845 and by the end of his career was to be called by Gen. McClellan, "the most magnificent soldier in the Army of the Potomac." From 1849 to 1855 Porter was an artillery instructor at West Point and from 1857 to 1860 served as Gen. Albert S. Johnson's adjutant in Utah. At the outbreak of the Civil War he became Colonel of the 15th Regular Infantry and on August 7 he was promoted to Brigadier General of Volunteers. He subsequently saw service in the Shenandoah, with McClellan training recruits in Washington, and in the Peninsular Campaign as head of a division of the III Corps. This however was only the beginning of his service as he also fought at the Battle of Seven Days, the Chickahominy, Mechanicsville, and Gaines Mill. After gallantry at Malvern Hill he was promoted to Major General of Volunteers and Brevet General in the Regular Army. Transferred to Pope's command, whom he despised, his criticism led to his downfall. He was relieved of command in November, 1862, arrested, tried, and dismissed from the Army. Porter spent the rest of his life trying to vindicate his name. In 1879 a board, headed by Gen. Schofield, exonerated Porter, restored him to his former rank, and called him the Saviour of the Army of Virginia at Second Manassas. In 1886 Grover Cleveland placed his name back on the rolls as a Colonel of Infantry. He died on May 21, 1901.

68 West 68th Street
New York, September 18th 1890

Dear General,

For the first time, with a mind free from outsides cares and worries long enough to reflect a little upon I read, I carefully read to say the copy of Genl. Pope's letter which you gave me and Don Piatt gave you for the Society of the Army of the Cumberland, I am very much obliged to Don Piatt. In the light of the present day—it shows how little Pope knew of his own positioning and the position of his army—and my relations to both; while all were fully known to me—and my actions were governed by a knowledge of those relations on the 29th of August 1862. His letter is, virtually, in the light of evidence since discovered and of my own despatches, proof of who was responsible for the losses, disasters & discomforts he complains of and wishes to place on other shoulders.

His letter & Piatts action reminds me of the faux-pas, innocently committed by Senator Hale in having published in the Rebellion Records the proceedings of my court martial, which had twice been printed by Congressional action and widely spread over the country. Desirous that the proceedings should be published as he desired, I purposely got my friends not to oppose or show any interest in his resolution—and when passed I quietly set to work and secured the publication at the and through the Secretary of war of the letter signed by the President of Jany. 12th' 63—but intentionally misquoted by Judge Advocate General Holt as of the 13th directing Holt to revise the proceedings & to report &c. General Halleck's letter of the 13th shows the proceedings were in his possession on the 13th and, of course, when forwarded to the Sec. of War met the President's order of the 13th and went directly to the J. Advocate. Thus is officially sustained what is otherwise known, that the proceedings *were never seen by the President,* who acted solely upon Holt's revision.

So it is, he who wishes to strike an unjust blow is sure to find it a boomerang. Stanton secured the order Piatt wishing to have Pope's blow only causes it to react upon Pope and himself. Perhaps Piatt would like to have proclaimed the generosity of the enemy who returned to him what he left when he fled from his temporary house at 1st Bull Run.

I believe you have the record of my court and of the advisory board—and if so my "statements of the services of the Fifth Corps" in Vol. 1. If these are not some written despatches (sic) in the latter I will send them to be inserted.

The translation of "Maj. Mangold's History of the Campaign in Northern Va. in Aug. '62" is now in the hands of the printer, who will decide this if he will publish it. Good reading for soldiers.

I hope you enjoyed—all of you—your annual gathering of a o/c.

Gen. H.M. Cist   Yours truly

F.J. Porter

---

68 West 58th Street
New York. September 18th 1890

Dear General,

For the first time, with a mind free from out-sides cares and worries long enough to reflect a little upon I read, I carefully read to day the copy of Genl Pope's letter, which you gave me and Don Piatt gave you for the Society of the Army of the Cumberland. I am very much obliged to Don Piatt. In the light of the present day- it shows how little Pope knew of his own positions and the position of his army. and my relations to both-; while all were fully known to me- and my actions were governed by a knowledge of those relations on the 29th of August 1862. His letter is, virtually, in the light of evidence since discovered and of my own despatches, proof of who was responsible for the losses, disasters & discom-forts he complains of and wishes to place on other shoulders. His letter & Piatts action, reminds me of the faux-pas, in-nocently committed by Senator Hale in having published in the Rebellion Records the proceedings of my Court Martial, which had twice been printed by Congressional action and widely spread over the country. Desirous that the procee-dings should be published as he desired I purposely got my friends not to oppose or show any interest in his resolution - and when passed, I quietly set to work and secured the publication, at the end, through the Secretary of War of the letter signed by the President of Jan'y 12th'63 - but intentionally misquoted by Judge Advocate General Holt as of the 13th directing Holt to review the proceedings &c report &c. General Hallecks letter of the 13th shews the proceedings were in his possession on the 13th and, of course, when forwarded to the Sec of War met the Presidents order of the 13th and went directly to the J. advocate. Thus is officially contained what is otherwise known, that the proceedings were never seen by the President, who acted solely upon Holts revision.

So it is, he who wishes to strike an unjust blow is sure to find it a boomerang. Stanton secured the order. Piatt wishing to strike an Opld blow only causes it to react upon Pope and himself. Perhaps Piatt would like to have proclaimed the generosity of the enemy who returned to him what he left when he fled from his temporary house at 1st Bull Run.

I believe you have the record of my Court and of the advisory Board - and if so my "Statement of the Services of the Fifth Corps" in vol 1. If there are not some written despatches in the latter I will send them to be inserted.

The translation of "Maj Mangolds History of the Campaign in Bohemia &c in Aug '62" is now in the hands of the printer, who will decide this if he will publish it. Good reading for soldiers.

I hope you enjoyed - all of you - your annual gathering 1/ a&c. Yrs Hm Cilt   Yours truly   F. J. Porter

Received Vera Cruz Mexico this Sixteenth day of November 1847 of Capt. M.R. Patrick Acting Commissary of Subsistence the Sum of One Hundred & Fifty Dollars Subsistence funds for which I am accountable for the Department $150.00

F. J. Porter
1st Lt. 4th Arty.
A.A.C.S.

JOSIAH GORGAS
BRIGADIER GENERAL, C.S.A.

Gen. Gorgas was born on July 17 1818 at Running Pumps, Pennsylvania. He graduated from West Point in the Class of 1841 and immediately joined the Ordnance Dept. of the Army where he served until the outbreak of the Civil War. Jefferson Davis appointed Gorgas Confederate Chief of Ordnance in 1861. He was promoted to Brigadier General on November 10, 1864 and continued in his capacity of supplying the Confederate Army with powder, caps, bullets, and arms. In order to secure many of these supplies from overseas sources Gorgas purchased five blockade-runners that brought many desperately needed supplies through the Federal blockade. At the conclusion of the Civil War until 1868 he was Superintendent of the Brierfield Iron Works in Alabama and then became Vice-Chancellor of the University of the South in Sewanee, Tennessee. In 1878 he assumed the Presidency of the University of Alabama dying at Tuscaloosa on May 15, 1883.

UNIVERSITY OF THE SOUTH,
Sewanee, Tenn., Mch. 19 1878.

Maj. E.A. Burke

Dear Sir

    I have received check on State Nat. Bk. of N.O. for $150. which I credit to account of *Meade*, altho'nothing is said of this check in your letter enclosing the P.O. order for $24.75.

Very truly yr.
J. Gorgas
V . C .

File Meades a/c

University of The South.

Sewanee, Tenn., Mch 19 1878.

Maj. E. A. Burke

Dear Sir—

I have received check on State Nat. Bk of N.O. for $150. which I credit to account of Meade, altho' nothing is said of this check in your letter enclosing the P.O. order for $24.""—

Very truly Yr
J. Gorgas—
V.C

LOVELL HARRISON ROUSSEAU
MAJOR GENERAL, U.S.A.

Gen. Rousseau was born on August 4, 1818 near Stanford, Kentucky. After studying law, he was admitted to the Indiana bar in 1840 and subsequently elected to the Indiana legislature in 1844. During the Mexican War he served as a Captain of the 2nd Ind. Volunteers. He was elected again as a member of the Indiana legislature from 1847-1849, after which he returned to Kentucky to practice law. Elected to the Kentucky Senate in 1860 as an opponent of secession, he resigned in 1861 to lead the 3rd Kentucky as its colonel. He was promoted to Brigadier General on October 1, 1861 and Major General on October 22, 1862. He commanded a brigade at Shiloh, led a division at Perryville, and served gallantly at Stone's River and Chickamauga.

From November 1863 to November 1865, Rousseau commanded the Districts of Nashville and Tennessee. He resigned in 1865 to assume a Congressional seat as a Republican from Kentucky. On March 28, 1867 President Andrew Johnson made Rousseau a Brigadier General and Brevet Major General in the Regular Army and sent him to Alaska to accept this future state from Alaska. In 1868 he took command of the Department of Louisiana and died shortly thereafter on January 7, 1869 while still in New Orleans.

It is said a yoke of oxen are taken from Mr. McCanlly. If so, they will be delivered to him on the fort stated on this paper.

> Lovell H. Rousseau
> Brig. Genl.

Author's Note: While this is undated, having been originally a part of a large document, Rousseau was promoted to Brigadier General on October 1, 1861 and to Major General October 22, 1862. Therefore, this document is most likely a field written order from the period Oct. 1, 1861—Oct. 22, 1862.

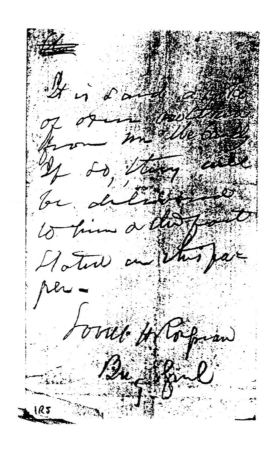

ANDREW ATKINSON HUMPHREYS
BREVET MAJOR GENERAL, U.S. ARMY

Gen. Humphreys was born on November 2, 1810 in Philadelphia, Pa. He graduated from West Point in 1831, and from then until the beginning of the Civil War spent most of his time with the Corps of Topographical Engineers in surveying the Mississippi Delta. At the outset of the war, he became an aide to Gen. McClellan, was promoted to Brigadier General of Volunteers in April of 1862, and served the Army of the Potomac as Chief Topographical Engineer. In September, 1862 he assumed command of a division of V Corps and led the assault on Marye's Heights and at Chancellorsville. Later his gallant service as part of Sickles III Corps at Gettysburg earned his promotion to Major General of Volunteers. He then joined McClellan as Chief of Staff until late 1864 when Grant placed him in command of the II Corps. He received his Brevet Major General, U.S. Army promotion for gallantry at Sayler's Creek. On August 8, 1866 he was made Brigadier General, U.S. Army and Chief of Engineers where he served until his retirement in 1879. He died in Washington, D.C. on December 27, 1883.

Camp of Head-Quarters, Army of the Potomac,

Jany. 2., 1864

Lt. Harrison Lambdin,
    A. D. C.

Dear Sir,

    I have been unable before this to reply to your note of the 31st. The subject of it has caused me much painful thought, for I find myself utterly powerless to aid or suggest any means by which aid could be afforded in procuring food for the Hon. Mr. Pendleton's animals.

    I noticed some time ago in riding beyond the pickets of the 3d. Corps on the road from Brandy Station to Rixeyville that there were farmers with stacks of fodder about the barns. These are now within our infantry picket lines and accessible to Mr. Pendleton. Perhaps from these or similar places, now within an infantry pickets forage may be obtained.

    Under the supervision of the War Dept. I learn that stores or a store is to be opened at Brandy Station for the purpose of trade with the inhabitants of this section of country, but I do not know whether it can afford any such facilities as those referred to in your note.

    Pray present my kindest regards to Mr. Pendleton and say to him that I have been unable to leave these Hd. Qrs. or I should before now have called to see him.

                  Very respectfully
                  Your obt. sert.
                  A.A. Humphreys
                  Maj. Gen.

JOHN WOLCOTT PHELPS
BRIGADIER GENERAL, U.S.V.

Gen. John Phelps was born on November 13, 1813 at Guilford, Vermont. He graduated from West Point in 1836, took part in the Seminole Wars of 1836-39. He fought in the Mexican War and subsequently on several Indian frontier posts. He resigned his commission in 1859 and devoted the next two years to crusading against abolition. He became a colonel of the 1st Vermont on May 9, 1861, and Brigadier General of Volunteers on May 17, 1861. His regiment captured Newport News, he commanded at Ship Island, and later achieved perhaps his greatest acclaim by organizing the first Negro troops on the outskirts of New Orleans. He resigned on August 21, 1862, the same day the Confederate government declared him an outlaw for his organizing and arming Negro slaves. After the war he ran for President on the Antimason Ticket in 1880. He died on February 2, 1885.

BRATTLEBORO VERMONT
May 14 1868

Charles F. Leonard Esqr.

Dear Sir.

    The report of Genl. Dodge of the Pacific Rail Road has come to hand, and is just what I wanted. Please accept my best thanks for your kind attention.
    You are doubtless kept advised of what is going on here in Brattelboro'. There will be put up from a dozen to twenty new buildings this year, large and small.

Very respectfully Yours,
J.W. Phelps

Annotated on obverse:

Maj. General—
    Memorable for his disagreement with Genl. Butler on the question of employing colored soldiers.

Brattleboro Vermont
May 14 1868

Charles F Leonard Esqr
   Dear Sir,
         The report of Genl Dodge
of the Pacific Rail Road has
come to hand, and is just what
I wanted. Please accept my
best thanks for your kind attention.
         You are doubtless kept advised
of what is going on here in Brat
tleboro'. There will be put up
from a dozen to twenty new
buildings this year, large and
small.
         Very respectfully Yours,
                    J.W.Phelps

ORLANDO METCALFE POE
BRIGADIER GENERAL, U.S.V.

Gen. Poe was born on March 7, 1832 at Navarre, Ohio. He graduated from West Point in the Class of 1856 and was subsequently appointed to the Corps of Engineers, serving northern lake areas. In 1860 he was promoted to 1st Lieutenant and the following year joined Gen. McClellan's staff, serving in Ohio, West Virginia, and Washington, D.C. In September 1861 he became Colonel of the 2nd Michigan, commanding his regiment in the Peninsular Campaign and at Second Manassas, when he commanded one of the brigades of Kearney's III Corps. At Fredericksburg he commanded a brigade of the IX Corps. On November 29, 1862 he was appointed Brigadier of Volunteers but never confirmed by the Senate reverting to his regular rank of Captain on March 4, 1863. He then served as Chief Engineer of the XXIII Corps and of the Army of the Ohio and was responsible for the defenses of Knoxville. In April 1864 he became Chief Engineer of the Military Division of the Mississippi and fought at Atlanta and in Sherman's March to the Sea. He was again brevetted Brigadier General at war's end. After the war he served as aide-de-camp to Sherman until his retirement in 1884 and later as a military engineer in various Great Lakes projects. He died on October 2, 1895.

Washn. D.C.
Decr. 23d 1869

My dear Professor

The two bottles of brandy herewith, were sent to me by Mr. Motley of New York, to be handed you as a Xmas present. The brandy is of the same quality as that you have tasted, and is quite "handy to have in the house" in case of sickness, though for such an emergency I trust it may be long before you or yours require it.

Yours truly
O. M Poe

Profr. Henry
Smithn Inst^{t}.

Wash.n D. C.
Dec.r 23d 1869

My dear Professor.
    The two bottles of
brandy herewith, were
sent to me by Mr. Motley
of New York, to be handed
you as a Xmas present.
The brandy is of the same
quality as that you have
tasted, and is quite
"handy to have in the
house" in case of sickness,
though for such an emer-
-gency I trust it may be
long before you or yours,
require it — yours truly
Profr Henry   O. M. Poe
Smith. Inst.

JULIUS STAHEL
MAJOR GENERAL, U.S.V.

Gen. Stahel was born on November 5, 1825 in Szeged, Hungary. He rose in rank in the Austrian army from private to lieutenant but after siding with the revolutionary cause in 1849 and losing, he fled the country spending time in London and Berlin. He finally came to America in 1859 working for a German language weekly in New York. In 1861 he was instrumental in recruiting the 8th New York (1st German rifles) becoming its colonel. He led his regiment at First Manassas and was promoted to Brigadier General on November 12, 1861. He fought under Fremont in the Shenandoah and at Second Manassas where he commanded the first division of Sigel's Corps. In the spring of 1863 he was assigned command of the cavalry in the defense of Washington where he was promoted to Major General on March 17, 1863. In the spring of 1864 Stahel led a division of cavalry under Gen. David Hunter in the Shenandoah and West Virginia. In the Battle of Piedmont (June 5, 1864) he greatly distinguished himself and was in 1893 awarded the Congressional Medal for his services there. He resigned his commission on February 8, 1865. After the war he served in the consular affairs department in Japan and China and, upon returning to the United States, became associated with the Equitable Insurance Company of New York. Gen. Stahel died on December 4, 1912.

New York, June twenty second, 1903.

Captain Isaac P. Gragg
Secretary, Committee on Dedication of the Hooker Statue
Boston, Mass.

My dear Comrade,

Since accepting the honor which was conferred upon me by the invitation of His Excellency the Governor and the Executive Council of the Commonwealth of Massachusetts to be present at the Dedication of the Statue of Major General Joseph Hooker, on Thursday, June twenty fifth, 1903, my old enemy, Sciatica, has taken its hold on me so badly, that I am forced to deprive myself of the great pleasure of attending the celebration in memory of my highly revered late commander and friend General Hooker, the General was one of the foremost commanders of our army, whose services for the restoration of our glorious Union will I am sure be only forgotten when mankind forget chivalry, valor and patriotism.

With most respectful regards, and sincere best wishes, to His Excellency the Governor, the members of the Executive Council, the Dedication Committee and all comrades, I am

Fraternally yours
Julius H. Stahel

Annotated on verso:

N.Y. City June 22/03
Maj. Gen. Julius H. Stahel
Unable to respond to invitation previously accepted by him.

New York, June twenty second, 1903

Captain Isaac P. Gragg
Secretary, Committee on Dedication of the Hooker Statue

Boston, Mass.

My dear Comrade;

I received the honor which was conferred upon me by the invitation of His Excellency the Governor and the Executive Council of the Commonwealth of Massachusetts to be present at the Dedication of the Statue of Major General Joseph Hooker, on Thursday, June twenty fifth, 1903, my old enemy, sciatica has taken its hold on me so badly, that I am forced to deprive myself of the great pleasure of attending the celebration in memory of my highly revered late commander and friend General Hooker. – The General was one of the best most commanders of our army, whose service for the restoration of our glorious Union, will I am sure, be only forgotten, when mankind forget chivalry, valor and patriotism. –

With most respectful regards, and sincere best wishes, to His Excellency the Governor, the members of the Executive Council, the Dedication Committee and all Comrades. I am,

Gratefully yours

Julius H. Stahel

ROBERT FREDERICK HOKE
MAJOR GENERAL C.S.A.

Gen. Robert Hoke was born in Lincolnton, North Carolina on May 27, 1837. After graduating from Kentucky Military Institute he managed his family's cotton mill and iron works until the outbreak of the Civil War. He enlisted in the Confederate Army as a 2nd Lieutenant with the 1st North Carolina Volunteers. After fighting at Big Bethel he was promoted to Lieutenant Colonel of the 33rd North Carolina and later Colonel of the 21st North Carolina. Fighting during the Seven Days campaign and at Chancellorsville, he was severely wounded at Marye's Heights. While recovering he learned of his promotion to Brigadier General. Transferred to North Carolina, he proceeded to capture Plymouth and the 3,000 man Union garrison for which he was promoted to Major General. He later fought at Drewry's Bluff and Cold Harbor, Fort Fisher and Bentonville. After the war Gen. Hoke returned to private industry and lived until July 3, 1912.

Raleigh N.C.
Jay. 1888

Genl. Marcus J. Wright

    Dear Genl.

    Genl. S.D. Ramseur was born at Lincolnton N.C. on the 30th day of May 1837. His middle name was Dodson, and when a boy was called "Dod."

               Yours truly
               R.F. Hoke

Raleigh N. C.
Jany 1888

Genl Marcus J Wright —
    Dear Sir —
            Genl S. D. Ramseur
was born at Lincolnton N. C. on the
30th day of May 1837 — His middle name
was Dodson, and when a boy was
called "Dod" —

                Yours truly
                R. F. Hoke

WILLIAM MAHONE
MAJOR GENERAL, C.S.A.

Gen. Mahone was born in Southhampton County, Virginia on December 1, 1826. He graduated from VMI in 1847 and practiced engineering until being named President of the Norfolk & Petersburg Railroad, a post he held until being appointed Colonel of the 6th Virginia Infantry. He took part in the capture of the Norfolk Navy Yard, aided in erecting the defenses at Drewry's Bluff, fought at Seven Pines and was continuously with the Army of Northern Virginia until Appomattox. He did spend a brief period recuperating from a severe wound gained at Second Manassas. He was promoted to Brigadier General on November 16, 1861 and to Major General for his part in the Battle of the Crater on July 30, 1864. Gen. Mahone returned to railroading after the war until his election to the United States Senate in 1880 on the Readjuster Ticket. He died in Washington on October 8. 1895.

U.S. SENATE CHAMBER

Washington   5. March 1883

My dear Sir.

I send you by mail which takes this note a photograph, in response to yr. request and I am gratified at the cordial approval you express of my public course.

Yrs. truly
Wm. Mahone

J. Caldwell Davis Esq.
Franklin
N.C.

U. S. SENATE CHAMBER

WASHINGTON 5? March 188*3*

My Dear Sir.

I send you by mail which takes this note a photograph, in response to yr request: and I am gratified at the cordial approval you express of my public course.

Yrs truly
Wm Mahone

J. Caldwell. Davis esq
Franklin
N. C.

JAMES BARNETT FRY
BREVET MAJOR GENERAL, U.S. ARMY

  Gen. James Fry was born on February 22, 1827 in Carrollton, Illinois. He graduated from West Point in 1847 and was sent to Mexico City for garrison duty. He then spent the next five years as adjutant of the Military Academy and at the outbreak of the Civil War was placed in command of a battery of light artillery in Washington, D.C. During the last year of the Civil War he was Provost Marshal General. Previous to that he served in staff capacities including terms as McDowell's chief of staff at First Manassas and Buell's Chief of Staff for the Army of the Ohio. After the war he served as Colonel in the adjutant general's department and in 1881 retired to write on military matters. He died on July 11, 1894.

Washington
5 P.M.

Col. Heintzelman
Alexandria

    The President has gone to Alexandria. Find him & the Secretary & say that the review will be ready at the Fall Track Long Bridge at half past 6. today. Genl. McDowell will be there.

                J.B. Fry
                A.A.G.

Washington
 ? 9 n.

Col Heintzelman
   Alexandria

        The President
has gone to Alexandria, find
him & the Secretary & say that
the steamer will be ready at
the rail track long bridge at
half past 6. today. Gen.
McDowell will be there.

                H D Fry
                Capt

SAMUEL PETER HEINTZELMAN
MAJOR GENERAL U.S.V.

General Heintzelman was born on September 30, 1805 in Manheim, Pa. He graduated from West Point in the Class of 1826 and spent the next twenty years in recruiting and Quartermaster duties. He was breveted a major for gallant service at Huamantla in the Mexican war and again breveted lieutenant colonel in 1851 for his services at Fort Yuma, California. At the outset of the Civil war he was commissioned a Colonel of the 17th Infantry on May 14, 1861 and three days later Brigadier General of Volunteers. On May 5, 1862 he was promoted to Major General. He fought at First Manassas, Bull Run (where he was wounded), Yorktown (where he commanded the III Corps), Seven Pines, Second Manassas, Groveton, and by the end of the war in the defenses of Washington. After Appomatox he commanded in Texas until his retirement in 1869. He died on May 1, 1880.

OFFICE OF
S.P. HEINTZELMAN,

No. 8 Broadway
New York, March 25, 1871

Geo. W. Reed Esq.
243 West 18th St. N.Y.

My dear Sir:

Your letter of the 9th, I delayed answering not being able to find the information you desired. After a search through my papers I find the annexed statement which must have been taken from the official returns.

On the 25th June the affair I have called the "Orchards" took place in which at my suggestion, under the orders of the Commanding General I with my Corps & I think one division of Gen. Keye's (4th Corps) drove back the enemy's lines & we secured an improved position. The next day the battle of Mechanicsville took place & we gradually fell back till we brought up on the James River. My Corps suffered but trifling loss, until the 30th June 1862, the day after we crossed the White Oak Swamp, when the battle I call "Glendale" took place in which my Corps (the 3rd) was heavily engaged. Gen. Sumner calls this, I believe "Schons Farm," Genl. Smith or Franklin "White Oak Swamp," & the Rebels I believe "Frasers Farm."

Yours truly,
S.P. Heintzelman

Loss in 3rd Corps between 26th June & 2 July 1862.

	Eff.	Present	Off.	Men	Off.	Men	Miss	Agg.
Hooker	289	7,307	"	24	"	113	3,303	433
Kearney	283	6,242	7	71	20	469	1,432	1006
	572	13,549	7	95	20	582	4,742	1449
		572		7		20	4	
		14,121		102		602	4,746	

Agg. 15,570 - probable force present 29 June 1862

Grand Agg. S.P. Heintzelman Major Genl.

New York, March 25, 1871.

Geo. W. Reed Esq.
243 West 18th St. N. Y.

My dear sir:

Your letter of the 9th, I delayed answering not being able to find the information you desired. After a search through my papers I find the annexed statement which must have been taken from the official returns.

On the 25th June the affair I have called the "Orchards" took place in which at my suggestion, under the orders of the commanding General

in the army corps, & I think
one division of Gen. Reg. (4th
corps) drove back the enemy
drives & we secured an important position. The next day the
battle of Mechanicsville took
place & we gradually fell back
till we brought up on the James
river. My troops suffered but fig-
ting on, until the 30th June 1862,
the day after we crossed the White
Oak Swamp, when the battle
call Glendale took place, in
which my corps (the 3rd) was
heavily engaged. Gen. Sumner
calls this "Nelson's Farm,"
Gen. Smith or Franklin, "White Oak
Swamp," & the Rebels, "Nelson
...

Loss in 2nd. Corps between 26th
June & 2. July 1862.

Eff. present off. men off. men cur. agg.
Hooker 269 7.307 " 24. " 113. 3.303 443
Kearny 263 6.242 7. 71 20.469 1.439.1006
       572 13.549 7. 95 20.562 4.742 1449
            572   20   4
            14.121   102   802   4746
Agg. —
Grand Agg. 15. 570 — probable force present 29 June 62

J. Dbl. M[...]man
(Corps Gen'l

JOHN McALLISTER SCHOFIELD
MAJOR GENERAL, U.S.A.

Gen. John Schofield was born on September 29, 1831 in Gerry, New York. He graduated from West Point in the Class of 1853 and began his career in Florida followed by a stint as an instructor at West Point. During the early part of the war he served as Missouri's mustering officer, as Major of the 1st Missouri Infantry and as Chief of Staff to General Nathaniel Lyon at the Battle of Wilson's Creek. On November 21, 1861 he was made a brigadier general of volunteers and charged with the command of all Union militia in Missouri. From October, 1862 to April 1863, he commanded the Army of the Frontier. He was promoted to Major General on May 12, 1863. Later he commanded a division of the XIV Corps in Tennessee, the Department of the Missouri, the Army of the Ohio, and the XXIII Corps forcing heavy losses on the Confederates at Franklin, Goldsboro and Durham Station. In 1868 he served as President Johnson's Secretary of War, and later served as Superintendent of West Point from 1876 to 1881. He was promoted to Lieutenant General in 1895 and died at St. Augustine in 1906.

Knoxville Tenn.
Feb. 16th 1864

Hon. Ira Harris,
U.S. Senate
Washington D.C.

My dear Senator

I find that Capt. is not in my command. His regiment is in the Department of the Cumberland. From what I have been able to learn he is in some trouble. Exactly what I do not know, but I fear of a serious character. I am told he is very intemperate and has been guilty of some act of disobedience of orders. I sincerely hope his case is not so bad as represented. I will endeavor to ascertain what it is and see if it is possible for me to do anything for the unfortunate Captain. I expect a considerable force from Chattanooga soon, and understand that the regular Brigade will form part of the force. If so I will probably be able to relieve the Captain from his trouble. At least I will do so if possible.

The prospect in East Tennessee is becoming brighter. Our position here is now secure and supplies are obtained in sufficient quantity by rail. I intend to drive Longstreet out of Tenn. very soon. The campaign will be an extremely difficult one. The country is exhausted and the roads nearly impassible. Yet I believe the difficulties great as they are, can be overcome. I shall at least make every possible effort to accomplish what seems now to be the most important part of the general plan of operations.

I see the Senate has not yet acted upon my nomination. Perhaps they have determined to wait and see what I will do here. Of this I am not disposed to complain. I have gone through too many severe ordeals already to care much for the addition of another. I have determined to leave the question of my confirmation in the hands of my friends in Washington, and content myself with doing what I can for the country.

Please present my highest regards to Mrs. Harris and your daughters, and believe me

Very truly
Your friend
J.M. Schofield

Knoxville Tenn.
Feb. 16th 1864

Hon. Ira Harris
U. S. Senate
Washington D.C.

My dear Senator

I find that
Capt. ███████ is not in
my command. His regi-
ment is in the Department
of the Cumberland. From
what I have been able
to learn he is in some
trouble, exactly what I
do not know, but I fear
of a serious character. I
am told he is very intem-
perate and has been guilty
of some act of disobedience

of orders. I sincerely hope his case is not so bad as represented. I will endeavor to ascertain what it is and see if it is possible for me to do any thing for the unfortunate Captain. I expect a considerable force from Chattanooga to join my Command ~~~~~~~~, and understand that the regular Brigade will form part of the force. If so I will probably be able to relieve the Captain from his trouble. At least I will do so if possible.

The prospect in East Tennessee is becoming brighter. Our position here is now secure and supplies are obtained in sufficient quantity by rail. I intend to drive Hindman out of Tenn. very soon. The campaign will be an extremely difficult one. The country is exhausted and the roads nearly impossible. Yet I believe the difficulties, great as they are, can be overcome. I shall at least make every possible effort to accomplish what seems now to be the most important part of the general plan of operations.

I see the Senate has not yet acted upon my nomination. Perhaps they have determined to wait and see what I will do here. Of this I am

not disposed to complain.
I have gone through too
many severe ordeals already
to care much for the addition
of another. I have determined
to leave the question of my
confirmation in the hands
of my friends in Washington,
and content myself with doing
what I can for the country.

Please present my highest
regards to Mrs Harris and
your daughters, and believe
me Very truly
Your Friend
JMSchofield

JM Schofield

THOMAS WILBERFORCE EGAN
BREVET MAJOR GENERAL, U.S.V.

Gen. Thomas Egan was born in Watervliet, New York on June 14, 1834. He enlisted and began his Civil War career as Lt. Col. of the 40th New York, also known as the Mozart Regiment in April, 1861. In 1862 Egan was commissioned Colonel after the Battle of Seven Pines where he arrested his own Colonel for misconduct. Fighting valiantly in all of the skirmishes of the Army of the Potomac, he was severely wounded at Petersburg, leaving his legs partially paralyzed. He returned to duty two months later and was promoted to Brigadier General on September 3, 1864. He was again severely wounded on November 14, 1864 and was disabled. He again however returned to active duty and was breveted Major General on October 27, 1864 for gallantry by Boydton Plank Road. After the war he was a deputy collector in the New York Customs House. He died in a charity hospital on February 24, 1887.

Washington, D.C.   Aug. 30, 1865

My dear General,

I received your very kind letter of 18th in due course, but have been incessantly on the wing ever since, and could not answer sooner.

Do not regard my delay as wilful, but excuse me on the premise of better doings in future.

If you will send the books to the Metropolitan, New York, or to 87 Bleecker St., care of P. Murphy, they will reach me immediately. I am anxious to procure a copy of your wish, as I have long regarded the present system of tactics as partially obsolete, & shall regard any improvement as a desideratum.

With many thanks for your great kindness,

I am sincerely yours,
T. W. Egan,
Bvt. Maj. Genl. U.S.V.

Brig. Gen. W.H. Morris, U.S.V.
Stapleton,
Staten Id.
N.Y.

Washington D.C. Aug. 30, 1865.

My dear General,

I received your very kind letter of 18th in due course, but have been incessantly on the wing ever since, and could not answer sooner.

Do not regard my delay as wilful, but excuse me on the promise of better doings in future.

If you will send the books to the Metropolitan, New York, or to 87 Bleecker St., care of P. Murphy, they will reach me immediately. I am anxious to procure a copy of your work, as I have long regarded the present system of tactics as partially obsolete, & shall regard any improvement as a desideratum.

With many thanks for your great kindness,

I am sincerely yours,

T. W. Egan,
Bvt. Maj. Gen. U.S.V.

Brig. Gen. W. H. Morris, U.S.V.
Stapleton,
Staten Id.,
N. Y.

GALUSHA PENNYPACKER
MAJOR GENERAL, U.S.A.

Galusha Pennypacker was born in Chester County, Pennsylvania on June 1, 1844. When only sixteen, he enlisted in the 9th Pennsylvania where he served as Quartermaster Sergeant. He became Captain of the 97th Pennsylvania, a company he recruited, on August 22, 1861 at the age of seventeen. He was promoted to Major of the same unit in October, 1861. His early war service was with the Department of the South, serving in both Florida and South Carolina. By 1864 Pennypacker had become the youngest Colonel ever to command a regiment of the Regular Army. At Petersburg he commanded a regiment of the XXIV Corps, was wounded four times, and took a major part in the attempted capture of Fort Fisher. Hospitalized at Fort Monroe for ten months he became on April 28, 1865, a month before his 21st birthday, a Brigadier General. By March 13, 1865 he attained his final brevet rank of Major General. Pennypacker stayed in the army until his retirement in 1883. He died on October 1, 1916 in Philadelphia.

300 South 10th St.,
Philadelphia,
May 16th, 1903

Dear Captain Grogg:

With many thanks for your kindness, and a full appreciation of your courtesy, I have the honor to acknowledge the receipt of your invitation to be present at the "Dedication Ceremonies—Major General Hooker," on the 25th of next month,and to inform you that I will do my best to honor myself by being with you on the occasion named.—and I remain,

Your obdt. Servt.
G. Pennypacker.

Capt. Isaac F. Grogg,
Secretary,
&c., &c., &c.

Annotated on Verso:
Philadelphia, Pa.
May 16/03
Maj. Genl. Galuha Pennypacker U.S.V.
Accepts invitation to be special guest
Surviving Genl. Army of the Potomac

300 South 10th St.,
Philadelphia,
May 16th, 1903.

Dear Captain Grogg:

With many Thanks
for Your Kindness, and a
full appreciation of Your
Courtesy, I have the honor
to acknowledge the receipt
of Your Invitation to be
present at the "Dedication
Ceremonies — Major General
Hooker," on the 25th of
next month, — and to in=
form You that I will do
my best to honor myself
by being with You on

the occasion named. —
And I remain,
    Your obdt. Servt.,
        L. Hennypacker.

Capt. Isaac F. Grogg,
    Secretary,
        &c., &c., &c.

JAMES ADAMS DIX
MAJOR GENERAL, OF VOLUNTEERS, U.S.A.

Gen. Dix was born in Boscawen, New Hampshire on July 24, 1798. During the War of 1812 he fought at Lundy's Lane as an Ensign and after the War remained in the Army until 1828. He then entered law, settled in New York, and became a leader of the Jacksonian Democrats, adjutant general of New York, Secretary of State and New York State School Superintendent. He was elected to the United States Senate in 1845 and served until 1849. He was appointed Secretary of the Treasury by President Buchanan. When President Lincoln assumed office he was appointed Major General of Volunteers on May 16, 1861. Being considered too old to fight during the war, he served in various garrison capacities and was responsible for suppressing the New York Draft Riots in 1863. He resigned in 1865, served as Minister to France under President A. Johnson and in 1872 was elected Governor of New York. He died in New York on April 21, 1879.

JOHN ADAMS DIX (1798—1879)
MAJOR GENERAL U.S.V.

HEAD QUARTERS DEPT. OF VIRGINIA,
SEVENTH ARMY CORPS
Fort Monroe   27. Jan. 1863.

Chas. C. Seigh Esq.

    Sir: There is no one who will make a more proper distribution of the woollen tippets than Mr. Milder, the Supt. of Contrabands here. If addressed to him at this post, they will come free of charge from Baltimore.

I am respectfully yours,
John A. Dix
Maj. Genl.

On verso:
Genel. Dix
Jay. '27/63
Mr. Decker
Mr. Rockwell

Head Quarters Dept. of Virginia,
SEVENTH ARMY CORPS.

Fort Monroe 27. Jan. 1863.

Chas. C. Leigh Esq.

Sir:
There is no one, who
will make a more proper dis-
tribution of the woollen tippets
than Mr. Wildn, the Supt. of Contrabands here. If addressed
to him at this post, they will
come free of charge from
Baltimore.

I am, respectfully yours,
John A. Dix
Maj. Gnl.

469

PART II

THE CIVIL WAR DIARY
OF CAPT. W.S. McCREADY
CO. G. 11TH WISCONSIN

"We have nothing for breakfast ... The Supply train is fast in mudd 5 miles off."

—*W.S. McCready*

INTRODUCTION

W.S. McCready served four years and fifteen days in the Civil War fighting with his Co. G. of the 11th Wisconsin. During this time he rose through the enlisted ranks to Captain of his company. His incredible story of the long days waiting for orders, the endless and tiring marches, and the illness of a soldier's life are vividly portrayed in this diary which spans the period January 1, 1863 to October 2, 1865. The whereabouts of Capt. McCready's earlier war diary (if one even existed) are unknown. But thanks to the loving care of his descendant, Patricia McCready, this invaluable glimpse into his life and exploits has been lovingly preserved.

Capt. McCready's accounts of the war, particularly the fall of Vicksburg, troop movements on the Mississippi steamboats, war activities on the Texas coast, and late war election festivities in Louisiana shed important details on these critical war maneuvers and events. Simultaneously, they provide insight into the fears, hopes, thoughts, and joys of the North's common soldiers performing uncommon feats of heroism. All of these tales are told in a vibrant and sensitive language which transports the reader to the banks of the Mississippi where they too can visualize standing in a battle line as Gen. Grant reviews his troops. The reader also experiences the long nights "sleeping on the ground," the "killed hogs skinned and cooked," the treking through snow "to a depth of 8 inches," and the brutal "marching 26 miles." These were the daily tribulations of McCready, the difficulties which he and his comrades endured while fighting the rebels in their home bayous, sugar cane fields, and muddy back roads. It was a slow, monotonous, dangerous four years but it preserved the Union. The 11th Wisconsin marched back to Madison proud at having contributed to the ultimate victory which had cost so many lives, mangled others, and dashed the hopes of the South. Historians can exult at adding this previously unpublished diary to their treasure trove of historical accounts that will assist them in understanding this defining moment of American history.

THE FALL OF VICKSBURG

Pemberton stared into that black July night
With a steadiness that belied his inner fright
Grant's battle lines were drawn up tight
As thousands awaited the order to march light

In town the rats roamed freer than men
Grain and pilot bread only a memory then
Starvation every Rebel's companion that day
As hope faded for promised troops in gray

Unconditional surrender the only proferred terms
To relieve the weary defenders behind the berms
Caves of shredded memories soon to expel
The denizens of Vicksburg at noon's church bell

The flag of truce a shredded white blouse
Greeted silent generals within the pockmarked house
That was soon to witness the valiant city's fall
Where again only the bone weary defenders yet stood tall.

—*Wayne L. Wolf*

Thursday, Jan. 1st, 1863.

New Years in camp is passing off very quietly. Capt. Partridge gave each squad of the Co. a canteen full of Whiskey. Supply train left for Pilot Knob. Day cloudy & ground very muddy.

Friday, Jan. 2d. 1863.

Gen. Davidson charged one one (sic) of our Piquet posts last night. I took it the picquets neither fired at nor halted him. He has placed them in arrest for such conduct. Day rainy & ground muddy.

Saturday, Jan. 3d. 1863.

Rained hard nearly all last night. There was a good deal of Artillery firing across the river to day. I have not learned the cause. Day fair with some sunshine.

Sunday, Jan. 4th. 1863.

Co. inspected today. Rained nearly all night. Day cloudy but dry.

Monday, Jan. 5th, 1863.

A detail of men are clearing off a new camp ground. We are upon 3/5 rations. Received a letter from my mother. Day clear and sunshine.

Tuesday, Jan. 6th 1863.

Our Co. went to Barnesville to day 25 miles guarding a supply train. The first 10 miles of road was the worst that I ever saw the other 15 was on a ridge and was good. We slept on the ground all night. We killed some hogs skinned & cooked them. Hall Spink was greatly enraged by some one putting one of the hog skins into bed with him during the night. Day pleasant.

Wednesday, Jan. 5th, 1863.

Ground froze hard last night. We loaded our wagons and started on our return at 11 A.M. We broke a wagon tongue and were delayed until 2 P.M. putting in a new one. A dragoon was shot by a Bushwacker a little in advance of us. 12 men of an Indiana regiment was taken towards Barnesville under guard. We halted at dark 7 miles from Van Buren when an order arrived from Gen. Davidson ordering us to camp. 3 teams soon after arrived and took some of the sugar and coffee from our train. At 9 we moved again and at 3 A.M. we had made 3 miles. We then lay down and slept till morning. Day pleasant. Was very sick all night. Lost my woolen and rubber blankets.

Thursday Jan. 1st 1863

New Years in camp is passing off
very quietly Capt. Partridge gave
each squad of the Co. a canteenful
of Whiskey Supply train left
for Pilot Knob Day cloudy ground very muddy

Friday Jan. 2nd 1863

Gen Davidson charged on one
of our Picquet posts last night
& took it The picque's neither fired
at nor halted him He has placed
them in arrest for such conduct
Day rainy & ground muddy

Saturday Jan. 3rd 1863

Rained hard nearly all last night
There was a good deal of Artillery
firing across the river to day I have
not learned the cause Day
fair with some Sunshine

Thursday Jan 1st 1863

Co. 42 Inspection to day Rained heavy
all night Day cloudy but dry

Monday Jan 5th 1863

A detail of men are clearing off a
new camp ground We our open
1/2 ration Received a letter from ____
Day pleasant day clear and Sunshine

Tuesday Jan 6th 1863

Our Co. Went to Booneville to day
While guarding a supply train the
just 10 Miles it said was the worst that
I ever saw the others 15 miles on a
blizzard was good. We slept on the
ground last night We killed some
Rebels & coa fed them Stole
Stand was greatly enraged to you
putting on of the horses offic into
during the Lance during the night

Wednesday Jan. 5th 1863

Ground froze hard last night
We loaded our wagons and started on
our return at 11 A.M. We had a
wagon tongue in and war old loyd with a
1 P.M. putting in a new one. A
wagon was sent by a Bushwhacker
6 of them advance of our Men of the
Indiana regiment was to the Pinnacle
Booneville under guard. We halted at
dark 9 Miles from Van Buren where an
orderly arrived from Gen. Davidson ordering
us to charge. I teams from of the enemy
and took some of the the Sugar and
Coffee from our train at Booneville
again and at 5 A.M. we had broke
8 miles in the hard day down and slept
till morning. Day pleasant. We very
sick all the night my Mother
Mother Blankets

Thursday, Jan. 8th. 1863.

Arrived in camp at 2 P.M. to day. All very tired. Day pleasant.

Friday, Jan. 9th. 1863.

Pleasant.

Saturday, Jan. 10th. 1863.

'Tis reported that the Mo. State Militia at Springfield have joined the rebels. Day pleasant.

Sunday, Jan. 11th, 1863.

Capt. Partridge left in charge of a forage train. Wrote to my Mother. Sergts. Adams of Co. K. and Day of Co. B. received their commissions as 2d. Lts. of their Cos. to day. Day pleasant & attended divine service at 33d. Ill. to day.

Monday, Jan. 12th. 1863.

We moved our camp across current river this forenoon. All of the company except 6 signed a petition for Capt. Partridge to resign. A copy of it was given to Col. Harris.

Tuesday, Jan. 13th, 1863.

Received a letter from my Sister. Capt. Oagley of Co. B. and Lt. Downs of this Co. resigned and left us for Wis. Day cloudy with some rain.

Wed. Jan 14th. 1863.

Rained all night. Struck tents and marched at 9 A.M. We left 2 Corpls. and 2 privates sick at Van Buren. We halted at 2 P.M. having marched about 7 miles. The road was very bad and day was very rainy. Our team did not arrive and most other men lay down beside large fires that we built among the Pines.

Thursday Jan. 15th. 1863.

Snow is about 3 inches deep on the ground this morning. We borrowed rations and camp kettles from Co. K. and got breakfast. Our team arrived at 10 A.M. when we pitched our tents and carried straw from a farm built large fires in front of our tents and felt more comfortable. Afternoon very cold. We are camped on a ridge covered with Pine trees. Snowed all day.

Friday, Jan. 16th 1863.

Last night was very cold. Struck tents and marched at 7. Road is frozen hard with 4 inches of snow on the ground. We marched about 7 miles on the Thomasville Road and camped in a field. Our train arrived when we scraped the snow off and pitched our tents. Private John T. Bradley was promoted to 5th Sergt. Day cold but pleasant.

Sat. Jan. 17th. 1863.

Marched at 7 and camped at Falling Springs at noon having marched 15 miles. Road was good country very hilly soil sandy and timber is mostly rich pine. We are camped by a mill that is worked by a spring that falls perpendicularly 35 feet from the side of a high bluff. Day pleasant. Sunshine but did not thaw much.

Sunday Jan. 18th. 1863.

Marched at 7. Road soon became muddy. It thawed all afternoon. We marched 10 miles through the roughest tract of country that I ever saw. The bluffs were high and steep the ravines narrow being some places only about 20 feet wide and the bluffs rising perpendicularly for 200 and 300 feet on each side. The most beautiful streams of water that I ever beheld flowed down some of those ravines. We captured 11 Bushwackers to-day. Thawed all day.

Monday, Jan. 19th 1863.

Marched at 7 A.M. Roads very bad having rained all night. We arrived at Alton having marched 9 miles at 1 P.M. I went back with 8 men to get our team through and got back to camp at dark. Our provisions are done until our supply train arrives sometime tomorrow. Rained nearly all day.

Tuesday, Jan. 20th, 1863.

We have nothing for breakfast. 10 boxes of Pilot Bread was carried by men to us in time for dinner. The Supply train is fast in the mudd (sic) 5 miles off. Day cloudy.

Wed. Jan. 21st, 1863.

Wrote to my Sister. Day cold & cloudy.

Wednesday Jan 13th 1863

Thursday Jan 22nd 1863

Friday Jan 23rd 1863

Saturday Jan 24th 1863

Sunday Jan 25th 1863

Day cold and cloudy

Thursday Jan. 22d. 1863.

Had division drill this forenoon under command of Gen. Davidson. The 33d. Ill. marched back towards Van Buren to bring up the rear of the supply train. Dry cloudy.

Friday Jan. 23d, 1863.

Day cloudy.

Saturday Jan. 24th, 1863.

Moved camp about 4 miles on the Batesville Road and camped at Cave Springs country is now more open and is partially cultivated. Regt. fired their guns this evening. Day cold and cloudy.

Sunday, Jan. 25th, 1863.

Visited a cave this morning close by our camp. A large Spring rises about 12 feet from the mouth of the cave and falls into it. We decended (sic) a pole about 30 feet and found an oblong chamber about 80 feet in length by 50 feet in breadth and 50 in height.

We explored a number of intricate passages from this chamber the largest was about 100 feet long 10 feet wide and 4 to 6 feet high. Day rainy.

Monday, Jan. 26th, 1853.

Rained all of last night and untill evening to day when it commenced to freeze.

Tuesday Jan. 27th, 1863.

Ground is frozen hard this morning. Cos. B. & G. went out and brought in 60 hogs for the regt. We are ordered to be ready to march to morrow morning. Day cold & cloudy.

Wed. Jan. 28th, 1863.

Marched at 9 A.M. to Alton then on the Batesville Road to Warm Fork where we camped having marched 15 miles. Roads were hard in the morning but thawed out during the day. Country is rolling and little improved. The stream here parts at right angles one branch running South the other East.

Sunday Jan 25th 1863

Visited a cave this morning close by
our camp a large spring rises
about 12 feet from the mouth of it,
came out & fell into it, the stream
is just about 3 feet and found an
opening chamber about 80 feet in length
by 50 feet in breadth and 50 in height
we explored a number of intricate
passages from this chamber the larges
was about 100 feet long that was an
L & 6 feet high. Day rainy.

Monday Jan 26th 1863
Rained all day that night and until
morning today when it cleared up for
a short time.

Tuesday Jan 27th 1863
Rained a large part this morning.
Lt. B. S. sick in [...] and brought in others.
[...] 3 reg[t] [...] are ordered to be ready to
march to move at a moments notice.

Wednesday Jan 28th 1863.
Marched at 5 A.M. to take the
the Bolton Rail road to [...] got
where we camped having marched
13 miles road were hard in the morn
ing but it became wet during the day

Thursday Jan 29th 1863
from this point the road very bad
[...] obtaining forage [...] of land[...]
search [...] south the other 60 [...]
Marched as [...] in [...] West course.
toward the N Plains & banks of the Mississippi
18 miles. We passed [...] good farms to day

Friday Jan 30th 1863
Marched at 8 [...] arrived at 12 M
Plains [...] Lewis marched to
the West Plains contain about
one dozen of dwelling houses and a court house

Thursday Jan. 29th, 1863.

Marched at 7 in a North West course towards West Plains & camped after marching 18 miles. We passed some good farms to day. Day pleasant.

Friday, Jan. 30th, 1863.

Marched at 9 and arrived at West Plains at noon having marched 7 miles. West Plains contains about one dozen of dwelling houses one store one grocery and a courthouse. The payroll arrived with the Supply train. Wrote to my father. Day pleasant.

Saturday Jan. 31st, 1863.

Our supply train left us this morning. We are on half rations.
Feel very unwell. One man died here today with small pox. Day
cloudy.

Sunday, Feb. 1st, 1863.

Had division drill to-day. This is the first time that we have drilled on the Sabbath. Feel very unwell to day.

Monday Feb. 2d, 1863.

The 2d. division marched away this morning. Dry cold.

Tuesday, Feb. 3d.

A flag of truce came in from the rebels. Paymaster arrived to day. This is the coldest day of the season. Some papers arrived and are sold at 25 cents apiece.

Wed. Feb. 4th, 1863.

Received a letter from my Sister and 2 papers from a friend. Day cold with snow falling at times.

Thursday Feb. 5th, 1863.

Snow fell last night to the depth of 8 inches. This is I think the coldest day that I ever saw.

Friday Feb. 6th, 1863.

We signed the payrolls this morning and we were paid off this afternoon. We drew full rations this afternoon for the first time since New Years. Day very cold.

Saturday, Feb. 7th, 1863.

Weather moderated last night. It has thawed all day to day.

Sunday, Feb. 8th, 1863.

We marched at 8 A.M. towards Eminence and camped by a pool of water made by melted snow. We marched 26 miles today and did not see a single house or drop of water except melted snow. The land was level and rolling and is one continuous bed of gravel. Day wet and rainy. Nearly half of the men are barefoot their shoes having been worn out by the gravel. The snow is nearly all melted. Hundreds of the men gave out on the march and the ambulances were sent back to bring the tired men in all of this Co. (G. 11th Wis.) had arrived at midnight except Jacob Lanngennechard. The men are all very tired.

Monday, Feb. 9th, 1863.

Marched at 8th and camped after marching 5 miles. Road is very muddy. We are camped by the first stream that I have seen since I left West Plains. Day pleasant. Road very bad.

Tuesday, Feb. 10th, 1863.

One of Co. F died very suddenly last night. Marched at 8 and marched 12 miles and overtook the supply train. We camped at Jack's Fork on Current River. We are amongst the high hills and pine trees again. Day cloudy. Road very muddy.

Feb. 11th, 1863.

I drew rations for the regt. the commisary being sick. Gens. Davidson and Benton have gone to St. Louis. Col. Harris now commands this army. Day cloudy.

Thursday, Feb. 12th, 1863.

Rained very hard last night. J. Langennechard returned to day. He found a horse and then succeeded in overtaking the regt. He fell behind through fatigue on the day that we left West Plains. Day cloudy.

Friday, Feb. 13th, 1863.

Marched at 8 in a northerly course and camped having marched 9 miles. Country hilly and but little improved. Day cloudy.

Saturday, Feb. 14th, 1863.

Marched at 8 in a North Easterly course & camped having marched 12 miles. Country hilly. Soil sandy and timber poor. We marched 9 miles out of our way to day making our march to day 21 miles. Day cloudy.

Sunday Feb. 15th, 1863.

Marched 9 miles to day. A rebel spy was shot by one of our scouts. Country rough. Soil poor & stoney. Day pleasant.

Monday Feb. 16th, 1863.

Marched to day to Current River and in one hour. We made a bridge of our wagons and crossed over then marched 4 miles and camped on a high ridge. Where we crossed the river rejoiceth in the name of Eminence. It consists of one log courthouse and a large spring over 100 feet wide and has been sounded to a depth of 400 feet without finding bottom. There are numerous caves here also one is 1 1/2 miles long. Afternoon rainey.

Tuesday, Feb. 17th, 1863.

Marched at 7 and soon came to a very high hill. The infantry stacked arms and pulled the wagons and cannon up with drag ropes. We camped at 4 P.M. having marched 18 miles to reach Centreville.

Country very rough. We passed some good farms. Day cloudy.

Wed. Feb. 18th, 1863.

We marched to Centreville and made a bridge over & crossed over Little Black River and camped 1 mile from it having marched 22 miles. We are very tired. Country very rough and but little improved. Day cloudy.

Thursday, Feb. 19th, 1863.

Marched towards Pilot Knob this morning and had to ford Little Black River 9 times today. Country rough but more improved. Road bad and Day rainey.

Thursday Feb. 12th 1863

Rained very hard last night.
Co. Commenced returned
to-day. We found a hive another.
received in a note this Esq of
all well & all through their
to-day. Tell us Esq Day Pleno
Day Pleno

Friday Feb. 13th 1863

Marched at 8 in a Northern dir.
and camped having marched this
Burn Co. In Esq. Pont ent. Little
arrived Day Pleno

Saturday Feb. 14th 1863

Marched 8 in a North Eastern dir.
Day after having marched this little, sunny
quite dirt and ridges and timber than
the Marchin Miller out of our march this
Batter here here to-day of Miller
Day Pleno

Sunday Feb. 15th 1863

Marched 9 Miles to-day Pleble.
They and started on of our march
Country roads tell from 8 they
Day Pleasant

Monday Feb. 16th 1863

Marched to-day to current river
and over this the made a bridge
of our wagons and crossed over then
marched to Miller and camped on a
high ridge. Where we crossed the
river opposite to the Mason of
Currence id current of by one
big turn are big Burs here and
a large spring over 100 feet wide
but has been over head to a depth
of 60 feet without finding bottom
there are numerous caves here also one is
1/4 Miles long of Numerous names

Friday, Feb. 20th, 1863.

Marched at 8 A.M. and marched to Belleville Valley and camped having marched 20 miles. We received orders to immediately draw all clothing that we required and go to Vicksburg Miss. Received a letter from Mr. J. Lovewell which informed me that my Brother Samuel was killed Jan. 11th, 1863 at the Battle of Arkansas post. He was a member of Co. K, 23d. Regt. Wis. Infantry. He He (sic) was just 19 years old 6 months old on the day of his death, He was killed by a cannon ball. Our team did not arrive. We slept on the ground. Day pleasant.

Saturday, Feb. 21st, 1863.

Teams arrived at 10 A.M. When we pitched tents I then went to Pilot Knob 10 miles and drew rations for the regiment. Day pleasant. I feel both sorry and unwell to day.

Sunday, Feb. 22d, 1863.

Wrote to my father. Day very cold.

Monday Feb. 23d, 1863.

Went to Pilot Knob. Found it full of drunken soldiers. Road very muddy. On my return to the Co. the men were all drunk but 3. Day pleasant.

Tuesday, Feb. 24th, 1863.

Wed. 25th, Thursday 26th at Bellville Valley. Weather pleasant. I made out our muster rolls during those three days.

Friday, Feb. 27th, 1863.

Marched and camped within 2 miles of Middlebrook. Day pleasant.

Saturday, Feb. 28th. (1863)

We were mustered for pay to day by Col. Harris. I received a letter from my Father which confirmed and gave an account of my Brothers death. Day cloudy some rain.

Sunday, March 1st, 1863.

Co. inspection to-day. Day fair.

Monday, March 2d, 1863.

Moved camp to Middlebrook to-day. Day cold and Blustering. Gen. Carr has arrived and has taken command of this army.

Tuesday, March 3d, 1863.

We marched to Iron Mountain and were reviewed by Gen. Carr to-day. He is a very intelligent and good looking man and about 30 years of age. Day pleasant.

Wed. March 4th, 1863.

Went to Ironton and got our blue flag repaired. Day cold.

Thursday, Mar. 5th (1863)

Last night and to-day is wet & cold.

Friday, March 6th (1863)

Wrote to my father and I received a letter from my mother. Day cold and blustering.

Sat. March 7th (1863)

Rained hard all of last night and most of to-day.

Sunday, March 8th, 1863.

Our cavalry left on a scout to-day. Day rainey.

Monday March 9th (1863)

I went to Iron Mountain. Saw our furnace in operation making Pig Iron. The 2d. division marched for St. Genevieve to-day. Our Sick are being sent to Gen. hospital preparatory to our march to-morrow. 2d. Lt. Peaslee was promoted to 1st. Lt. to-day and 1st Sergt. Wynn to 2d. Lt. Day pleasant.

Tuesday, March 10th, 1863.

Marched 15 miles to wards St. Genevieve on a good plank road. Day pleasant.

Wednesday March 11th (1863)

Marched at 8 A.M. and soon arrived at Farmington—a very pretty town of 300 inhabitants. We have marched 17 miles to-day on the Turnpike. Capt. Partridge is very sick. Day pleasant. Country well improved.

Regt. from the 2d division marched
for St. Genevieve to-day. Our Reg't
are being sent to Gen. hospital
preparatory to our march to-morrow
Reg't Roll be was presented to—
to-day and 1st Serg't Wyman to 2nd Lt.
Day pleasant

Tuesday March 10th 1863
Marched 15 miles towards St Genevieve
on a good pleasant road Day pleasant

Wednesday March 11th
Marched at 6 A.M. and soon arrived at
Farmington – a very pretty town of
300 inhabitants – we have marched
17 miles to-day on the Turnpike
Capt. Partridge is very sick Day
pleasant country well improved

Thursday March 12th
Marched to St Genevieve and camped

looking from the about 3 years
Regt. Day pleasant
Wed. March 4th 1863
Went to Boston and got our
Blue flag was marched Day cold
Thursday Mar. 5th
Est Regt and to-day marched & cold
Friday March 6th
Note to my father and received
a letter from my mother
Day cold and blustering
Sat March 7th
Remained here all of last night and
Mar to-day
Sunday March 8th 1863
Our Cavalry left on a scout to-day
Day pleasant
Monday March 9th
moved to from mountain saw
Service in operation marching

Thursday March 12th (1863)

Marched to St. Genevieve and camped one mile above town on the Miss. River bank. I saw the end of a house in St. Genevieve covered with Ivy the first Ivy that I have seen in America. Day pleasant.

Friday March 13th, 1863.

Went to St. Genevieve to-day. It is a town of about 1000 inhabitants. It is one of the oldest towns on the river. Some of the monuments in the cemetery date 1790. Day pleasant. The inhabitants are mostly French.

Saturday March 14th (1863)

Capt. Partridge has resigned to the great joy of his company. Day pleasant.

Sunday, March 15th, 1863.

Wrote to my father the right wing of our regiment sailed down the river to-day. Day pleasant.

Monday March 16th 1863.

We went on board of the Steamer Illinois with all of our baggage to-day and sailed for Memphis at 1 P.M. The 33d. Ill. Infy. and 1st Ind. Battery of artillery are on board with us. Day pleasant.

Tuesday, March 17th 1863.

Tied up all night & 20 miles above Cape Girardeau. Arrived at the Cape at 9 and landed some soldiers of the 1st Nebraska Infantry. Arrived at Cairo at 2 P.M. found the Ohio River very high and muddy. Most of the streets of Cairo is covered with water. 6 companies of the 25th Wisc. Infy. are in garrison at Cairo. Sailed from Cairo at 9 P.M. Day pleasant.

Wednesday, March 18th, 1863.

Arrived at New Madrid at daylight. Passed Fort Pillow at 4 P.M. At dark took in wood. Arrived at Memphis at midnight. Day pleasant.

Thursday, March 19th, 1863.

Cooks cooked up 3 days rations on shore. Some of the 12th, 32d, 33d, & 23d. Wis. Infantry and 2d Wis. Cavalry came on board. I met with some old acquaintances amongst them. We were permitted to go on shore and visit Fort Pickens. Cos. E.H. and myself with the colors were put with the right wing on the Steamer White Rose. Wrote to my father. Sailed at 8 P.M. Day pleasant.

Friday, March 20th, 1863.

We awoke at Helena this morning. We then went down the river 8 miles to Yazoo Pass and went on board of the Steamer Metropolitan. Found the 8th Wis. Infantry and 6th Wis. Batt. camped at the pass. Day very warm.

Saturday, March 21st, 1863.

Our boat steamed up to Helena and coaled, then went back to Yazoo Pass then went up the river and tied up to the Miss. bank opposite to Helena. Day pleasant.

Sunday, March 22d and 23d (1863)

Went over to Helena and found Cos. G. K. and B. They arrived from Memphis during the night the(y) came on board. We drew new rubber blankets of good quality. Went back across the river and tied up for the night. Day rainey.

Tuesday, March 24, 1863.

Rained all last night. Day cold and wet. Sailed down the river at 2 P.M.

Wednesday, March 25th, 1863.

Tied up within 5 miles within of Lake Providence. Found the 14th & 15th, 16th. and 18th Wis. Infantry there. sailed from Lake P. at one P.M. and tied up at Thompson's Landing. One of Co. F. died last night. Day pleasant.

Thursday, March 26th, 1853.

We took everything on shore and camped when we were ordered to Milliken's Bend. We carried our baggage on board and arrived at Milliken's Bend. Found the 23d. Wis. saw a no. of acquaintances in that regiment. There is a great deal of sickness in it at present. Day pleasant.

Friday, March 27, 1863.

Landed and camped 1/2 mile from the river. Day pleasant.

Saturday, March 28th, 1863.

Co. drill in forenoon and Battallion drill and Parade in afternoon. Day warm.

Sunday, March 25th, 1863.

There was a great storm of Wind and rain here last night blowing down most of our tents. Day cold and rainey.

Monday, March 30th, 1863.

Troops continue daily. Day wet and cold.

Tuesday, March 31st, 1863.

Wrote to my father. Day warm and pleasant.

Wednesday April 1st, 1863.

We have been reorganized. The 18th and 8th Indiana Inf'y. and 33d. and 99th Illinois Inf'y. comprises the 2nd Brigade. Our regt. with the 21st., 22d., and 23d., Iowa form the 2d. Brigade commanded by Col. Harris. Day pleasant.

Thursday, April 2d. 1863.

Review and Inspection to-day by Col. Harris and Brigade drill in the afternoon. Our division is the 14th of the 13th Army Corps div. is commanded by Gen. Carr and corps by Gen. army by Gen. Grant. Appointed 2d. Sergt. to-day. Day pleasant.

Friday, April 3d, 1863.

7 Cos. of the regiment are away on fatigue duty. Day pleasant.

Saturday, April 4th, 1863.

Day warm.

Sunday, April 5th (1863).

Co. inspection. Day pleasant.

Monday April 6th, 1863.

Division Sutler Shop was pillaged last night. We are preparing for review tomorrow. Day pleasant.

Wednesday, March 25th 1863

Tied up within 3 miles within of Lake Providence as found the 16th and 18th Wis Regt on their... Sailed down Lake P at one P.M. and tied up at Humphreys Landing at one oclock last night Day pleasant

Thursday, March 26th 1863

We took everything on board and camped when we were ordered to Milliken's Bend We corralled our baggage on board and arrived at Milliken's Bend at one oclock Wed saw a no. of acquaintances in the 76th regiment There is a great deal of sickness in it Day present

Friday, March 27th 1863

Landed and camped 3 miles from the river Day pleasant

Saturday, March 28th 1863

Co. drill in forenoon and Battallion drill and Parade in afternoon

Sunday, March 29th 1863

There was a great stir in a minor and rain here last night blowing down several of our tents Day Cold and rainy

Monday, March 30th 1863

Troops continue daily Day somewhat

Tuesday, March 31st 1863

Weather fine Day warm and pleasant

Wednesday April 1st 1863

We have been reorganized The 18th and 83rd Indiana Regts and 93rd and 99th Illinois Regts compose the 18th 8th Brigade Our regt north the 19th 97th and 23rd Wis regt from the 2nd Brigade commanded by Col. Head Day pleasant

Tuesday, April 7th, 1863.

Held an Election for Chief Justice Co. G. Gave Dixon Union candidate 20. The regiment gave Dixon Union 374 majority. Co. is on picquet. Review is postponed. Day pleasant.

Wednesday, April 8th, 1863.

Were inspected today by Maj. General McClernerd. Day warm and pleasant.

Thursday, April 9th, 1863.

Reviewed by McClernard to-day. Day pleasant.

Friday, April 10th, 1863.

Were mustered today by Col. Wood. Day pleasant and the flowers are out again.

Saturday, April 11th, 1863.

We are preparing to march to morrow. Day pleasant. Spring is opened. The country is well cultivated. Houses large and the gardens full of flowers.

Sunday, April 12th, 1863.

Rained all of last night. We marched at 9 A.M. today towards Richmond. We left our tents. Road very muddy. Arrived at Richmond 10 miles from Milliken's Bend. Day pleasant. Country is level and interspersed by numerous bayous with large banks of earth built on each side to prevent the land being overflowed during high water. Soil is rich. Land is nearly all cultivated. Cotton is the principal product and Fleas are more numerous than Grant's Army.

Monday, April 13th, 1863.

Rained all night. We slept dry beneath our rubber blankets. Richmond is a town of about 200 inhabitants. It contains a Hotel, Printing Office, Courthouse, 2 stores. Ground very muddy. Day cloudy.

Tuesday, April 14th, 1863.

1st Iowa Battery was attached to our Brigade to-day. Day Rainy.

Wednesday, April 15th (1863).

Received a letter from my sister. Wrote to her. Feel very unwell. Day pleasant.

Thursday, April 16th (1863).

Marched 12 miles towards Carthage to day. We passed the large plantation of the rebel Gen. Holmes. It is the best plantation that I have seen. Feel unwell to-day. Day pleasant.

Friday, April 17th (1863).

Heard a very heavy cannonade last night in the direction of Vicksburg last night. Signed the payrolls to-day. Day warm. We are camped at Smith's Plantation on Roundaway Bayou.

Saturday, April 18th, 1863.

A steamboat came up the Bayou within a mile of us to-day. Day pleasant.

Sunday, April 19th (1863).

Rained all of last night. Day pleasant.

Monday, April 20th (1863).

Were Paid off to-day. Day pleasant.

Tuesday, April 21st (1863).

Showery.

Wednesday, April 22d. (1863).

1st Lt. Pearlee promoted to Capt. 2d. Lt. Wynn to 1st Lt. 1st Sergt. Law to 2d. Lt. and myself to 1st Sergt. I have been Color Sergt. 14 months. Sergt. Bradley is appointed color Sergt. Day very sultry. Marched at 5 P.M. down the levee of Bayou De Ville for 2 miles then crossed over the Bayou in a barge then marched 1/2 mile on a levee and then went 2 miles on little flat boats down a slough through a large Cypress swamp. We landed on a levee again. Marched 1/2 mile farther then slept on the Levee until daylight.

Thursday, April 23d, 1863.

6 of our steamboats and 8 barges ran past the Batteries of Vicksburg last night. The Henry Clay was sunk. The others are all loaded with rations. The cannonade was terrific when the fleet ran past. We marched to Carthage 1 mile. Day pleasant. Carthage contains only a few houses.

Friday, April 24th, (1863)

Marched about 5 miles down the river bank. The fields are all overflowed with water. Day very warm.

Saturday, April 25th, (1863)

A large cotton gin and steam saw mill was burnt down last night by the soldiers. Day warm. We are camped on Perkin's Plantation.

Sunday, April 26th, 1863.

All of the houses on this plantation were burnt by the soldiers. Our first Brigade had a sham fight in presence of Gov. Yates of Ill. Gen. McClernard and others. Our flat boat arrived with our tents and cooking utensils. Day showery.

Monday, April 27th, 1863.

Rained hard all of last night. My tent was blown down. Got up in the rain and put it up again. Received a letter from my sister. Wrote to my mother. 80 rounds of cartridges were issued to each man. At 6 P.M. we were ordered to march the men gave three cheers. We marched down to the river. The band playing Hail Columbia and went on board of a large barge alongside of the Steamer Horizon. Day cloudy and rainy.

Tuesday, April 28th, 1863.

The barge is so crowded with men that only a few could lay or sit down last night. At last all lay down making about 3 deep. Those below crowded for the to & in this way the night passed off more could sleep. Some curseded the boat some the General and some the country. All agreed that we were in a bad place. Sailed down the river at noon and landed at Hard Times on the La. shore within 2 miles of Grand Gulf. the boats returned for more troops. Day pleasant.

Wednesday, April 29th, 1863.

The Gunboats dropped down the river near the Rebel batteries of Grand Gulf. The Gunboats opened a furious bombardment at 8 A.M. which was as briskly replied to from the Rebel batteries from boats to the forts from the forts to the boats the shell flew carrying death and destruction to both parties. This continued until 2 P.M. when all of the rebel guns were silenced but one large gun that the shot from the gunboats could not break is badly disabled (the Tuscumbia) the loss on both sides is pretty heavy. At 2 P.M. our gunboats returned Genls. Grant & McClernard witnessed the engagement from a little tug steamboat at at (sic) 3 P.M. we marched down the levee and camped at De Shron's Plantation and camped after dark. Our gunboats and transport ran past the batteries in safety. The rebel battery opened fire and for 1/2 an hour the fight between the gunboats and batteries was brisk with shell which looked like comets flying back and forth each screaming an unearthly scream and each scream different from those that preceeded it. Day pretty warm.

Thursday, April 30th 1863.

Reveille at 4 A.M. and went on board of the boats at 6 all in good spirits and sailed down the river and landed without molestation at Bruimburg at noon. We then marched for Port Gibson 16 miles distant the 1st 5 miles was level. We then struck into a hilly country where it required nearly as much labor to make a wagon road as it does to build a Railroad. We were detained 2 hours of the afternoon building a bridge over a creek. We then continued our march our brigade in advance. We rested often. The road was very hilly and we were all very drowsey. It was almost impossible to keep awake. Day very warm.

Friday, May 1st, 1863.

Battle of Port Gibson or Magnolia Church. We arrived within 4 miles of Port Gibson when we came upon the Rebel picket which fired and retreated. We followed them up for a mile when a battery opened on us. The first Iowa Batt. was put in position and a brisk fight was kept up from 2 to 3 oclock A.M. when the firing ceased and we lay down and slept untill morning. We were on Dr. Shafer's Plantation. The road forks here and each leads to Port Gibson. The Rebel line crossed each road about 1/2 mile from Shafers house. Magnolia Church is on the South Road in a grove of Magnolia trees. The Rebel Battery was planted at that place last night at day break. The Rebels open 'd their Artillery upon us at all points seeming confident of victory. The 1st Iowa Battery was planted on a ride in a field in front of Shafer's house.

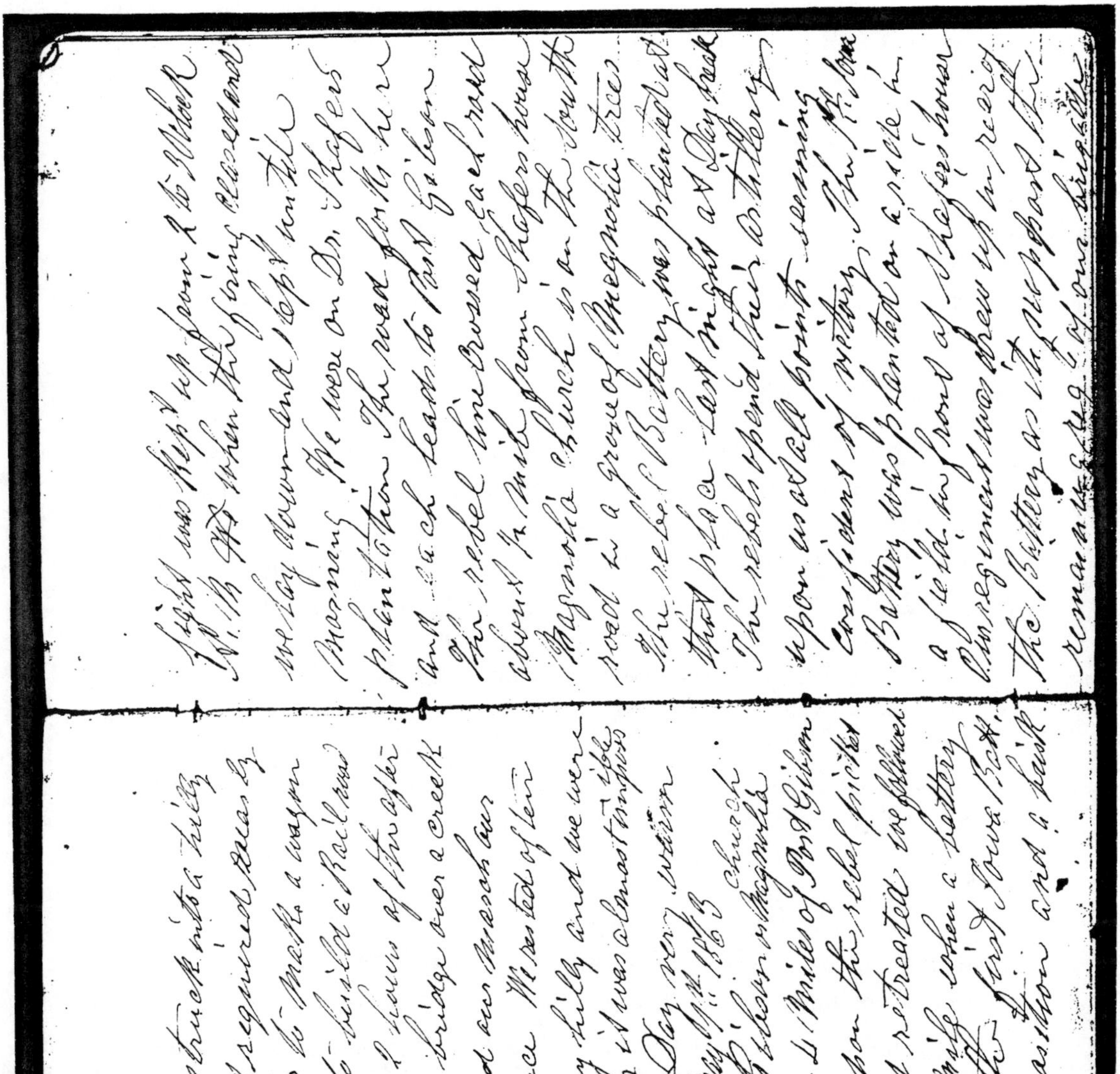

Friday, May 1st 1863

Battle of Port Gibson Church

Our regiment was drew up in rear of the Battery as its support. The remaining regt. of our brigade was formed on our left. Our first brigade was on our right and Gen. Hovey's division was formed on the left of our division. Gen. Osterhaus formed on the North road supported by Smith's div. It was 9 oclock before the lines were formed as described in the mean time a fierce artillery duel was fought between the batteries. The shell flew and burst through our regt. in every direction and to the surprise of us all not one of our regiment was hurt. At 9 Oclock infantry firing commenced on our right which continued to increase for half an hour when we were ordered to advance. We marched over the ridge then marched 1/4 mile through a piece of timber and cane brak(e) where the cane vines and underbrush was so thick and entwined that the place was almost impossible. The Artillery continued to throw shell over our heads after going through the cane brake we found a ridge in our front. It was planted in corn. The rebel line was on the top. Car(r)'s whole division was formed in line along the edge of the brake. The charge was sounded and the whole division fixed bayonet and charged up the hill. The cheering never ceased untill we had ascended the hill and had routed the rebel line and took their Battery and turned it on their flying columns. We took about 500 prisoners. The firing was terrific as we advanced up the hill. We were about 10,000 strong on each side and when about 200 yards apart we fired about 20 rounds on each side the Chatter of the musketry was similar to the drops of hail on a house top in a hail storm and the bullets whizzed about us thick as bees when the(y) are swarming. At first we all dodged when ehen (sic) they passed but after a few rounds were fired there was no dodging. We followed the rebels about a mile when they received reinforcements from Vicksburg and reformed for another attack. The enemy had now tried to turn our right and amassed his forces there accordingly we were on the extreme left on the South Road for 1 hour. We were not engaged but sat on the fences and watched the battle on our right. The Infantry on booth (sic) sides were drew up in three lines about 100 yards apart on the hill side on the rebel side of the valley their troops were pretty concealed by trees and brush on our side. The hill side was cultivated. The cannon were planted on the top of the ridges and fired over the Infantry. For one hour we watched the infantry lines firing a steady fire and the artillery throwing case shot that burst over the infantry. It was the grandest sight that I ever saw. At 2 P.M. Col. Landrum rode a little to our left and was immediately fired upon. Our brigade and 2 Kentucky regts. form into line and immediately met a division that attempted to turn our left flank. For half an hour the battle raged furiously between us when the rebel division ran away. On our right the battle raged until sundown. Osterhaus on the North Road drove the rebels 3 miles and took 1000 prisoners. Our Co. lost none killed or wounded. Regt. lost 2 killed and 18 wounded. Day very warm. Capt. Whittlesey behaved with the greatest bravery during the day. Our total loss is about 800. The rebel loss is about 2000.

Saturday, May 2d, 1863.

We slept soundly last night on the field of battle. We formed into line of battle this morning at sunrise and advanced 1/2 mile and found that the rebel army had retreated during the night. We marched into Port Gibson and camped. the rebels burnt the Suspension Bridge over Bayou Pere outside of the town when the(y) retreated. Our Prisoners had built a new bridge by 4 P.M. and McPherson's Corps had started in pursuit of the rebels. We found 400 rebel wounded in town which we paroled and found over 1000 stand of arms and the road is lined with arms, accoutrements and other things that the rebels threw away in their retreat. Our regiment is appointed Provost Guard. Gen. Lawler is assigned to command our brigade. He arrived to-day. Day very warm.

Sunday, May 3d, 1863.

We found a large quantity of Powder today. Port Gibson is the prettiest town that I ever saw. The gardens are very beautiful. Day pleasant.

Monday May 4th, (1863)

We took a large quantity of cornmeal bacon &c. to day. Straglers continue to arrive from the Rebel army daily and give themselves up prisoners to us. We foraged a team to draw our knapsacks. Wrote to my father. Day very warm.

Tuesday, May 5th, 1863.

Marched at 4 P.M. 9 miles to-wards Vicksburg. Encamped near a bayou which is bridged by an excellent wire suspension bridge. Country is very hilly and is mostly cultivated. Day very warm.

Wednesday, May 6th (1863).

5 of our ambulances were captured yesterday near Port Gibson. We marched 8 miles back to-wards Port Gibson then marched back to camp road very dusty. Day cool and pleasant.

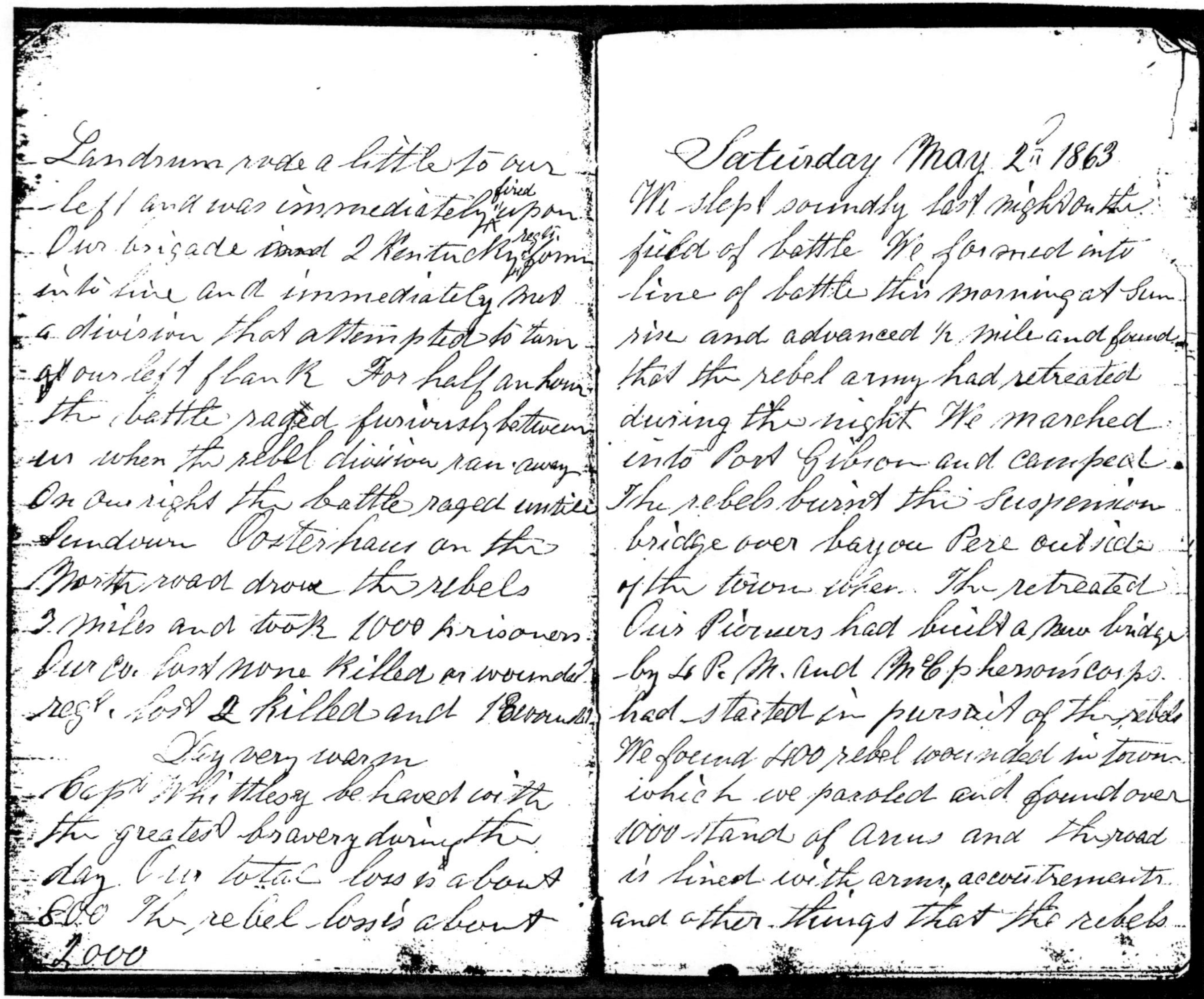

Saturday May 2nd 1863

Thursday, May 7th, 1863.

Marched at 3 A.M. and camped within 5 miles of Big Black River. Road very dusty. Day cool and pleasant. We eat our last rations for breakfast. Tonight we feel anxious for more.

Friday, May 8th, 1863.

We received some flour today. We were reviewed by Maj. Gen. Grant. Day very warm.

Saturday, May 9th, (1863).

Warm.

Sunday, May 10th, (1863).

Marched 8 miles towards Jackson to-day. Land mostly cultivated. Train arrived from Grand Gulf loaded with ammunition. Day warm. Water scarce.

Monday, May 11th (1863).

Very warm.

Tuesday, May 12th (1863).

Marched at 5 A.M. and halted about an hour near the Mile Creek. Then moved about one mile to the edge of a wood and camped. Day very warm road dusty. Our advance had a sharp skirmish here this morning.

Wed. May 13th, 1863.

Marched at 5 A.M. towards Raymond. We passed within 3/4 of a mile of the rebel line of battle. They thought that we were going to attack them untill after we had passed them when they attacked our rear and were repulsed. The main body of our army is marching on Jackson the Capitol of the State. Our Corps was sent round this way to deceive the enemy. Sherman's Corps defeated the enemy at Raymond yesterday. Rained hard for 2 hours of the afternoon wetting everything. Our train arrived at 8. We pulled down a board fence and built huts with the board and slept till morning.

Thursday, May 14th (1863).

Marched to Raymond 5 miles. Found Osterhaus' division there. We continued our march to Mississippi Springs when we halted 2 hours in a large house that sheltered 2 regiments. These are mineral springs and have been a place of resort for the Southern Gentry. The Hotel is large enough to accomodate nearly 500 guests. The houses are poor and the grounds are not ornamented but we were glad to gain the shelter of the houses from the furious rain storm that raged all forenoon. At 2 P.M. we continued our march towards Jackson. The roar of Artillery was incessant from 10 Oclock to 2 towards Jackson. We met an aide camp when within 7 miles of Jackson. He stated that the city was taken. We then halted and camped for the night. We took 400 prisoners and 17 cannon. To-days march was the severest of the Campaign. Rain fell in torrents all day. The roads were knee deep with mud in some places yet we marched at least 20 miles and would have marched 7 miles farther to Jackson cheerfully if our presence had been needed there. We have been on short rations since we left Port Gibson receiving little more than we could gather upon the march.

Friday, May 15th, 1863.

We marched back to Raymond and camped 2 miles from it towards Cham(p)ion Hill. Day pleasant.

Saturday, May 16th, 1863.

We marched at 6 towards Champion Hill. A heavy cannonade soon commenced about 5 miles off on our left at 9 A.M. Skirmishing commenced in our front. Hovey's Division was formed in line. Osterhaus went in next. Carr's div. in reserve. At noon the firing was terrific. The Artillery was sent back to us. They said that they could not use the cannon. At 2 P.M. Carr's div. went forward except our regiment that was left to guard the Artillery. Blairs and Smiths divisions now went forward at 4. We were relieved by the 17 Wis. Infantry and we went forward with 4 batteries of Artillery. The battle was fought in a growth of underbrush and timber on a succession of narrow ravines and ridges where a person could not see over 100 feet in advance. After the Rebels were drove from their position the(y) fled. Our div. in close pursuit. We followed them to Edwards Station. The road was st(r)ewed with dead and wounded men broken wagons, horses, Cannon and all kinds of small arms that the rebels threw away in their flight. Even the letters from their friends were cast away to lighten them in their retreat. There was a great many explosions to-wards Black River during the night. The battle between those engaged to-day was very severe. Hovey's division is badly cut up. I hear his loss is at least 1600. We took 37 pieces of cannon and a large number of prisoners. The killed and wounds is not far from 3000 aside. We found some corn meal and bacon at Edwards Station where we made some porridge. It was the first that we eat to-day. Day very warm.

Morning Thursday May 14th
Marched to Raymond 5 miles
Several Osterhaus division
then. We continued our march
to Mississippi Springs then
we halted 2 hours a large
house that sheltered 2 regiments
These are Mineral Springs and
have been a place of resort for
the Southern Gentry. the hotel
is large enough to accommodate
nearly 500 guests the houses are
poor and the grounds are not
ornamented but we were glad
to gain the shelter of the houses
from the furious rain storm
that raged all afternoon
at 3 P.M. we continued our
march towards Jackson
the river of on the Muddy water

incessant from 10 o'clock
to 1 towards Jackson. We met
an advance camp taken within
Miles of Jackson he stated
that the city was taken. We
then halted and camped for
the night. We too took prisoners
and 18 cannon. To days March
was the severest of the campaign
rain fell in torrents all day the
roads were three deep with mud
in some places. yet we marched
over 20 miles and arrived
have marched 5 miles farther
to Jackson cheerfully if our
presence had been needed then
We have been an hour picturing
since we left Port Gibson
declaring little march then
we could get farther to march

Sunday, May 17th, 1863.

Reveilee at 2 and marched at 3 at sunrise the skirmishing commenced when we continued to advance slowly untill within 1/2 of Big Black River bridge when we found the rebels were strongly entrenched at the bridge. Our brigade was formed in line on the right of the road our regt. in advance. We threw off our knapsacks and advanced through the timber and soon came in sight of the entrenchments. Each flank of them ran to the river and fields of at least 300 yards breath (sic) in front of their works. It was a very strong position. As we came out of the timber in to the open field the rebels rose up from behind their works and poured a volley into us. One man was instantly killed and Capt. Hough mortally wounded. Towards the bridge our regiment changed front to the right and charged on the brigade formed there. Some swam the river. We took 1705 of them prisoners and one stand of colors and brought them all of(f) the field. It is Greens' Missouri brigade the(y) were armed with new Enfield rifles. We had the old muskets which we threw down and marched three times our own number of Prisoners off the field with their own arms. The whole rebel line was now charged and taken but the(y) succeeded in destroying the bridges which took all of the afternoon for us to replace them. Our total loss is not over 300. While we took over 3000 prisoners and 17 cannon from the enemy. Day very warm during the afternoon our brigade was detailed to gather up the arms off the battle field.

Monday, May 18th, 1863.

Our Co. lost none killed or wounded yesterday. Our regt. only lost 2 killed and 12 wounded. The dead are being buried to-day. At sunset we marched across Big Black River and camped on the West side. Our brigade is the rear guard of the army. Haines Bluff was taken to-day by Sherman's Corps. Day very warm.

Tuesday, May 19th (1863).

Marched at 7 A.M. towards Vicksburg. A heavy cannonade is going on in that direction. We arrived in front of their entrenchments at 2 1/2 P.M. and rested about 3/4 mile from their breastworks behind a ridge. The breastworks are on the top of a succession of ridges and will be difficult to take. At 4 P.M. we marched about 3 miles to the left and remained there all night. Day very warm.

Wednesday, May 20th, 1863.

Marched towards the center this morning and drew up beside a seige battery as its suppor(t). We are about 400 yards to the left of the Rail Way and about 1/2 mile from the rebel forts. Day very warm.

Thursday, May 21st, 1863.

After dark last night we moved for within 600 yards of Fort Beauregard and worked all night making a rifle pit at day light this morning the pit was large enough to conceal the regiment. At day light the rebels discovered us and commenced to load their cannon but we sent such a shower of rifle bullets through their embrasures that they could not fire a single shot from their cannon all day. While our batteries poured an incessant stream of shot and shell into their work all day. We received full rations of bread today for the first in 3 weeks. Day very warm. We had 2 wounded to-day.

Friday, May 22d, 1863.

Our Brigade moved forward about 400 yards at daylight this morning. The Rebel works are in the form of a Crescent with a fort on each wing and one in the center. A ridge runs along from wing to wing like the string of a cross bow behind this ridge we were formed. The 21st and 22d. Iowa on our right and the 97th Ill. Infantry in our rear as our support. At 10 A.M. the charge was sounded when we fixed bayonets and charged the Iowa regiments charged on the fort to our right and our regt. charged the center fort. The 97th ran away and left us. We crossed the ridge and crossed the ravine and ascended the ridge to the rebel forts about 450 yards under a front and enfilading fire on both flank of Infantry and Artillery. Our men fell at every step. We then had not more than 300 men left in our regiment. We sheltered ourselves in ruts that the heavy rains had made on the hill side and there we opened fire on the enemy and we soon beat them down where they would load their pieces and hold up their arms and fire over their breast works without exposing their bodies. We then fired at their arms. Our Artillery threw shell over our heads all day which burst over our heads and the fragments fell inside of the rebel works. We we (sic) thus 10 hours in the midst of a continued storm of Musketry and Artillery and bursting shell. At dark we were ordered to return to our rifle pit which we done bringing off nearly all of our wounded. Our Co. has lost 4 killed and 15 wounded out of 32 who charged and our regiment has lost 18 killed and 106 wounded out of 400 who charged in the morning. the dead are left on the field of battle. Our Capt. is killed and 2d Lt. wounded. Day very warm untill 2 P.M. when a smart shorter of rain fell that cooled the atmosphere very much.

Saturday, May 23d, 1863.

A flag of truce was sent over to the rebels. They fired on it and the officers returned. Day pretty warm.

Wednesday May 20th 1863

Thursday May 21st 1863

Friday May 22nd 1863

Sunday, May 24th (1863).

We were making rifle pits all night. Wrote to my father at dark our Co. was sent to drive in the rebel Picquets and bury the dead. We went near the picquets and were fired on and returned when we were put on picquet all night. Day very warm.

Monday, May 25th, 1863.

A flag of truce came over from the rebels. I took 3 men and went over and buryed our dead. Festus Daily, Jacob A. Michael and Jacob Langennachard. There was no firing untill dark. Day very warm.

Tuesday, May 26th, 1863.

Very warm. Lay all of last under arms in the rifle pits.

Wednesday, May 27th, 1863.

I am 27 years of age to-day. The gunboats have bombarded the enemy furiously all day. Day very warm.

Thursday, May 28th, 1863.

Received a letter from my sister and one from Uncle George. Day very warm.

Friday, May 29th, 1863.

A heavy cannonade commenced at 6 this morning along our entire line and continued untill 6 1/2. Every gun was loaded and fired as fast as the gunmen were able to fire them. Feel very unwell today. There was a smart shower of rain during the afternoon.

Saturday, May 30th, 1863.

Went to our division hospital to-day and went to Corps head qrs. and obtained a leave of absence for Lt. Law. The total loss of our Corps since we crossed the river April 30th is 1235. Day very warm.

Sunday, May 31st, 1863.

Went to division hospital. Wrote to my father. Day very warm. Siege continues regul(ar)ly.

Monday, June 1st, 1863.

Went over to the 23d. Wis. Day very warm.

Tuesday, June 2d, 1863.

Gov. Salamon and Adjt. Gen. Gaylord of Wis. arrived in our camp today. They came to care for the sick and wounded of our state. All of our sick and wounded have been sent to Gen. Hospital. Day cool and pleasant. Siege continues regularly.

Wednesday, June 3d, 1863.

Went to the 6th Wis. battery. The rebels fired a good many shell over us today, without doing us any damage. Our Co. is on picquet to-night. Day very warm.

Thursday, June 4th, 1863.

2 deserters came in this morning. They give a dolefull account of affairs in Vicksburg. Our baggage and sick men arrived from Grand Gulf. Day very warm.

Friday, June 5th, 1863.

We were mustered today by Maj. Platt for March and April. Day warm.

Saturday, June 6th, (1863).

Made out our muster rolls to-day. Day warm.

Sunday, June 7th, (1863).

Very warm.

Monday, June 8th, (1863).

Dr. Boyce of our Regiment has resigned. We now have 2 lines of rifle pits round the enemies works and we have batteries planted on every little eminence along the lines. Day very warm.

Tuesday, June 9th (1863)

Another deserter came over last night. Co. is on picquet. Day very warm.

Wed. June 10th, 1863.

Col. Harris left us for Wis. to-day on sick leave of absence. Charles Baywater was wounded this morning while eating breakfast. Rain has been falling all day.

Monday June 1st 1863

West over to the 23rd Wis. Day very warm

Tuesday June 2nd

Gov. Salomon and Adjt. Genl. Gaylord of Wis. arrived in our camp to day, they came to care for the sick and wounded of our state. All of our sick and wounded have been sent to Genl. hospital.

Day cool and pleasant siege continues regularly.

Wednesday June 3rd 1863

Went to the 6th Wis. battery the rebels fired a good many shell over into to day. without doing us any damage. Rebels in in prospect to enjoy. Day very warm

Thursday June 4th

Rebels came in this morning they give a — full account of affairs in Vicksburg river across from Grand Gulf.

Day very warm

Friday May 29th 1863

A heavy cannonade commenced at 6 this morning along our entire line and continued until 6½ every gun was loaded and fired as fast as the gunner were able to fire them feel very unwell today there was a almost shower of rain along the afternoon

Saturday May 30th

Went to our division hospital to day and went to Corps head quarters and obtained a leave of absence for S. Law. The total body of our corps since we crossed the river April 30th is 11,235. Day very warm

Sunday May 31st 1863

Went to division hospital to see my father Day very warm Siege continues regularly

Thursday, June 11th, 1863.

On Picquet today. Day cloudy.

Friday, June 12th (1863)

The rebels opened a battery of 8 large guns upon us this morning. They were soon silenced by our batteries. Regiment went to the rear to wash. Day very warm.

Saturday, June 13th (1863)

Wrote to my father. All has been quiet along the lines. To-day hot.

Sunday, June 14th (1863)

There was a sharp action on our right and center to-day. Received a letter from my sister. Day hot.

Monday, June 15th (1863)

On fatigue duty last night. The rebels opened two new batteries on us this morning without doing us any damage. Day very warm.

Tuesday, June 16th 1863.

On Picquet in the advance rifle pit. At 4 P.M. the Rebels threw a shell into our rifle pit which burst within 6 feet of me. Corpl. Tiernan was mortally wounded by it and Corpl. Fisher and myself were knocked down by it but were not much hurt. Day very warm.

Wednesday June 17th (1863)

2, 8 inch Columbiads were put in position here to-day. I made out the Descriptive rolls of our Sick and wounded men. Day very warm.

Thursday June 18th, 1863.

There was a large fire in Vicksburg last night. We worked all night in an approach to Fort Beauregard. We worked within 40 feet of the rebel Picquet. Day very warm.

Friday, June 19th, 1863.

Regiment march 2 miles to the rear to a pond and washed our clothes. I received a letter from my sister. Day very hot.

Saturday, June 20th, (1863)

A heavy bombardment was kept up from 4 A.M. to 11 A.M. Day very warm.

Sunday, June 21st (1863).

Day warm. The enemy has not replied to our fire with artillery during the last 48 hours. Our approaches are made nearer to their works every night.

Monday, June 22d, 1863.

Our regiment was paid for March and April today. Day hot.

Tuesday, June 23d (1863).

Lieut. Law of our Co. is dead. On Patrol last night. Wrote to my brother James. Day very warm.

Wednesday, June 24th, (1863).

A brisk action of 1/2 hours duration occured on our left last night. The mortar boats shelled the town all night. Rained all night. To-day is cloudy.

Thursday, June 25th (1863)

All of our troops were moved into the rifle pits at 2 P.M. and a heavy fire of Artillery and Infantry was opened on the enemy. A fort in front of Logan's division was blown up and all of its garrison killed except a negro who was sent 300 feet through the air and alighted in our rifle pit. He say that he was working in the fort when the mine was lighted and he asked a white man where they were going and the next moment he was blown into our rifle pit. Four regiments of our troops charged on the rifle pits adjoining the destroyed fort and held them an hour when they were driven out. A.L. Stroud was wounded to-day. Day very warm.

Friday, June 26th (1863).

Lay all of last night under arms in the advance rifle pit. Our gun and mortar boats have poured a continuous shower of shell into their forts during the last 36 hours. Day very warm.

Saturday, June 27th, 1863.

I drew clothing for the co. to-day. Day very warm.

Saturday June 27th 1863

I have nothing for this to day

Sunday June 28th warm

Day very warm

Monday " 29th "

Tuesday " 30th "

Wednesday July 1st 1863

Sergt Maj Dudley the Thurman received
his commission as Capt of our company

To day Day very warm

Thursday July 2nd 1863

It were were up till midnight
And got our days rations and
fell in ready for an inspection and
On marched towards Big Blackriver
We halted at 5 P.M. and eat breakfast
and rested until 11 when we com-
menced our march 6 miles farther
This the hottest day that ever

Friday July 3rd 1863

We returned to camp and rested
nearly a much in the hot sun we
also yesterday all was intollerable
hot as was in camp A flag of truce
offered to surrender and asked that
commissioners might be exchanged
to draw up the terms of capitulation
Gen Grant refused all but an unconditional surrender Gen Pemberton tha
requested an interview with Gen Grant
which Grant readily granted. they

saw a great many of our regiment was
Churchdieut in never suffered much
from heat and fatigue before as to day
Gen Pawk did not seem enough
We camped in the most beautiful
meadow that I ever saw

Sunday, June 28th.
    Warm

Monday, " 29th
    Warm

Tuesday, " 30th
    Warm

Wednesday, July 1st, 1863.
    Sergt. Maj. Dudley C. Wyman received his commission as Capt. of our company to-day. Day very warm.

Thursday, July 2d, 1863.
    We were woke up at midnight and took one day's rations and 80 rounds of ammunition and marched towards Big Black River. We halted at 5 A.M. and eat breakfast and rested untill 11 when we continued our march 6 miles farther. This is the hottest day that I ever saw. A great many of our regiment was sunstruck. We never suffered so much from heat and fatigue before as to-day. Gen. Lawler did not rest enough. We camped in the most beautiful meadow that I ever saw.

Friday July 3d, 1863.
    We returned to camp and suffered nearly as much in the heat as we done yesterday. All was still when we arrived in camp A flag of Truce had arrived from the rebels which offered to surrender and asked that commissioners might be appointed to draw up the terms of capitulation. Gen. Grant refused all but an unconditional surrender. Gen. Pemberton then requested an interview with Gen. Grant which Grant readily granted. They met midway between the lines Grant smoking a cigar during the interview. It was agreed between them that Gen. Pemberton would march out the garrison and stack their arms outside of their works at 10 A.M. tomorrow, the Anniversary of our Independence. The generals seperated and all was quiet during the night.

Saturday, July 4th, 1863.

Our Co. are on rear Picquet guard. Vicksburg was surrendered to-day at 11 A.M. The garrison numbers about 32,000 men and there are 227 pieces of cannon in the fortification and 60,000 stand of small arms. The taking of Vicksburg is the most important victory of the war. Received a letter from my mother. We are ordered to be ready to march tomorrow morning at 4 A.M. for Jackson. Wrote to my mother. Day very warm.

Sunday, July 5th, 1863.

Marched at 6 along the Rail Road towards Black River bridge where we arrived at 2 P.M. Day very warm.

Monday, July 6th (1863)

Remained in camp untill 4 P.M. when we marched across the river and camped near Edwards Station. The Rail Road track has been destroyed here for three miles by the rebels. Day very warm.

Tuesday, July 7th (1863).

Marched at 7 towards Jackson. Road very dusty. Marched 13 miles and camped.

Wednesday, July 8th (1863).

There was the greatest storm of rain, thunder, lightning here last night that I ever witnessed. We marched at 5 P.M. and camped at 10 P.M. having marched 5 miles. Day very warm.

Thursday, July 9th (1863).

Marched through Clinton and camped within a few miles of Jackson. Day very warm.

Friday, July 10th (1863).

Arrived in front of the rebel works at Jackson. Day very warm.

Saturday, July 11th (1863).

Some of our batteries were planted to-day and shelled their works. They replied with their artillery. Co. B. lost 2 killed and one wounded to-day. The rebels made three charges and were repulsed every time. Day very warm.

Wednesday July 8th
There was the greatest storm of rain
Thunder & Lightning here last
night that I ever witnessed.
We marched at 5 P.M. and camped
at 10 P.M. having marched 5 mile
Day very warm

Thursday July 9th
Marched through Clinton and
camped within a few miles of
Jackson. Day very warm

Friday July 10th
Arrived in front of the rebel works
at Jackson. Day very warm

Saturday July 11th
Some of our batteries were planted
to-day and shelled their works. They
replied with their artillery &c.
Had 2 killed and one wounded to-day.

The rebels made three charges and
were repulsed every time.
Day very warm

Sunday July 12th
We formed in line with a strong
force of skirmishers in front We
advanced 1 mile and came in sight
of the rebel works our artillery were
then put in position and a sharp
artillery duel was fought during the
afternoon Gen Lauman ran into
to-do an ambuscade and his division
badly cut up. I hear that our
forces have gained a decided victory
at Helena Ark. Water is very scarce
Here each company has a mule
and one man detailed to carpenter
to the respective companies
Day very warm

Sunday, July 12 (1863).

We formed in line with a strong force of skirmishers in front. We advanced 1/2 mile and came in sight of the rebel works. Our Artillery were then put in position and a sharp artillery duel was fought during the afternoon. Gen. Lauman ran his div. into an ambuscade and his division is badly cut up. I hear that our forces have gained a decided victory at Helena, Ark. Water is very scarce here. Each company has a mule and one man detailed to carry water to their respective companies. Day very warm.

Monday, July 13th, 1863.

We pulled down the houses on Lynches' plantation and built breast works. There was a sharp action in the afternoon without any decisive result. Day very warm.

Tuesday, July 14th, (1863).

There was a truce from 2 P.M. to 4 and by agreement each side was to remain within their respective lines but the curiosity of some of our boys led them out towards the rebels breastworks and were fired upon by the rebels. Our men returned the fire. Several little fights of this kind occured. On Picquet today. Day cloudy but warm.

Wednesday, July 15th (1863).

Received a letter from my sister. Wrote to my father. Day warm.

Thursday, July 16th, 1863.

A sharp fight occured on our front and left. Regt. lost none. Day very warm.

Friday, July 17th (1863).

We found this morning that the rebels had evacuated their works during the night. We marched over to the city and we found that their works were well planned and well made. The rebels burnt the houses of all of the Unionists before they retreated. Over one hundred woman and children were wandering in the streets when we entered the city the soldiers set fire to the town in a number of places. The officers detailed several regiments and made every effort to extinguish the flames but without effect. By sunset nearly all of the city and suburbs were in ashes. Day very warm. The rebel army retreated across Pearl River and they buried torpeadoes by the way. Some of our men were killed and wounded by their explosions.

Saturday, July 18th, 1863.

   The city continued to burn all night. Marched about 5 miles South and tore up the track of the Rail Road burnt the ties and heated and bent the rails. Afternoon rainey.

Sunday, July 19th (1863).

   Continued to tear up the track and destroy it all day. Day very warm.

Monday, July 20th, 1863.

   Ret. to camp near Jackson. Day very warm.

Tuesday, July 21st, 1863.

   Marched at 8 A.M. and camped at Raymond at sunset having marched 18 miles. Road very dusty. Day very warm.

Wednesday, July 22d (1863).

   Marched to and camped at Bakers Creek 12 miles. There was a heavy shower of rain at evening.

Thursday, July 23d (1863).

   Marched at 7 A.M. and camped within 6 miles of Vicksburg. There was a heavy shower of rain in afternoon.

Friday July 24th (1863).

   Marched to our old camp at Vicksburg. Then marched in search of a camp south of the town. Our officers lost their way and after marching till 4 P.M. we marched into the Town of Vicksburg and camped on the river bank. Day very warm. It just lacks 2 days of being 3 most since we crossed the Mississippi River at Bruinsburg. During that time we have slept with our clothes on and our guns loaded by our sides every night untill tonight.

Saturday, July 25th, 1863.

   Our tents and baggage arrived and we are in our tents again for the first time in three months. Day very warm.

By sunset nearly all of the city had sunk down here in to the
river.

Day very warm.
The rebel army retreated across
the river, and they burned
the bridges by the river. some of
our men re took on the railroad
by their expression.

Saturday July 18th 1863
The city commenced the funeral
last marched about 5 miles
south and tore up the track of
the Rail Road burnt the Road
heaters and burnt tents the rails

Afternoon Rainy
Sunday July 19th
Continued to tear up the track
destroyed it all the day very warm
Monday July 20th 1863
Day very warm.

Tuesday July 21st 1863
Arrived marched at 8 A.M. and camped
at Raymond at sunset having
marched 15 miles marching day by
day very warm

Wednesday July 22nd
Marched to and camped at Bolton
over 14 miles there was a heavy
shower of rain at Evening

Thursday July 23rd
Marched at 4 A.M. and marched
within 6 miles of Vicksburg, then
was a heavy shower when in afternoon

Friday July 24th
Marched down railroad at morning
then marched in march to a camp
within by the town. Our officers lost
their way and got marching till
late this we marched into town

Sunday, July 26th (1863).

Wrote to my father. Made out the inventories and final statements of the deceased men of our Co^{1}y. There was a heavy rain during the afternoon.

Monday, July 27th, 1863.

Merit Whitmore was hurt last night by an axe flying off its helve and hit him on the head last night rainey. To-day is very hot.

Tuesday, July 28th (1863).

Moved camp to the bluff south of the town. Afternoon rainy.

July 29th, 30th and 31st.

Very warm.

Saturday, Aug. 1st, 1863.

Our division is ordered to Natchez. Day very warm. There are severer (sic) Negro regiments here. A great deal of sickness prevails amongst them.

Sunday, August 2d, 1863.

Wrote to my Sister. Day very warm.

Monday, August 3d (1863).

Day oppressively hot.

Tuesday, August 4th (1863).

Received a letter from my sister. Day very warm.

Wed. August 5th (1863).

We were paid for May and June. Inspection by Corps inspector. Day very warm.

Thursday, Aug. 6th (1863).

Battallion drill in afternoon. Day very warm.

Friday, Aug. 7th (1863).

Sickness is increasing among the troop here. Chronic Diarreha and Bilious fever are the prevailing complaints. Day very warm.

Saturday, Aug. 8th, 1863.

Very warm.

Sunday, Aug. 9th (1863). Monday 10th and Tuesday 11th.

Very warm.

Wednesday Aug. 12th (1863).

Feel very unwell to-day. Day very warm.

Thursday, Aug. 13th (1863).

At 1 P.M. we were ordered to pack up and at 5 P.M. we went on board of the steam boat Autocrat and sailed down the river at 8 P.M. Day very warm.

Friday, Aug. 14th (1863).

Arrived at Natchez at 8 A.M. and remained there untill 10 A.M. and then sailed down the river. Natchez is built on a high bluff and little of the town can be seen from the river. Those who went on shore report it to be a very pretty town. About 5 P.M. a barge which was loaded with Gov. wagons, Sutlers goods &c. and was towed by one of our Marine boats struck a snag and stove its bows. We lay too and lowered the boats and recovered most of the cargo. Day very warm. Tied up to the river bank all night.

Saturday, Aug. 15th (1863).

Sailed at day light and passed Port Hudson at 7 A.M. We saw a number of large batteries but we did not land. I saw the first alligator to-day that I ever saw. He followed our boat a little way. We passed Baton Rouge the capitol of Louisiana at 3 P.M. The capitol and assylum for the blind are beautiful houses as seen from the river. We arrived at Carrollton at 9 P.M. There was several thunder showers during the afternoon. The country from Baton Rouge to Carrollton (about 100 miles) is the richest and most beautiful that I ever saw. It is a succession of sugar plantations on each side of the river with beautifull houses all of the way. The plantations are lower than the river and are protected from inundation by large artificial banks of earth called Levees.

Sunday August 2d 1863
Wrote to my sister day
very warm

Monday August 3d
Day unusually hot

Tuesday August 4th
Received a letter from my
sister Day very warm

Wed. August 5th
We were paid for May and
June Inspection by Corps
inspector Day very warm

Thursday Aug. 6th
Battalion drill in of forenoon
Day very warm

Friday Aug. 7th
Sickness is unreasing among
the troops here. Chronic Diarrhea
and Bilious fever are the prevailing complaints Day very warm

---

Saturday Aug. 8th 1863
very warm

Sunday Aug 9th
Monday 10th and Tuesday 11th
Very warm

Wednesday Aug. 12th
feel very unwell to-day
Day very warm

Thursday Aug. 13th
At 7 P.M. we were ordered to pack
up and at 9.5 P.M. we went on
board of the steam boat Autocrat
and sailed down the river till 8
P.M. Day very warm

Friday Aug. 14th
Arrived at Natchez at 8 A.M. and
remained there until 10 A.M.
and then sailed down the river
Natchez is built on a high bluff

Sabbath Aug. 16th, 1863.

We landed at Carrollton at 9 A.M. and remained there untill evening when we marched and camped about one mile from town. The men drank pretty freely of Lager Beer during the day and several fights occured. A(ll) kinds of eatables are for sale and cheap a not very common thing to us. For we have been skinned by the Sutler's during the last 2 years. Carrollton contains perhaps 2000 inhabitants. Its site is lower than the bed of the river and it is protected from inundation by a levee. The town contains many beautiful residences and gardens. It was a place of resort for the gentry of New Orleans before the war commenced. Day very warm.

Monday, Aug. 17th, 1863.

One of Co. F. was shot dead last night by one of the Provost guard. Day very warm.

Tuesday, Aug. 18th (1863).

I went to New Orleans this morning and rambled over a good deal of the city. There was a fleet of men of war and some merchant vessels in the port. The city is very clean and contains some beautiful residences. The houses are mostly two and 3 stories high. The streets are narrow but the cleanness of the city gives it a very good appearance. Canal Street is one of the finest in the world. A Bronze Statue of Henry Clay is in this street. There is a Bronze Statue of Gen. Jackson in Jackson Square by the Cathedral.

The Custom House is yet unfinished. It is very large and is built of Granite. It is used for a prison at present. The Medical College and Marine Hospital a good buildings. We returned to Carrollton at evening having spent the day very pleasantly.

Wednesday, Aug. 19th, 1863.

Day wet and rainy.

Thursday, Aug. 20th (1863)

Day wet and rainy.

Friday, Aug. 21st (1863).

Very sick today. Day very warm.

Saturday, 22d. Aug. 1863.

This army corps was reviewed by Maj. Gen. today. Day very warm. I am sick to-day. Day very warm.

Sunday, Aug. 23d (1863).

Troops continue to arrive from Vicksburg. Very sick yet. Day very warm.

Monday, Aug. 24th (1863).

I feel better today. Day warm.

Tuesday, Aug. 25th (1863).

Received a letter from my sister. Making out our muster rolls. Day very warm.

Wednesday, Aug. 26th, 1863.

Day very warm.

Thursday, Aug. 27th (1863).

Finished the muster and Pay rolls. Day very warm.

Friday, Aug. 28th (1863).

Went to New Orleans to-day. Day cool and pleasant.

Saturday, Aug. 29th. 30th and 31st (1863).

Very warm.

Tuesday, Sept. 1st, 2d and 3d. (1863).

Very warm. Lt. Northup of Co. F. died to-day of congestive chill.

Friday, Sept. 4th (1863).

We struck tents and marched to the Champ de. Mars at 9 A.M. and were reviewed there by Maj. Gens. Grant and Banks. Gen. Grant was received with three rousing cheers by the troops. We marched to the boat from the review ground and were taken and landed at Algiers opposite New Orleans where we took the cars and went to Bayou Boeuf where we bivoucked at midnight. Day pleasant.

Wednesday Aug. 26th 1863
Day very pleasant

Thursday Aug. 27th
Finished the Muster and Pay
rolls Day very pleasant

Friday Aug. 28th
Finished the Muster and Pay
rolls Day very pleasant
Thursk it hurt Orders to-day
Day Cool and pleasant

Saturday Aug. 29th 30th
and 31st very cooler

Tuesday Sep. 1st, 2nd and 3rd
very warmer
A about to-day of congestive fever

Friday Sep. 4th
The think tents and marched to
the church De. than at 9 A.M.
and were received here by Maj.
Genl. Grand and Ban of Genl.
Grand was received with

three morning cheer by the troops
He marched to the boat form the
review General and were taken
and landed at Algien opposite
New Orleans where we took the
Cars and went to Bayou Boug
Where we bivouacked at Midnight
Day pleasant

Saturday Sep. 5th 1863
Genl. Grant was reviews by his troops
getting at New Orleans by a fall
form his horse Day very warm

Sunday Sep. 6th
Rained all afternoon

Monday Sep. 7th
Received a little from Day inter
Day very warm

Tuesday Sep. 8th
Wrote to Big Sister Day warm

Saturday, Sept. 5th, 1863.

Gen. Grant was seriously injured yesterday at New Orleans by a fall from his horse. Day very warm.

Sunday, Sept. 6th (1863).

Rained all afternoon.

Monday, Sept. 7th (1863).

Day very warm.

Tuesday, Sept. 8th (1863).

Wrote to my Sister. Day warm.

Wednesday, Sept. 9th, 1863.

Very unwell. Day very warm.

Thursday, Sept. 10th, (1863).

The country along Bayou Boeuff is low, The soil is rich and the principal product is sugar. The water of the Bayou is very bad. It is almost bitter. The plantations have mostly been confiscated and are worked by lessees of the government. Day very warm.

Friday, Sept. 11th (1863).

Marched 7 miles to and camped at Brashear City. Water is very scarce and weather very warm.

Saturday, Sept. 12th (1863).

The men are mostly fishing for crab fish in the Bayou. Day pretty warm.

Sunday, Sept. 13th (1863).

A detail of 200 men who were unloading commisary stores at the R.R. depot last night. Broke open some Sutler shops and took Beer and Whiskey. 40 of them have been arrested. Col. Whittlesy left us for Wis. on furlough. Day pleasant.

Monday, Sept. 14th (1863). Tuesday 15th, Wednesday 16th, Thursday 17th.

Weather pleasant.

Friday, Sept. 18th (1863).
Lt. Wynn returned to Co. to-day.

Saturday, Sept. 19th (186^).
Our army corps. is crossing Berwick Bay to Berwick. Day cool and pleasant.

Sunday, Sept. 20th, 1863.
Day cool and pleasant.

Monday, Sept. 21st (1863).
Maj. Gen. Washburne came to see our regiment on Dress Parade. Day cool and pleasant.

Tuesday, Sept. 22d, 1863 and Wednesday, Sept. 23d.
Pleasant.

Thursday, Sept. 24th (1863).
We sent our baggage to Berwick. Day pleasant.

Friday, Sept. 25th (1863).
We crossed Berwick Bay to Berwick and camped about 1 mile from Berwick. Day pleasant.

Saturday, Sept. 26th (1863).
Water is very scarce and sickness is on the increase. Day pleasant.

Sunday, Sept. 27th, 1863.
A runaway horse ran through our ranks while on parade yesterday and injured Merit Whitmore of our Co. severely. Day cloudy.

Monday, Sept. 28th (1863).
Very unwell. Wrote to my father. Day cloudy.

Tuesday, Sept. 29th (1863).
Rained hard all night and has continued during to-day. Feel very unwell to-day.

Sunday
Wednesday Sept. 24th 1863
? marched away three miles then
Night the rattle while on parade
this day and injured them if will
- have been severely

Day cloudy
Wednesday Sept 18th
very ... wrote to my
father Day cloudy
Tuesday Sept 24th
rained had all Richmond has
returned during today feel
very unwell to-day
Wednesday Sept 90th
Rained the greater part of last
night and to-day feel very unwell
to-day
Thursday Sept 1st 1863
Capt. Forward, Baker and Parks

Day at Berwick Day cool and pleasant
Sunday Sept 20th 1863
Day cool and pleasant
Monday Sept 21st
Brig. Gen. Washburne came to re-
-view regiment no Dress Parade
Day cool and pleasant
Tuesday Sept 22nd 1863 and
Wednesday 23rd present
Thursday Sept 24th
We sent our baggage to Berwick
Day pleasant
Friday Sep 25th
We crossed Berwick Bay to Berwick
and camped about 1 mile
from Berwick Day pleasant
Saturday Sept 26th
Water is very scarce and sickness
is on the increase Day pleasant

Wednesday, Sept. 30th (1863).

Rained the greater part of last night and today. Feel very unwell to-day.

Thursday, Sept. 1st (1863).

Corpls. Farwell, Baker and Parks who were wounded at Vicksburg returned to the company. Day showery.

Friday, Oct. 2d, 1863.

Received a letter from my Mother. We are ordered to march tomorrow. Day pleasant.

Saturday, Oct. 3d (1863).

Marched at 6 A.M. and marched about 14 miles nearly West. We passed a rebel fort and the hull of a rebel gunboat that the rebels had burnt and placed across the bayou to obstruct the passage by boats but it does not quite reach across the Bayou. Bayou Teche is the name of this Bayou an(d) it is about 300 feet wide here. Day pleasant.

Sunday, Oct. 4th, 1863.

Marched at 6 1/2 A.M. Our Co. is rear guard. We camped at Franklin having marched 12 miles. This country is well improved. Sugar is the principal product but few of the plantations are worked. Day pleasant.

Monday, Oct. 5th (1863).

Marched 12 miles up Bayou Teche. Day pleasant.

Tuesday, Oct. 6th (1863).

Marched at 6 A.M. and camped near New Iberia having marched 12 miles. Day pleasant. Country around is mostly prairie.

Wednesday, Oct. 7th (1863).

Wrote to my mother. Day pleasant.

Thursday, Oct. 8th, 1863.

One of Co. B. was buried today. There is a great many mules, horses and cattle on the plantations here. Day pleasant.

Friday, Oct. 9th, 1863.

Marched at 6 to H. Martin's 15 miles and were appointed Provost guard and remained in town untill 4 P.M. when we marched 6 miles farther to a creek and camped. Day pleasant.

Saturday, Oct. 10th (1863).

We are 2 years in the U.S. service today. Marched to Vermillion Bayou 10 miles and camped there. We found the 19th army corps. Day pleasant.

Sunday, Oct. 11th, 1863.

The Bridge over the Bayou was burnt by the rebels. A new one is being built. Day pleasant.

Monday, Oct. 12th, 1863.

Dress parade. Day pleasant.

Tuesday, Oct. 13th (1863).

Col. Shunk of 1st Brigade was sent to New Orleans to-day under arrest for permitting his men to forage on their own account. We were inspected at Dress Parade this evening by Gen. Ord. Day pleasant.

Wednesday, Oct. 14th (1863), Thursday 15th & Friday 16th.

Pleasant.

Oct. 17th to 20th (1863).

Pleasant. Have been unwell during the time.

Wednesday, 21st & Thursday 22d (1863).

Pleasant. Lieut. Wynn resigned.

Friday, Oct. 23d, 1863.

Marched at 6 and marched 12 miles to Carrion Crow Bayou in the coldest rainstorm that I ever experienced.

Saturday, Oct. 24th, 1863.

Marched to Oupolousas (Opelousas) 10 miles. We passed the skeleton of a human being hanging to a tree. Day pleasant.

Sunday, Oct. 25th, 1863.

Pleasant. Some of our boys were taken by the rebel scouts to-day.

Monday, Oct. 26th, 1863.

We were inspected by Division inspector. Day pleasant.

Tuesday, Oct. 27th, 1863.

Marched back 12 miles to Grand Chataw Bayou. Day pleasant.

Wednesday, Oct. 28th, 1863.

Making out our muster rolls to-day. Day pleasant.

Thursday, Oct. 29th (1863).

Marched to Vermillion Bayou. Rained during the forenoon making the road very muddy. Mail arrived and we received some letters and papers.

Friday, Oct. 30th, 1863.

Marched to New Iberia 22 miles. Rained part of the afternoon.

Saturday, Oct. 31st, (1863).

Were mustered to-day by Col. Harris. Day pleasant.

Sunday, Nov. 1st, 1863.

A number of our men were arrested today for forageing and were compelled to carry they foraged all day under guard. Day pleasant.

Monday, Nov. 2d, 1863.

Pleasant.

Tuesday, Nov. 3d (1863).

Election to-day for the officers. Lewis Union received 264 votes in this regiment to 3 for the Copperhead. Day pleasant.

Wednesday, Nov. 4th (1863).

Wrote to my father. Day pleasant.

Thursday, Nov. 5th (1863).
>Sick with ague to-day. Day pleasant.

Friday, Nov. 6th, 1863.
>Marched 1 mile beyond the town and remained in line of battle untill 9 A.M. expecting an attack from the rebels when we camped. Day pleasant.

Saturday, Nov. 7th, 1863.
>Went to hospital at New Iberia and visited some acquaintances who are there wounded. Day pleasant.

Sunday, Nov. 8th (1863).
>Marched 24 miles towards Franklin. Day pleasant.

Monday, Nov. 9th (1863).
>Marched to within 6 miles of Berwick and camped. Pleasant

Tuesday, Nov. 10th (1863).
>Marched to Berwick. Day pleasant.

Wednesday, Nov. 11th, 1863.
>There was a hoar frost on the ground this morning. Day pleasant.

Thursday, Nov. 12th (1863).
>Received some letters from home. Day pleasant.

Friday, Nov. 13th (1863).
>A part of our 1st Brigade left on Gulf boats to-day. Day pleasant.

Saturday, Nov. 14th (1863).
>A part of our brigade left us for New Orleans today. Day pleasant.

Sunday, Nov. 15th (1863), & Monday Nov. 16th.
>Pleasant.

Bismarck and went by R.
R. to Algiers near New Orleans
Day Pleasant

Wednesday Nov 18th 1863
Here to New Orleans the
sugar and cotton trade
Learned very fast. &
Large amounts of cotton and
sugar is brought from the
back country Day Pleasant

Thursday Nov 19th
Regiment orders on board the
Steamboat R.C. tents and went
over to New Orleans and returns
to the wharf and foot of street
returns on board. A great
many went to the Theater
Wrote to my father
Day Pleasant

Wednesday Nov 11th 1863
There was to have first on
the ground this morning
Day Pleasant

Thursday Nov 12th
Received Minie letters
from home Day Pleasant

Friday Nov 13th
A part of our 1st Brigade
left on Gulf boats to the
Day Pleasant

Saturday Nov 14th
A part of our Brigade left
for New Orleans today
Day Pleasant

Sunday Nov 15th

Monday Nov 16th & 17th

Tuesday Nov 17th
We crossed the bay to

Tuesday, Nov. 17th (1863).

We crossed the bay to Berwick and went by R.R. to Algiers near New Orleans. Day pleasant.

Wednesday, Nov. 18th, 1863.

Went to New Orleans. The Sugar and Cotton trades seemed very brisk. A large amount of cotton and sugar is brought from the Teche Country. Day pleasant.

Thursday, Nov. 19th (1863).

Regiment went on board of the Steamboat T. A. SCOTT and sailed over to New Orleans and tied up to the wharf and took 50,000 rations on board. A good many went to the Theater. Wrote to my father. Day pleasant.

Friday, Nov. 20th, 1863.

'Tis 2 years to-day since we left Wis. Sailed down the river at 12 M. Day pleasant.

Saturday, Nov. 21st (1863).

Crossed the bar at the mouth of the Miss. River and were soon out of sight of land with a fine breeze of wind. The steamer commenced to role making a good many sick.

Sunday, Nov. 22d (1863).

Spied a vessel that tried to keep from us. We soon overhauled here. She proved to be a prize of our blocade squadron and is loaded with cotton. She is in charge of a prize crew and is bound for New Orleans.

Monday, Nov. 23d, 1863.

Arrived at the mouth of the Rio Grande at noon and found a large fleet of merchant ships at anchor outside of the bar. The water over the bar is so shallow that the vessels trading with Matamoras lay outside of the bar and the merchandize is carried over the bar in small steamboats. 2 Co. of our regiment and all but 4 men of our co. and myself were taken ashore in a small steamer. We must wait untill morning. The land looks sterile and sanday (sic). Sea is rough but no wind.

Tuesday, Nov. 24th, 1863.

A strong breeze spring up this morning which soon increased to a gale. We were compelled to weigh anchor and run clear of land when the boat was laid too. At 2 P.M. the storm somewhat abated when a man of war came to us from Point Isabel and ordered us to Aramas Pass.

Wednesday, Nov. 25th (1863).

We arrived at Aramas Pass at noon and were transferred to a small steamer and were landed on Mustang Island. Day windy. Sea rough. The coast from the Rio Grand here is a windy desert all of the way 110 miles.

Thursday, Nov. 26th, 1863.

Gen. Banks is here. Oysters are plenty around these Islands. Day blustering.

Friday, Nov. 27th (1863).

Our baggage was brought off the steamer and our regiment having taken 5 days rations were crossed over to St. Joseph's Island and marched to join a force that has preceeded us. I'm left here untill the company arrives. Day windy.

Saturday, Nov. 28th (1863).

A norther commenced at dark last night. Some of our tents were blown. A cold rain fell in torrents during the night. Near morning the rain ceased but a cold north wind continued all day drifting the sand in clouds filling our eves with it making all but the guards keep within their tents. All of the victuals that we attempt to cook were almost instantly filled with sand.

Sunday, Nov. 29th, 1863.

Last night very cold. The wind rose to a hurricane and the wet sand was frozen this morning to the dept(h) of 2 inches. At day break a weather moderated but the sand was drifted all day.

Monday, Nov. 30th (1863).

The Norther still continues.

Tuesday, Dec. 1st, 1863

The storm is over and a calm prevails once more which is a great relief from the sand storm of the last few days. Day pleasant.

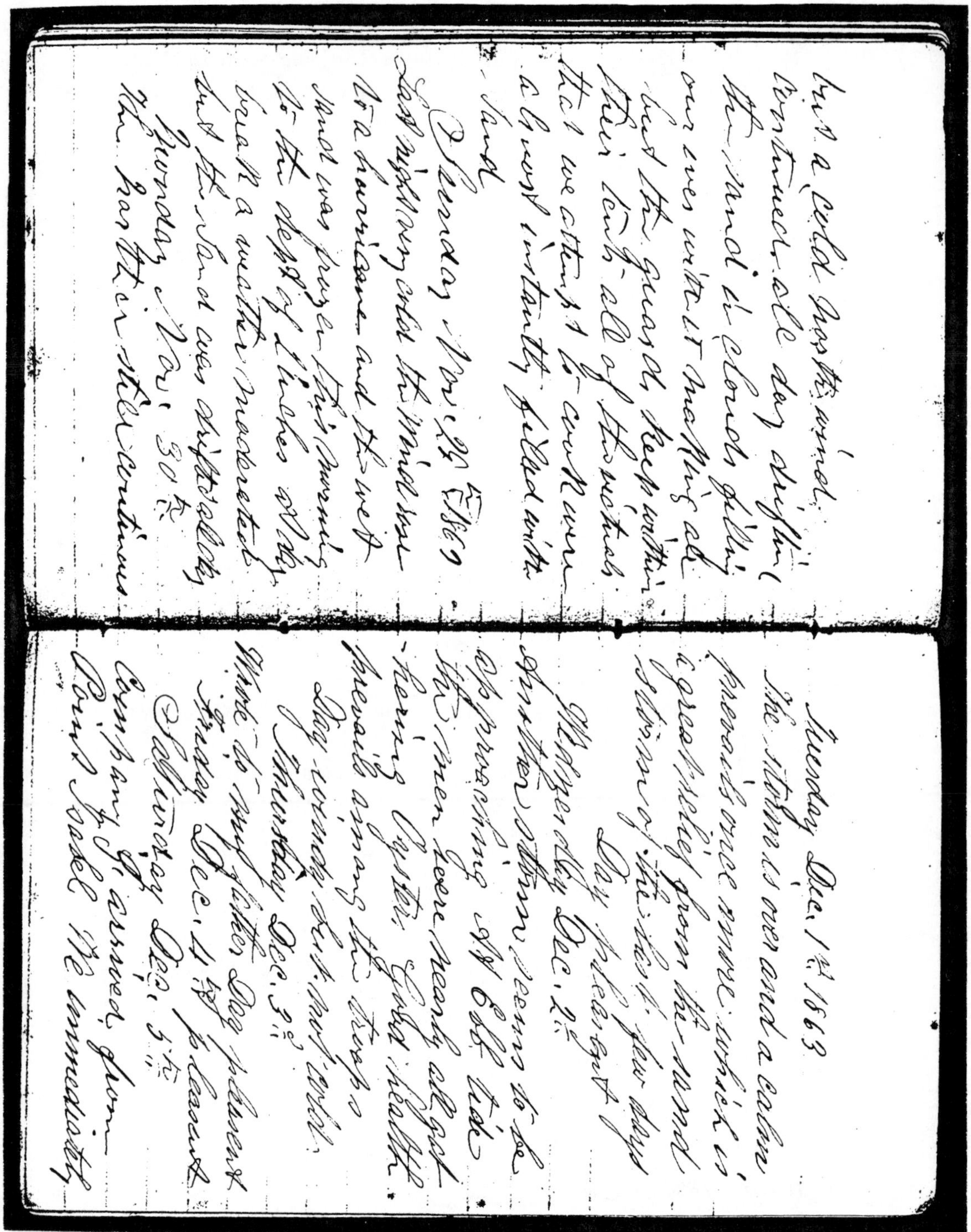

Wednesday, Dec. 2d (1863).

Another storm seems to be approaching. At Ebb tide the men were nearly all gathering oysters. Good health prevails among the troops. Day windy but not cold.

Thursday, Dec. 3d. (1863)

Wrote to my father. Day pleasant.

Friday, Dec. 4th (1863).

Pleasant.

Saturday, Dec. 5th (1863).

Company G. arrived from Point Isabel. We immediately put all of our baggage and 20,000 rations on the Steamboat Alabama. The companies then went on board where we remained all night. Day pleasant.

Sunday, Dec. 6th, 1863.

We sailed at 6 A.M. and were soon sea sick. We arrived at Matagorda Inlet at 2 P.M. There is a strong fort on Matagorda Island that commands the inlet. It is called Fort Esperenza. We landed at Decrows Point on Matagorda Peninsula. Afternoon rainy.

Monday Dec. 7th (1863).

The regiment came over from Fort Esperanza. We then camped. Day pleasant.

Tuesday, Dec. 8th, 1863.

Wrote to my father. Day pleasant.

Wednesday, Dec. 9th (1863).

Batt. drill in forenoon and a drill and parade in afternoon. Day pleasant.

Thursday, Dec. 18th (1863).

Gen. Lawler drilled the regt. an hour this forenoon. He is a good regimental commander. Day pleasant.

Friday, Dec. 11th (1863).

Pleasant.

Saturday, Dec. 12th (1863).

Moved camp about 1/2 mile this forenoon. Went on board of the Steamboat Alabama at dark and anchored in the inlet. Day pleasant.

Sunday, Dec. 13th, 1863.

We weighed anchor and sailed up the bay to Powderhorn 25 miles and landed. The rebels left the town at our approach. It is a town of about 500 inhabitants. We remained some time in the courthouse and broke open the jail but found nothing of importance. The houses of the town are poor and the wharfs are nearly all burnt by the rebels. We returned to the Steamer and then to camp. Day windy.

Monday, Dec. 14th (1863) to Dec. 16th (1863)

Weather pleasant.

Thursday, Dec. 17th, 1863.

Another Norther is blowing. Day very cold.

Friday, Dec. 18th, 1863.

Regiment was inspected by corps inspector. Day pleasant.

Saturday, Dec. 19th (1863).

Our company was detailed to unload a steamboat. Day cold.

Sunday, Dec. 20th (1863) and Monday Dec. 21st (1863).

Pleasant.

Tuesday, Dec. 22 (1863).

Received a letter from my sister. Day pleasant.

Wednesday, Dec. 23d (1863).

Our quarters and camp was inspected to-day by the Div. Medical inspector. Day pleasant.

Thursday, Dec. 24th, 1863.

Making out our muster rolls. Day pleasant.

Thursday Dec 31st 1863

Nearly all of our tents were
blown down last night
Were mustered today by Lt
Col. Whittlesey. Back nearly to
March at 3 P.M. to return the
Orders were countermanded
Day very cold

I marched to Poughkeepsie this
morning escorted by our Brigade
they gave us three cheers as we
passed. We went on board of
the steamer Powell and
arrived here and came
on the Provost duty directly

Thursday Dec 24th 1863
Making out our Musterrills
Day pleasant
Friday Dec. 25th
A number of letters have
arrived bringing writing
Papers Paces &c which
have been much needed
Christmas has passed very
quietly Day pleasant
Saturday Dec. 26th
Sunday " 27th pleasant
Monday " 28th pleasant
Tuesday Dec. 29
Received a letter from my
Wife Day pleasant
Dec. 30th and 31st
pleasant

Friday, Dec. 25th (1863).

A number of Sutlers have arrived bringing writing materials Tobacco &c. which have been much needed. Christmas has passed very quietly. Day pleasant.

Saturday Dec. 26th to Monday Dec. 28th (1863).

Pleasant.

Tuesday Dec. 29th (1863).

Received a letter from my Sister. Day pleasant.

Dec. 30th (1863).

Pleasant.

Dec. 31st, 1863.

Nearly all of our tents were blown down last night. Were mustered to-day by Lt. Cole Whittlery. Made ready to march at 5 P.M. when the orders were countermanded. Day very cold.

Friday, Jan. 1st 1864.

Last night was very cold. Ice froze thick enough on a pond here for men to walk on it this morning. The 23d. Wis. Infy. arrived from New Orleans. New years has passed very quietly. Day pleasant.

Saturday, Jan. 2d, 1864.

Regiment went on board of the Steamboat Warrior this morning and reported to Maj. Gen. Washburne at Fort Esperanza and were ordered back to camp. Day rainy.

Sunday, Jan. 3d (1864).

A detail is making rifle pits. Day wet and rainy.

Monday, Jan. 4th, 1864

Packed up this morning and went on board of the Steamboat Matamores and sailed to Powder-Horn where we arrived at dark but we could not land at the wharf. Day rainy and windy and very cold.

Tuesday Jan. 5th (1864).

The cold last night was intense. The boatmen went to the wharf this morning and lashed a ladder to it then rigged a block and tackle between the boat and wharf by which the yawl was propelled back and fort(h). The regiment was then landed on the wharf in this manner 6 at one trip. The waves broke over the little boat threatening to swamp it and wet us to the skin. The day was exceedingly cold. The water froze almost the instant it touched us. We were quartered in the houses. The oldest inhabitants say that this is the coldest weather that has been in Texas during 19 years. We are on half rations. The stormy weather prevents the small steamers going over the bar to bring rations off the transports.

Wednesday Jan. 6th (1864).

Marched to Indianola 3 miles and were quartered in tenantless houses. The town contained before the war probably 1000 inhabitants all of the men able to bear arms are in the ranks of the rebel army. The wharfs here have all been destroyed. The inhabitants are mostly German. Day very cold.

Thursday, Jan. 7th and Friday Jan. 8th (1864).

Cold.

Saturday, Jan. 9th (1864).

Our Co. went about 3 miles out on the Prairie and pulled a house down and hauled it into town for firewood. The land around is all prairie with thousands of cattle grazing on it. There is no timber in sight of the town. There is a large oyster bed in the bay in front of the town from which we obtain all the oysters that we choose to eat. Day pleasant.

Sunday, Jan. 10th, 1864.

A number of rebel horsemen approached the town when our regiment marched out to meet them when they galloped off. A number of our regiment have signified their intention to reenlist for 3 years more. Day pleasant.

Monday, Jan. 11th (1864).

A large number of rebel cavalry made their appearance to-day and threatened to attack us. The 22d Iowa Inf. with 2 pieces came to our assistance from Powderhorn. The rebels kept out of range of our rifles but the first shot from the Artillery started them off. Wrote to my sister. Day pleasant.

Wed. Jan. 13th & Thursday 14th (1864).
    Pleasant.

Friday, Jan. 15th (1864).
    A German commited suicide to-day by cutting his throat with a razor. He leaves 2 children. Day pleasant.

Saturday, Jan. 16th (1864).
    The division was reviewed by Gen. Benton. Day pleasant.

Sunday, Jan. 17th (1864).
    Brigade inspection this forenoon. Attended divine service at the M.E. Church at evening. Day cold.

Monday, Jan. 18th & Tuesday 19th
    Cold

Wednesday, Jan. 20th, 1864. Thursday Jan. 21st, Friday Jan. 22d.
    Pleasant. Received a letter from my sister.

Saturday, Jan. 23d (1864).
    Adjutant Hunt commenced to enlist those who desire to serve 3 years longer in the army.

Sunday, Ja. 24th (1864).
    Sergt. Dodge and Privates A. Calkins, Moore and Johnson returned to Co. from Generel (sic) Hospital. Day pleasant.

Monday, Jan. 25th to Friday 29th (1864).
    Pleasant. 246 men have enlisted from this regiment. Col. Whittlery has gone to New Orleans to obtain leave for the regt. to go to Wis. on furlough as that is one condition of the enlistment. The 33d. Ill. Inf'y. has departed for New Orleans on their way to Ill. on furlough as they have reenlisted. There is a good deal of sickness in our Co. but not much in the other companies of the regiment. The following order was read on parade to-day.

Head Quarters U.S. Forces Texas
Pass Cvallo Jan'y 28th 1864.

General Order
No 12

The field officer of the day for Jan. 23d 1864 has called the attention of the Major General commanding to the perfection of instruction discovered in the Picket line and records of the Eleventh Wisconsin Volunteers. The Commanding General acknowledges the great pleasure he feels at recognizing in these soldiers the qualities which he has heretofore heard they possessed. Such proficiency reflects honor on the officers and proves the existence of an espirit du corps which not only makes their own state but the whole North West feel proud. By order of Maj. G. N.J.T. Dana

(signed) H.G. Brown Assistant Adjutant General

Saturday, Jan. 30th, 1864.
Pleasant.

Sunday, Jan. 31st, 1864.
Pleasant. Received a letter from my brother James.

Monday, Feb. 1st, 1864.
Day pleasant. Gen. Hamilton Military Governor of Texas has arrived and has established the Capitol of the State for the present at Powderhorn.

Tuesday Feb. 2d, 1864. and Wed. 3d.
Pleasant.

Thursday, Feb. 4th (1864).
Were on fatigue duty to-day making breastworks. Day pleasant.

Friday, Feb. 5th (1864).
Our 1st Brigade marched for Lavaca this morning. Day pleasant. Rebel scouts hover around us every day.

Saturday, Feb. 6th, 1864.

    Pleasant. We are ordered to New Orleans 3/4 of the regiment having reenlisted we will receive a furlough of 30 days in Wisconsin.

Sunday Feb. 7th (1864).

    We were reviewed to-day by Maj. Gen. Ord. Day warm.

Monday Feb. 8th (1864).

    Wrote to my sister. Making out our muster out rolls. Day pleasant.

Tuesday, Feb. 9th (1864).

    Making out our muster in rolls. Day pleasant.

Wednesday Feb. 10th (1864).

    Pleasant. Went to PowderHorn. All of our regiment who did no(t) reenlist were transferred to the 23d. Wis.

Thursday, Feb. 11th and Friday Feb. 12th (1864).

    Pleasant.

Saturday, Feb. 13th, 1864.

    We were mustered into the service of the U.S. to-day by Lt. Minehold for 3 years more. Day pleasant. I feel very unwell to-day.

Sunday, Feb. 14th, 1864.

    We marched to Powderhorn escorted by our brigade. They gave us three cheers at parting as we are leaving for Wis. We went on to the Steamboat Planter & sailed to De Krows Point where we landed and bivoucked on the ground. Day cold & windy.

Monday, Feb. 15th, 1864.

    I saw some acquaintances in the 22d Wis. Our left wing went on board of the Steamer Sophia & sailed for N.O. at 12 M. with a good sailing breeze which continued till dark. Day pleasant.

Tuesday Feb. 16th (1864).

A strong breeze is blowing from the North. Our boat is from the Chesapeake Canal is of iron but is not a fast sailor. We are making but little progress to-day. Have been very sea sick today. Day windy.

Wednesday, Feb. 17th (1864).

The wind is blowing a perfect Hurricane. Our vessel is laid too and she rides the waves beautifully. Sea sick to-day yet.

Thursday Feb. 18th, 1864.

The storm is furious to-day. Its equal has been seldom seen by the oldest marines.

Friday, Feb. 19th (1864).

Storm is over and our boat is on her course once more. Feel better to-day. Day pleasant.

Saturday Feb. 20th (1864).

Arrived at the mouth of the Miss. River at 8 A.M. and soon got a Pilot who guided us over the bay and then left us and we are steaming up the Miss. with a pleasant breeze. Day pleasant. The water of the Mississippi is very muddy and does not unite with the water of the sea for many miles from its mouth. The muddy water of the river floats along the top ten miles from the bar and the paddles of the Steamer would bring up the clear water of the Gulf beneath showing the river water to be about 1 foot deep on the surface. We arrived at Fort St. Philip and Jackson at 3 P.M. They have been greatly enlarged and improved since they were taken from the rebels. They are now very formidable forts. They mount about 200 guns and are garrisoned at present by a regiment of Negroes.

Sunday, Feb. 21st, 1864.

We arrived and landed at the wharf at New Orleans at daybreak where we remained untill 3 P.M. when we marched to a barracks in a cotton press where we have very comfortable quarters. Day pleasant.

The color of the water of the Mississippi is very muddy and does not unite with the water of the sea for many miles from its mouth. The muddy water of the river forms a belt along the top ten miles of the sea and the line would be distinctly seen could it be clearly seen...

Monday Feb. 11th 1844

We anchored and landed at the wharf at New Orleans at very early hour...

Monday, Feb. 22d (1864).

This is the anniversary of Gen. Washington's birthday. A large number of cannon have been fired in honor of the occassion. An election is being held today in this State for State officers preparatory to the state reentering the Union. No disturbance has occured during the forenoon. Day very pleasant. Hahn will probably be elected.

Tuesday, Feb. 23d, 1864.

Day pleasant. Our left wing of our regiment arrived last night. Wrote to my father to-day. Went to the Charles Theatre this even(ing). The principal performance is a panorama of the war.

Wednesday, Feb. 24th (1864).

Day pleasant. Saw the play of Romeo and Juliet at Varieties Theatre.

Thursday, Feb. 25th (1864).

Day pleasant. Went to the theatre tonight and saw Othello played.

Friday, Feb. 26th (1864).

Went to the Varieties Theatre this evening. Day pleasant.

Saturday, Feb. 27th (1864).

24 recruits were mustered into our regiment to-day. Day pleasant.

Sunday, Feb. 28th (1864).

Went to Sabbath School at the Baptist Church and to the Episcopal Church in forenoon and to vespers in the Catholic Church in the afternoon. Day pleasant.

Monday, Feb. 29th (1864).

Made out our musterrolls to-day. Day pleasant.

Tuesday, Mar. 1st, 1864.

Rained all day.

Wednesday, Mar. 2d (1864).

Made out our company report and receipts to our Quarter Master Gen. Day cool but pleasant.

Thursday, March 3/64.

Turned over to ordnance office our damaged ordinance. Day pleasant.

Friday, March 4th, 1864.

Michael K. Hahn Gov. Elect of Louisiana will be inaugurated to-day with great ceremony at sunrise. A salute was fired by Artillery and all of the bells in the city were rung at 10 A.M. We were marched to Lafayette Square where we found a large platform erected and seats built in a semi circle to seat at least 6000 persons. The park was adorned with appropriate flags Laurels &c. about 5000 school children soon arrived and were seated. the 1st Regt. Regular Infantry the 30th Massachusetts, 37th Illinois and the 11th Wis. were drew up in 8 lines. 50 pieces of artillery were formed in a semicircle and were fired by Electricity. Gov. Hahn was sworn in as Gov. and delivered an inaugural address and was followed by a short speech by Maj. Gen. Banks neigther (sic) of which could I hear our line being so far from the speakers. All of the musicians in the city were present forming a band of fully 300. Those were accompanied by 40 beaters on anvils the firing of 50 pieces of cannon and regiments of Infantry the singing of 5000 children and the ringing of all of the bells in the city. We returned to our camp at 2 oclock P.M. having witnessed the grandest celebration that was ever seen in America.

Day cool and pleasant. At evening our regiment marched to the St. Charles Theatre Lafayette Square was illuminated and looked very beautiful. The plays at the theatre were the little treasure and the Frensh (sic) Spy. Miss Emma Madden received her benefit to-night. The houses were crowded & Miss Madden played her part well.

Saturday March 5th, 1864.

Pleasant.

Sunday, March 6th (1864).

Went to the Baptist Church on Camp Street to an ordination to-night. Day pleasant.

Saturday March 5th 1864
Pleasant

Sunday March 6th
Went to the Baptist church
on Camp Street to a Ordination
returned to our camp at
2 o'clock P.M. having witnessed
the ordinates Day Pleasant
Monday March 7th
Pleasant

Tuesday March 8th
preparing to leave tomorrow
Day very rainy
Web. March 9th
We were paid off to day
and will our leave until
to morrow Day very rainy
Thursday Mar. 10th
We marched from town off
Steamer Empire city — a
sailed from a fine St
3 P.M. Day Pleasant

2nd Regiment of Infantry
the singing of school children
and the ringing of all
the bells in the city. We
returned to our camp at
2 o'clock P.M. having witnessed
the grandest of celebration
that was ever seen a America
Day Col. and Pleasant
at reviewing our regiment
marched to the St Charles
Theatre — Lafayette Square
to an illuminated and looked
very beautiful the Square
the Theatre were too little
Treasure and the French
Lay. Miss Emma Matthew
received her being 3 to-night
this house were crowded
Miss Matthew played her part

Monday, March 7th (1864).
Pleasant.

Tuesday, March 8th (1864).
Preparing to leave to-morrow. Day very rainy.

Wednesday, March 9th (1864).
We were paid off to-day but will not leave untill to-morrow. Day very rainy.

Thursday, Mar. 10th (1864).
We marched on board of the Steamer Empire City & sailed from N.O. at 5 P.M. Day pleasant.

Friday, March 11/64.
We passed Baton Rouge at 9 this morning and Port Hudson soon after. Our Steamer is a very fast sailer and the men are all in comfortable quarters. The atmosphere here already feels cooler than at N.O. This boat is one of those that ran the blockades of Vicksburg & Grand Gulf last spring and assisted to carry our army across the Miss. River April 30/63.

Saturday, March 12/64.
Passed Grand Gulf at 2 P.M. and arrived at Vicksburg at 8 P.M. Day pleasant.

Sunday, March 13th, 1864.
Coaled and took a number of mules & wagon on board. The(re) is a large movement of troops from Vicksburg to Memphis. Day pleasant. There is no business at Vicksburg except unloading &c. of army supplies. Day pleasant.

Monday, March 14th (1864).
Sailed from Vicksburg at 2 A.M. Our boat is heavily loaded a(nd) does not sail very fast. Day pleasant.

Tuesday, March 15th (1864).
The atmosphere feels much colder here than at New Orleans. Day pretty cold.

Wednesday, March 16th (1864).

Arrived at Helena at 12 P.M. and coaled. Sailed from Helena at day light. Day pretty cold. Arrived at Me(mphis) at 8 P.M. and unloaded mules, wagons and then coaled. Day pleasant.

Friday, March 18/64.

Sailed from Memphis at noon. Day pleasant. Some of our men became intoxicated and were left at Memphis. Only one of our Co. Private Sharkey.

Saturday, March 19/64.

Arrived at Cairo Ill. during last night and landed at 8 A.M. and remained in the town during the day. At 8 P.M. we departed by the Ill. Cen. R.R. for Chicago. Day pleasant.

Sunday, March 20th, 1864.

Our train did not run fast during the night but is doing very well to-day. Day pleasant.

Monday, March 21st (1864).

Arrived in Chicago at 8 A.M. and received a good breakfast at the Soldiers rest when we marched to the Depot of the North Western Rail way and took the cars for Madison Wis. where we arrived at 9 1/2 P.M. and were received at the Depot by Gov. Lewis and other and we then partook of a good supper at the R.R. Hotel. Our regiment was then quartered at the City Hall and Fairchelds' Block. Day and evening was pretty cold. The lakes are frozen. The snow is mostly thawed off.

Tuesday, March 22d, 1864.

We marched to the Eastern front of the Capitol this morning and returned our Flags to the Governor and be presented with new colors. We were then addressed by Gov. Lewis, Sec. Fairchield and Maj. Morgan. I received a commission as 1st Lieut. of my company to-day. Day pleasant.

Wednesday, March 23d, 1864.

Took the cars to Spring Green this afternoon where I met my father in waiting and arrived at home after an absence of 2 years 4 mos. and 10 days and found our family all well. Day pleasant.

Thursday March 24th, 1864.

Author's Note: A gap exists in the diary until Sept. 12, 1865 at which point the following entries are made which span the period Sept. 12, 1865 to Oct. 1, 1865.

Sept. 12, 1865 (Tuesday).

Frank Herseman of my Co. G. died today, on the steamboat. I left his remains in the dead house of the Gayoso Hospital at Memphis, Tenn. from which he will be interred to-morrow.

Thursday, Sept. 14 (1865)

Passed Cairo, Ill. at midday.

Friday, Sept. 15 (1865).

Arrived at Illinois town at 3 P.M. where we remained all night.

Saturday, Sept. 16 (1865).

Left at noon on the Terra Haute R.R. Changed to the Ill. Cent. R.R. about midnight at Puca, Ill. Weather pleasant.

Sabbath, Sept. 17 (1865).

Arrived at Freeport at 3 P.M. where we obtained refreshments. Arrived at Beloit Wis. at 10 P.M. The men are quartered in the city hall and the officers at Saulsbury Hotel. Corporal Samuel Robinson was killed by falling between the cars while in motion.

Monday, Sept. 18 (1865).

Citizens of Beloit furnished us with breakfast. At 8 1/2 P.M. we left by N.W. R.R. and arrived at Madison at noon. We met many friends at the depot. My father was one of the number. After a speech from Gov. Lewis we were furnished a dinner at the R.R. Hotel. We then found quarters at Camp Randall.

Thursday, Sept. 19 (1865).

Our last rolls were signed to-day when we were dismissed to our houses till the 29 inst.

Wednesday Sept. 20 (1865).

I turned over all public property which I yet retained and left by R.R. at 4:30 P.M. for Spring Green, and arrived at home at 9 P.M. after an absence of 1 year & 5 months.

Wednesday, Sept. 27th (1865).

Went to Madison, Wis. to-day.

Thursday, Sept. 28 (1865).

Obtained a final settlement of my accounts to-day.

Saturday, Sept. 30 (1865).

Gen. W.T. Sherman visited Madison to-day and received an ovation. Senator Doolittle spoke in the Assembly Room during the evening. Nearly all of our men were paid to-day, and left for their houses.

Sabbath Oct. 1 (1865).

Went to Presbyterian Church.

Monday, Oct. 2, 1865.

Paid off to-day and arrived at home at 9 P.M. My part in the war is over. The Eleventh Wisconsin Infantry is now known only in history. I served 4 years and 15 days and was paid untill Sept. 30/65.

Thursday Sept. 19,
Our first Bell was rung
to day, when our men advanced
to our lines till the 29 inst.

Wednesday Sept. 20,
I turned over all Public
Property which I yet retained,
and left by Rd. at 4.30 P.M. on
Spring River Rd. arrive at
home at 9 P.M. after
an absence of 1 year & 6 months.

Wednesday Sept 27,
Went to Madison Wisconsly.

Thursday Sept. 28,
Returned & final settlement
of my accounts to day.

Friday Sept 30
Went in to Eau Sept. 30
Gen. W. T. Sherman visited
Madison to day and received
an ovation. Senator Doolittle

Spoke in the Assembly room
during the evening,
We lay all of our men were
paid to day, and left for their
homes.

Sabbath Oct. 1,
Went to Ross by Iowa Church.

Monday Oct. 2, 1865,
Paid off to day and mine
I came at 9 P. M.
My Post in Tennesee were
the Eleventh Wisconsin
Infantry known to fame
early in history.
Received 4 years and 13 days
and was paid up to Sept. 30/65.

PART III

THE CAMP LETTERS OF
JEROME B. SETTERLEE
44TH REGIMENT NEW YORK VOLUNTEERS

"Men are strange creatures and war is a very tantalizing game."

—*Jerome B. Setterlee*

INTRODUCTION

Jerome B. Setterlee served his nation as a volunteer with the 44th N.Y. Regiment of Volunteers during the War Between the States. Surviving from those years of marching, camping and fighting are this wonderful series of camp letters running from March 2, 1862 at Camp Butterfield, Halls Hill, Virginia to July 17, 1863 at the McVeigh House Hospital. These letters, never before published, shed a fascinating light on the daily toils, dreams and disappointments of one of America's unsung heroes.

Jerome Setterlee maintained an active correspondence with his parents, brother and sister throughout his fighting days and later imprisonment and hospitalization. He shared with them the readiness of his unit to fight for a cause he deeply believed in, his ardent dislike for Secesh former countrymen, the health of his fellow comrades, and the reactions of Southern folk as his Yankee troops passed through their towns. Each of these he describes in a "folksy" manner, e.g. "Enjoying himself eating hominy," "Bacon that tasted like mouldy soap grease," "Contrabands congregated around the Fort," and "How every house of worth had been burned and but little of anything better than Slave Cabins is to be seen." This was a soldier who cared for not only his fellow soldiers but the small Negro children, old white-haired men, and beautiful young women he met along Virginia's backroads. These letters form a moving and heartwarming account of one Yankee's journey through the South during the difficult years of 1862 and 1863. Reading these letters help the historian of today truly "live" the experiences of the men who saved the Union.

BYSTANDER TO DESTINY

The old black man with beard of gray
Stopped to stare and in silence pray
As columns of blue slowly marched by
Knee deep in mud beneath Virginia's sky

His freedom in the balance hung
Not yet certain it would ever be won
Yet he helped with whispers of camps and men
And Rebels to be captured where and when

Then with withered hands again gripped his hoe
To slowly till the endless cotton row
Of acres he could only dream to one day own
If Honest Abe's success could be sown

A bystander to destiny in homespun pants
Murmuring hidden messages in spiritual chants
The Old Massa's gaze seemed to say
What secrets passed North this August day?

—Wayne L. Wolf

Camp Butterfield
Halls Hill, Va.
March 2nd 1862

Dear Parents.—Brother & Sister

The time is so short since I last wrote to you that I have but little to write but as I was foolish enough to write that I expected to go on some expedition I shall now have to write that in the rouse of doing anything of the kind we are here still at the old camp and there is no more prospect of our going away now than there has been at any time since my arrival here. The fact of the business is (as I suppose) that Gen. Banks was about to cross the river to move upon the Rebels at Leesburgh and our Division was got in readiness to go to his assistance in case the enemy was too strong for his colums to manage and that is the only reason we can see why we were packed up and furnished with 100 rounds of ammunition kept on the tiptoe for two or three days and finally ordered to make ourselves comfortable again—when the news came that Gen. Banks was victorious and that we should not be needed in that direction. At present all is quiet in camp again and except the fact that the boys are some of them infinitely disgusted at the thought that some of them lost the best part of two nights sleep things go on harmonious as ever. Men are strange creatures and war is a very tantalizing game at the best so great in fact has become the soldiers or rather a certain class of them that they are or seem to be actually miserable over what seems to them to be the present prospect viz. that they will have to go home without ever seeing a fight but of one thing you may be sure it is not the ones who blow the loudest because we did not move at the time expected who were best prepared for a real advance and I think for my own part that we shall all see war enough before this scrape is ended to satisfy the most warlike. I have just received & read your letter. I was very glad to hear from home for I began to think that you must have failed to get my first letter. You speak of my enjoying myself in eating hominy. I wish I could always be sure something as good for it be known that nothing but the last extremity of starvation will ever drive me to eat that horrible Bacon which our commissary persists in furnishing for the men notwithstanding the fact that none of them will on my account eat it and that the only earthly use we can make of the awful stuff is to use it for kindling wood. Bacon such as they deal out to us is prepared as near as I can find out in this way viz: piled up in heaps and sprinkled with dry salt until it gets a little salt taste then smoked and sowed up in cloth to keep the flies from foreclosing on such valuable property the taste of which when cooked is very like mouldy soap grease. The most of our fodder however is very good. We get good pork tolerably good beef first rate rice hominy beans & bread and the sugar and molasses is also first rate no cheap poor stuff of the kind being brought into camp. We also have plenty of pilot bread or sea crackers which are hard enough for better teeth than mine but very good if a person can have patience and teeth sufficient to eat them. So on the whole we get plenty to eat as a general thing and can not reasonably find much fault with quantity or quality. It has been snowing some since noon today and the ground is covered with snow about two inches in depth. The first I have seen since I left Baltimore and the look of the thing is very like our country when the ground is covered with what we call a sugar snow and notwithstanding the fact that it is Sunday the boys are having a great time snowballing while I write hitting the tents in all directions. I dont want to try to guess when we shall move from this place for after I have trusted to appearances and got all ready once I have but little confidence in orders or appearances but of one thing I am certain that is as certain as I wish to be that when we go we go for the purpose of taking Mannassas not in the front but for the purpose of drawing the attention of the Rebels and perhaps drawing them into a battle outside of their works while Banks & perhaps Burnside take the liberty to attack them in the rear. The Anaconda is tightening his folds and I think if the Rebels do not leave Mannassas voluntarily they will be destroyed if they do not prove too strong for us and beat us back again as they did at Bull Run. The position of our Army is such that we could easily surround them at any time if it should be deemed expedient so to do, but of expediency we shall have to leave our commanders to judge. But my letter is long enough

I guess to tire your patience so I will close for the present.

Your Son & Brother
Jerome B.Setterlee

Camp Butterfield
Halls Hill. Va.
March 2nd 1862

Dear Parents.—Brother & Sister

The time
is so short since I last wrote
to you that I have but little to write
but as I was foolish enough to write
that I expected to go on some exped-
-ition I shall now have to write
that in the room of doing anything
of the kind we are here still at
the old camp and there is no more
prospect of our going away now
then there has been at any time
since my arrival here. The fact
of the business is (as I suppose) that
Gen. Banks was about to cross
the river to move upon the Rebels
at Lusburgh and our Division
was got in readiness to go to his
assistance in case the enemy
was too strong for his Column
to manage and that is the

only reason we can see why we were packed up and furnished with 100 rounds of ammunition kept on the tiptoe for two or three days and finally ordered to make ourselves comfortable again — when the news came that Gen Banks was victorious and that we should not be needed in that direction. At present all is quiet in camp again and except the fact that the boys on some of them infinitely disgusted at the thought that some of them lost the best part of two nights sleep things so on harmonious as ever. Men are strange creatures and war is a very tantalizing game at the best so great in fact has become the mania for a fight among the soldiers or rather a certain class of them that they are or seem to be actually miserable over what seems to them to be the present prospect viz. that they will have to go home without ever seeing a fight but of one thing you may be sure it is not the one who blow the loudest because we did not move at the time expected who were best prepared for a real advance and I think for my own part that we shall all see war enough before this scrape is ended to satisfy the most warlike. I have just received & read your letter I was very glad to hear from home for I began to think that you must have failed to get my first letter. You speak of my enjoying myself in eating Hominy I wish I could always be sure of something as good for be it known that nothing but the last extremity of starvation will ever drive me to eat that horrible Bacon which our commissary persists in furnishing for the men notwithstanding the fact that none of them will on any account eat it and that the only earthly use we can make of the awful stuff is to use it for kindling wood. Bacon such as they deal out to us is prepared as near as I can find out in this way viz piled up in heaps and sprinkled with dry salt until it gets a little salt taste then smoked and sewed up in cloth to keep the flies from foreclosing on such valuable property the taste of which when cooked is very like mouldy soap grease The most of our fodder however is very good we get good pork tolerably good beef first rate rice hominy beans & bread and the sugar and molasses is also first rate no cheap poor stuff of the kind being brought into camp we also have plenty of pilot bread or sea crackers which are hard enough for better teeth than mine but very good if a person can have patience and teeth sufficient to eat them so on the whole we get plenty to eat as a general thing and can not reasonably find much fault with quantity or quality. It has been snowing some since noon today and the ground is covered with snow about two inches in depth the first I have seen since I left Baltimore and the look of the thing is very like our country when the ground is covered with what we call a sugar snow and notwithstanding the fact that it is sunday the boys are having a great time snowballing while I write hitting the tent in all directions. I dont want to try to guess when we shall move from this place for after I have trusted to appearances and got all ready once I have but little confidence in Orders or appearances but of one thing I am certain that is as certain as I wish to be that when we go we go for the purpose of taking Mannasas not in the front but for the purpose of drawing the attention of the Rebels and perhaps drawing them into a battle outside of their works while Banks & perhaps Burnside take the liberty to attack them in the rear. The Anaconda is tightening his folds and I think if the Rebels do not leave Mannasses voluntarily they will be destroyed, if they do not prove too strong for us and beat us back again as they did at Bull Run. The position of our army is such that we could easily surround them at any time if it should be deemed expedient so to do, but of expediency we shall have to leave our commanders to judge. But my letter is long enough I guess to tire your patience so I will close for the present

Your son & brother

Jerome B. Settle

44th Regiment   New York Volunteers,
Col. S.W. STRYKER, Commanding.

Camp Near Hampton Va.   March 24th, 1862

Dear Parents. Brother & Sister.

I again sit down to let you know something of my whereabouts for as we are almost continually on the move now I must write when I can or not at all. We that is our Division and I dont know how many other troops left Alexandria for down the River (on steamboats) last Friday or rather Saturday for we did not make our final set out till Saturday morn, and this morning landed at Fortress Monroe whence we proceeded to this place just west of where the old village of Hampton stood before it was burned by the Rebels. How then you are no doubt curious to know when we are going but I can tell you nothing certain. I presume however we are to advance toward Richmond and the talk is we start tomorrow to fight if there is fighting to be done so you need not be surprised if the next news from this way is to the effect that we have had a battle of magnitude. Perhaps you would like to hear something of the voyage down the Potomac and the Chesapeake so I will try to tell you a little. The first day out I passed very well. The scenery on the banks of the Potomac is generally speaking very common place there being but little in the line of farms or buildings of any account. I had a first rate view of Mt. Vernon the home of Washington and although I always expected to see something nice I was not prepared to see anything in Virginia equal in beauty to this lovely spot where lived died and now in the beautiful quiet of this delightful scene reposes the Father of his Country. It stands upon a sort of Bluff overlooking the River for miles and you might look the World over and not find another spot equal to Mt. Vernon. You may think me extravagant but if you could see as I did you would say like me it is the spot of all spots for the residence of a Washington. I was very sea sick during the later part of my trip and so did not enjoy anything for I could hardly stand without leaning against something but since I landed I feel like a new person "all right." Ft. Monroe you will of course expect to hear something of so I will merely say for this time that it looks like a very formidable piece of war machinery and could you see the tremendous stacks of cannon balls, shell and also cannon lying in the yards outside the Fort, you would start with astonishment and wonder what Uncle Sam ever expected to do with them. The Village of Hampton is among the things that were but it was built in a beautiful spot and the land here is rich as any I ever saw resembling the flats of the Mohawk in looks and the soil is also much the same. I must also say something of the crowd of Contrabands congregated round the Fort for twas my fortune to get a good sight of a pretty good crowd of them and you may be sure it was a sight worth seeing for they were of all dimensions from the sise (sic) of a small Woodchuck up to that of a full grown man from the infant in his mothers arms black as the ace of spades and woolly enough to funny up to the gray haired Patriarch. The babies poor little rats grinned and crowed at us as if they liked the sight and I am not so prejudiced against color but that I could see beauty in this (to me) novel scene. I would write more but it is bedtime and I must close. I enclose a piece of Black Flag one of several found in the Rebel Forts at Centreville by our boys. I wish you to preserve it and if any Secesh has anything to say in favor of the Pirates we are engaged in trying to subdue show then a piece of the No. Quarter Flag found in the Camp of their Southern Friends by a Yankee soldier. Direct your letters the same as before untill further orders.

With much love I remain

Your son & Brother
J. B. Setterlee

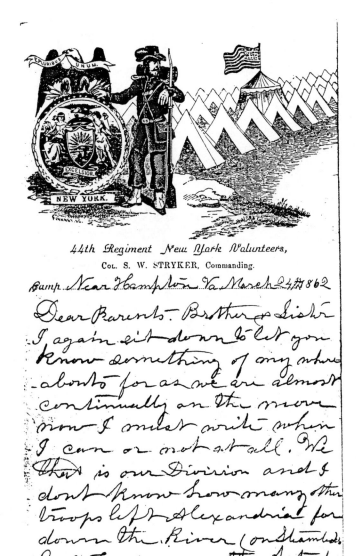

44th Regiment New York Volunteers,
Col. S. W. STRYKER, Commanding.

Camp Near Hampton Va March 24th 1862

Dear Parents- Brother & Sister
I again sit down to let you
know something of my where
-abouts for as we are almost
continually on the move
now I must write when
I can or not at all. We
that is our Division and I
dont know how many other
troops left Alexandria for
down the River (on Steamboats
last Friday or rather Saturday

but if you could see as I did you would say like me it is the spot of all spots for the residence of a Washington. I was very sea sick during the latter part of my trip and so did not enjoy anything for I could hardly stand without leaning against something but since I landed I feel like a new person "all right". Ft Monroe you will of course expect to hear something of so I will merely say for this time that it looks like a very formidable piece of war machinery and could you see the tremendous stacks of cannon balls, shell and also cannon lying in the yards outside with astonishment and wonder what Uncle Sam ever expects to do with them. The village of Hampton is among the things that were but it was built in a beautiful spot and the land here is rich as any I ever saw resembling

NEW YORK. EXCELSIOR.

The flat ——— the ——— the ——— in looks and the soil is also much the same. I must also say something of the crowd of Contrabands congregated round the Fort for I was my fortune to get a good sight of a pretty good crowd of them and you may be sure it was a sight worth seeing for they were if all dimensions from the size of a small Woodchuck up to that of a full grown man from the infant in his mothers arms black as the ace of spades and oddly enough to look first up to the gray haired Patriarch the babies poor little rats grinned and crowed etc as if they liked the sight and I am not so prejudiced against color but that I could see beauty in the (to me) novel scene. I would write more but it is bedtime and I must close. I enclose a piece of a Black Flag one of several found in the Rebel Forts at Centerville by our boys. I wish you to preserve it and if any Secesh has anything to say in favor of the Pirates we are engaged in trying to subdue show them a piece of the No Quarter flag found in the Camps of their Southern Friends by a Yankee Soldier. Direct your letters the same as

before untill further order.
With much love I remain
Your Son & Brother
J. B. Setterlice

44th Regiment   New York Volunteers,
Col. S.W. Stryker, Commanding.

Camp In Woods near Hampton March 29th, 1862

Dear Parents, Brother and Sister.

I will again commence a letter to you. I have nothing to do and as I expect to see the time at no very distant day when I shall have more to do I will begin now and forward when I can. We moved from the position we were in when I last wrote last Tuesday and after a march of about four miles camped in a piece of pine woods. The next day we did nothing but were held in readiness as the enemy was said to be near but of course as they could not effect a surprise they staid away. Wednesday night we had orders to fill our canteens and be in readiness for a call at any time but were not called out till morning when the order came for us to be ready to march without knapsacks in the direction of Great Bethel the spot where our troops were so sadly handled last summer. We were ready and in line in good season when we found that the movement was one of magnitude for all the troops in the neighborhood were stirring and prepared or preparing to march. And here for the first time I had a fair view of Brig. Gen. Butterfield who commands our Brigade and who looks just as near like pictures of Napoleon the Great as one man ever looks like any other and judging from his looks and the reputation he bears he is a regular little Napoleon in military matters and I predict he will distinguish the name of Butterfield before the end of this war. But to return to our trip (to Great Bethel) after forming in line in the road we had to wait for Griffin's Battery of Artillery to pass by. This is a regular Battery of Rifle cannon and the barkers look as if they would be apt to do good business in case of a fight. We marched very cautiously with skirmishers ahead and on both flanks to guard against a surprise for the country is very much covered with second growth pine and other evergreens and affords the best of hiding places for those who love sneaking so well as the Rebels seem to and our leaders did not mean that this Great Bethel should come out just like the other so we had a good opportunity to look around. The country is very level and the land is good but almost every house of any worth has been burned and but little of any thing better than Slave Cabins is to be seen. A few cattle and hogs indeed were generally to be seen roaming round the deserted farms and trying to get something to support nature but if their looks is any criterion of the quantity or quality of their fare they fare poorly enough. In one place we saw a cow with two little calves running with her and they were as wild as if they had never seen a man. I presume they never had or at least known anything of man's care. In a few cases however far toward Bethel the houses were left standing and they (the Farmers) had commenced to plough for Spring grain their Secesh sympathies I presume had saved them when their Union neighbors were burned out of houses and home. About noon we reached the clearing near the spot where was fought the disastrous Battle of Great Bethel and the first notice that we got of the fact our Brigade was forming in line of Battle. We drew up in line and the Pioneers were ordered to clear away the fence which was soon done and we moved forward toward the Rebel Batteries. But lo! and behold! no roar of cannon met us for the Sneaks had gone and taken all their goods with them so Great Bethel fell into the hands of the Mud-sills without a struggle. They were however (a few of them) at work on their entrenchments when our skirmishers came in sight and two or more of them fell victims to the skill of a few Berdan Sharpshooters who were with us. Our Band mounted the deserted works of the Rebs and the air was made to ring with the sound of Hail Columbia Red White & Blue, Star Spangled Banner & Yankee Doodle. So if there was a Rebel within any common distance they had to hear the "detested music." We rested some time here and while doing so we saw the smoke of houses &c. that the Rebels were burning as they ran. While we were resting other troops (a large number of them) came on and filed round ahead of us so after a little we formed and retraced our steps to camp where we arrived just before sundown disappointed because we had no fight but it will probably be different when it comes to the reality of a Battle. I will here say that although all of us expected a desperate fight not a man quailed on although we could hear the firing of the skirmishers ahead of us. Our Regt. formed in line with as much readiness as if on drill and marched forward in as good order as they are in the habit of doing when nothing more than common is occurring. We are lying still now for some purpose best known to our leaders and our Pioneers are at work building a bridge across a large Creek just west of our Camp.

Sunday 30th. I again resume my pen to write an addition to an already long letter. The day is quite rainy today and our camp is not very comfortable yet we manage to get along very well. I tent with M.H. Bliss, P.C. DeLong and another Herkimer Co. boy of the name of P.T. Broadway. I think we have the best tent in camp for some of the boys only have two pieces of tent cloth and where only two go together the tents are very small but four pieces make a very comfortable and roomy tent. This difference is mostly to the fact that some of them can not agree long at a time and so will not hitch together to make out a tent of respectable size. A soldier's life is a lazy life on the average though we have now and then a day of hardship yet most of the time there is only too much time for lounging playing cards and other sports of the same kind and Sunday in camp is as unlike Sunday as it ought to be as can well be imagined. Yet I have seen but few cases of wanton Sabbath breaking most of the kind being partly necessary. I have managed however to keep from work on Sunday and have always tried to have the Sabbath what it should be at all times the day of rest. I am heartily glad of one thing that is our Leaders have come out very strict against all plundering or disturbing the property of any and they have affixed severe penalties on any violation of this rule. You may think all this unnecessary with civilized soldiers but I assure you if it were not for

Military Law every Pig, Hen or even Cow in the country we pass through would go to help fill the stomachs of our Army not because they are actually needed but the fare they give us is not of the kind to satisfy those used to better and so all of a certain class would grab at anything eatable very quick and without stopping to inquire to whom it belonged so they have to be checked or the country would be entirely stripped and the men no better off. They almost always get as much and often more rations than they can eat and that too good enough to answer the purpose of substantial food. I do not know as you had better look for another letter very soon for I shall probably be very busy so you need not be concerned but if I do not write as often as I have you may think I have less time to spare from other duties. And so hoping this may find you as it leaves me in the enjoyment of health. I will bring this long letter to a close. Our mail goes from here regularly but we have received none lately. Write to me when you can get time and do not wait for me for I shall write as often as I can spare time. Think of the soldier for he thinks often of you.

Your son & Brother
J.B. Setterlee

44th Regiment New York Volunteers,
Col. S. W. STRYKER, Commanding.

Camp In Woods near Hampton March 29th 1862

Dear Parents, Brother and Sister

I will again commence a letter to you. I have nothing to do and as I expect to see the time at no very distant day when I shall have none to do I will begin now and forward when I can. We moved from the position we were in when I last wrote last Tuesday and after a march of about four miles camped in a piece of pine woods. The next day we did nothing but were held in

for those who love sneaking as
well as the Rebels seem to and
our leaders did not mean that
this Great Bethel should come
out just like the other so we
had a good apportunity to look
around. The country is very level
and the land is good but almost
every house of any worth has been
burned and but little of anything
better than I saw above is to be
seen. a few cattle and hogs indeed
were generally to be seen roaming
round the deserted farms and
trying to get something to support
nature but if their looks is any
criterion of the quantity or quality
of their fare they fare poorly enough
In one place we saw a cow with
two little calves running with
her and they were as wild as if
they had never seen a man I
presume they never had or at
least known anything of mans
care. In a few cases however
far toward Bethel the houses were
left standing and the farmers
commenced to plough for Spring
grain their slaves

E PLURIBUS UNUM

EXCELSIOR

NEW YORK.

Col. _____ W. STRYKER, Commanding   186_

when their Union Regiment ~~New York Volunteers~~, and

come. About Owen eve reached

the Clearing near the Spot

where was fought the disastrous

Battle of Great Bethel and the

first notice that we got of the

fact our Brigade was forming

in line of Battle. We drew

up in line and the Pioneers

were ordered to clear away the

fence which was soon done

and we moved forward toward

the Rebel Batteries. But lo! and

behold! no roar of Cannon

met us for the enemy had

a large Creek just west of our
Camp. Sunday 30th. I again resume
my pen to write an addition to another
long letter. The day is quite rainy today
and our camp is not very comfortable
Yet we manage to get along very well
I tent with M. F. Bliss, L. C. Delong and
another Herkimer Co. boy of the name
of P. T. Broadway. I think we have the
best tent in Camp for some of the
boys only have two pieces of tent cloth
and where only two go together the
tents are very small but four
pieces make a very comfortable
and roomy tent. This difference
is mostly owing to the fact that
some of them can not agree long
at a time and so will not hitch
together to make out a tent of
respectable size. A Soldiers life is
a lazy life on the average though
we have now and then a day of
hardship yet most of the time
there is only too much time for
lounging playing Cards and
other sports of the same kind
and Sunday in camp is as much
Sunday as it ought to be as can

well we imagined yet I have seen
but few cases of wanton Sabbath
breaking most of the kind being
partly necessary. I have managed
however to keep from work on
Sunday and have always tried
to have the Sabbath what it sho-
-uld be at all times the Day of rest
I am heartily glad of one thing
that is our Leaders have come
out very strict against all
plundering or disturbing the property
of any and they have affixed severe
penalties on any violation of this
rule. You may think all this un
-necessary with Civilised Soldiers
but I assure you if it were not
for Military Law every Pig, Hen or
even Cow in the Country we pass
through would go to help fill the
Stomacks of our Army not because
they are actually needed but the
fare they give us is not of the kind
to satisfy those used to better and

so and of a certain class would grab at anything eatable very quick and without stopping to inquire to whom it belonged so they have to be checked or the country would be entirely stripped and the men no better off for they almost always get as much and often more rations than they can eat and that too good enough to ——— ——— of ——— ——— food. I do not know as you had better look for another letter very soon for I shall probably be very busy so you need not be concerned but if I do not write as often as I have you may think I have less time to spare from other duties. And so hoping this may find you as it leaves me in the enjoyment of health I will bring this long letter to a close ——— ——— ——— regularly but we have received none lately. Write to me when you can get time and do not wait for me for I shall write as often as I can spare time. Think of the Soldier ——— ——— ——— ——— for he thinks often of you. Your Son & Brother
J. B. Setterlee

44th Regiment   New York Volunteers,
Col. S. W. STRYKER, Commanding.

Camp Near Yorktown Va.   Apr. 8th 1862

Dear Parents, Brother & Sister.

I received your letter this morning and I need scarcely add I was very glad to hear from you. I am well and although surrounded by warlike preparations and by war in fact I am enjoying myself as well as can be expected. My health is very good much better than it has been in years past and I manage to go through with the duties and hardships of a Soldiers life as well as most men and even better than a great many. I have been unwell enough to mention only once since I came here and that was owing I suppose to the change of food & water which set me into a diarreha but I soon cured myself with the medicine I brought along from L. Falls and have since been well as any. I have always managed to have plenty to eat by taking care to save what was given to me and have been able to divide with some less fortunate and I think of all the boys took care of their food as they ought to there would be less complaint and all would have enough to keep them comfortable. As to clothing I am still wearing the same suit I left home in and none of them have come to mending. You will expect to have me say something of the prospects of our Army but I can tell you but little. We expect to fight at Yorktown and the time is not far distant when the fight will commence (I think but of the strength of the Rebels I know nothing and therefore can say nothing) about how much we have to do to conquer for we must conquer and shall probably have to fight hard to do it. Our force here is very large and McClellan is here with us. His reputation as a General is at stake and now is his time. In addition to the large land force here we have a fleet of Gunboats on York River and when we move there will a combined move by land and water which must not fail. Prof. Lowe is here with his Balloon and he has taken a thorough view of the Rebel works so our Generals know all about their situation and strength and are thus prepared to direct each move so that it will be successful. There has already been some cannonading between our Field Batteries and their works resulting to the advantage of our men three of their Forts being entirely silenced for the time by Griffins Battery on Friday last and that without the loss of a man on our side the enemys shell and gunnery being poor. Martins Battery (3d. Mass.) was less lucky losing two killed and two wounded and also four horses killed. Since then we have had but little firing on either side for our heavy guns have not yet come up and the Rebels seem to be afraid to come out which is probably owing to the fact that Griffins and other guns and also the Sharpshooters stand ready to give them fits the moment that they show their heads.

Our Army is hopeful without being inclined to boast and victory we must have though we have to fight long and fight hard to gain it. The fighting seems likely to be

Artillery fighting mostly but of course we may have something to do before Yorktown is taken and from present appearances I think our men enough in earnest to do the fair thing. I think you would be astonished to see the coolness of our men during the engagement of last Friday for though some of the enemy's shell struck within a short distance of us all seemed perfectly cool and I doubt not had we been called on we should have done well for the honor of Uncle Sam. I will here say that the body of the Army have perfect confidence in McClellan and will I think do better under his command than they would under any other man and the Tribune although it may be able to sway the minds of the people can not break the hold that this young Chieftan has on the hearts of his soldiers. For myself I will say that I do not think so highly of him as many seem to yet I believe he is a deep thinking & careful if not a brilliant military man and I believe he will come out all right in the end notwithstanding the opposition of the Tribune and the say of the Tribune and other journals that it was known that Centreville and Mannassas were evacuated is only bosh for they were not really evacuated till the march of our Army compelled their evacuation. You may think it strange that I should contradict such a strong report but when I tell you that the Rebels had a force as far north as Fairfax C.H. only the day before our Regt. got in there and that a Company of N.J. Cavalry killed and took prisoners twenty four of their men in a skirmish near that place and the fact that their pickets retreated but a few hours before we marched on to Centreville added to the fact that they left flags swords knives guns knapsacks and clothing in their haste to get away from the latter place you will perhaps have a mind to think that those who sit in their closets in N.Y. or Washington and write articles for the Tribune know less about the whereabouts of the Rebels than those N.J. boys who felt them with their Sabres and when they had defeated them saw them streak it for the woods. No I tell you there was no truth in that report. The Rebels were leaving Mannassas when we were in Centreville for I saw with my own eyes the smoke of the buildings that they were burning as they left the place and Horace Greely can find better business if he tries hard than telling such lies to weaken the confidence of the people in their leaders because the leaders happen to differ with him on some trifling points. Gen. McClellan has shown himself a man of ability in getting up and preparing so large an army to take the field and it is simply mean to try to detract from his justly earned reputation. I notice one fact with reference to him that is when he is present with us the Sabbath is more respected and things generally move much more smoothly than when we are away from his presence which of course argues well for his influence with those under his immediate command. The weather is rainy and chilly to day but we have had much pleasant weather and the peach trees have been in blossom for some ten days yet they say that the spring here is a very late one. On our march here I had an opportunity to see some of the innocent causes of this war I mean the negroes some of whom I presume had never seen such a thing as a Yankee before and they were as much pleased to see us as if they expected great things of us which most of them probably do. One old fellow his head white with years seemed almost beside himself with joy. He fairly could not stand still and when asked where the Rebels were he said "day lef here bout ten clock massa an dey wen for Lord know where and I guess dey's running yit" so let the Slaveholders tell as much as they chose about the faithfulness of the slaves one thing is very certain they always seem very glad to see Yankee soldiers and they are always more than willing to tell all they know likely to result to our advantage.

My hands are cold so you must expect to find poor writing even poorer than usual if that were possible. Another thing I wish to speak of I hear that you were all very much alarmed by the report that so large a body of our men had been blown up at Mannassas. I hope you will not give yourself more trouble than is necessary about such reports for they always are to large to be true. 60,000 men cover a piece of ground larger than the Rebels will be likely to dig up in some time and by the time the last powder was planted the first would need drying and so on and my opinion is they would get sick of the speculation. Such stories are never to be believed for they are never true. I hope you will give yourself no uneasiness about our present position for although I will not try to disguise the fact that there is a probability of some hard fighting here there may not be any engagement of consequence in which the Infantry will have to take part. I feel that I am ready and willing and I hope you will give yourself as little uneasiness as possible. Write soon and write a long letter. Amos I want you to write some in the next letter. You can write something of interest to me for you will write of things that Martha does not mention.

Apr. 9th

We have just received news of the taking of Island No. 10. and the defeat of Beauregard and you may be sure our soldiers feel decidedly well over the good news and we hope to make some good news ourselves one of these days. But I have written very long already and must close. Should you not hear from me again so soon as usual you may think I am more than usually busy. I can not always get time to write when I wish but will write when I can. If you hear of a battle here soon you need not be disappointed nor need you be disappointed if you hear from me again before we have any for the roads are very bad now and the troops necessarily move slow but in any event give yourself no uneasiness about me for there is no present danger and there may never be any. Hoping that this letter may find you all enjoying a good degree of health

I remain now as ever with much love
Your son & Brother
J.B. Satterlee

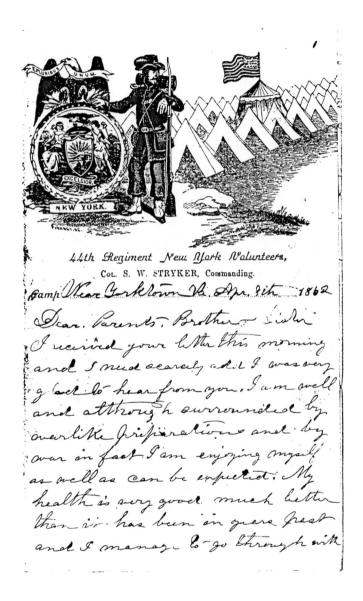

44th Regiment New York Volunteers,
Col. S. W. STRYKER, Commanding.

Camp Near Yorktown Va. Apr. 9th 1862

Dear Parents, Brother & Sister

I received your letter this morning
and I need scarely add I was very
glad to hear from you. I am well
and although surrounded by
warlike preparations and by
war in fact I am enjoying myself
as well as can be expected. My
health is very good much better
than it has been in years past
and I manage to go through with

view of the Rebel works so our
Generals know all about their
situation and strength and are
thus prepared to direct each move
so that it will be successful.
There has already been some
Cannonading between our Field
Batteries and their works resulting
~~to the advantage of our one the~~
of their Forts being entirely silenced
for the time by Griffins Battery on
Friday last and that without
the loss of a man on our side the
enemys shell and gunnery being
poor. Martins Battery 3 d. Mass
was less lucky losing two killed
and two wounded and also four
horses killed. Since then we have
~~had but little~~ firing on either
side for our heavy guns have not
yet come up and the Rebels seem
to be afraid to come out which is
probably owing to the fact that
Griffins and other guns and also
the Sharpshooters stand ready to
give them fits the moment that
they show their heads.

Our army is hopeful without being
too ... and ... victory we
... we have to fight
...
...
...
...
... appearance
...
earnest to do the fair thing I think
you ...

the
Coolness of our men during the
engagement of last Friday for
though some of the enemy's shell
struck within a short distance
of us all seemed perfectly cool
and I doubt not had we been called
on we should have done well for
the honor of Uncle Sam. I will here
say that the body of the Army have
perfect confidence in McClellan
and will I think do better under
his command than they would
under any other man and the Trib...

& though it may be able to sway
the minds of the people can not
break the hold that this young
Chieftain has on the hearts of
his soldiers. For myself I will say
that I do not think so highly of
him as many seem to yet I believe
he is a deep Thinking & careful
if not a brilliant military man
and I believe he will come out all
right in the end notwithstanding the
opposition of the Tribune and the
say of the Tribune and other journal
that it was known that Centreville
and Mannasses were evacuated is
only bosh for they were not really
evacuated till the march of our army
compelled their evacuation. You
may think it strange that I should
contradict such a strong report but
when I tell you that the Rebels had
no force as far north as Fairfax C.H.
only the day before our regt got

in them and that a Company of N.J.
... killed ... took prisoners
...
...
...
...
...
...
... knives
...
their haste to get ...
latter 44th Regiment New York Volunteers
Col. S. W. STRYKER, Commanding
Camp .... N.J. 186
have a mind to think that those
who sit in their closets in N.J.
or Washington and write articles for
the Tribune know less about the
whereabouts of the Rebels than
those N.J. boys who felt them
with their Sabers and when defeated
sur them chased them
Strak it for the woods. No I tell you
there was no truth in that report
the Rebels were leaving Manassas
when we were in Cen'rville for
I saw with my own eyes the smoke
of the burning that they were

burning (as they left) the place and
Horace Greely can find better business
if he tries hard than telling such
lies to weaken the confidence of the
people in their leaders because the
leaders happen to differ with him
on some trifling points. Gen.
McClellan has shown himself a man
of ability in getting up and preparing
so large an army to take the field
and it is simply mean to try to
detract from his justly earned reputation. I notice one fact with
reference to him that is when he
is present with us the Sabbath is
more respected and things generally
move much more smoothly than
when we are away from him, since
which of course argues well for his
influence with those under his
immediate Command. The weather
is rainy and chilly to day but we
have had much pleasant weather
and the peach trees have been in

blossom for some ten days yet they
spread here very little
our much her head
be see
response far
in negro and
her rather
a task
very much
pleased to see us as of very

expect the Regiment of New York Volunteers,
a Lieut Col W. STRYKER Commanding. Probably
not. One old fellow his head white[?]
with years seemed almost beside
himself with joy he fairly could
not stand still and when asked
where the Rebels were he said "dey
lef here bout ten oclock massa an dey
run for Lord know where and I
guess deys running yit, & so let the
Slave holders tell as much as they
chose about the faithfulness of the
slaves one thing is very certain
they always seem very glad to see

ourselves one of these days. But I have written very long already and must close. Should you not hear from me again so soon as usual you may think I am more than usually busy I can not always get time to write when I wish but will write when I can. If you hear of a battle here so you must not be disappointed nor need you be disappointed if you hear from me again before we have any for the roads are very bad now and the troops necessarily move slow but in any event give yourself no uneasiness about me for there is no present danger and there may never be any. Hoping that this letter may find you all enjoying a good degree of health.

I remain now as ever

With much love Your Loving Brother

J. B. Satterlee

Camp Winfield Scott
April 25th 1862

Dear Parents

I sit down to write a letter to you. I received Martha's letter yesterday and was most happy to hear from home. Indeed I was getting quite anxious for I had been without direct news from home longer than at any time since I left and when I dont get my regular letter from you I am almost lost. I am well and hope you may be enjoying the same blessing. We dont have much to do now or nothing great enough to make hard work of it a little drill and now and then a day of Piqueting (sic) or work on the road being about all we have to do. Yet you must not suppose that matters are dragging because we don't have to work very hard for there is a large force here to work and many hands make light work and when directed by as skilled brains as those who are directing the siege of Yorktown many hands make the work move. The Rebel works are skillfully made and there is a deep miry (sic) stream runs between their works and our Army so we must have a number of bridges built for the transportation of Artillery and that our forces may pass over with the necessary expedition when the time comes and this is part of the work we are now doing so when you consider that these bridges are from twenty to thirty rods in length you can see at once that a safe bridge of that length costs some labor. Then we have roads to make around the hills so that we can get quite close to the Enemy's works without being seen and being seen of course exposed to their fire. Day before yesterday our regt. worked on the road and I think I did more real work than I have done in eight months before. We worked under the supervision of an Engineer and did a splendid job and one too that will be of great use even after the close of the war. Five hundred men well directed can do a good deal of work in a day and I am informed by one of our Lieutenants that eighteen thousand of our troops are at work every day and night before the Rebel works at this place. Last Sunday we were on Piquet and as the day was somewhat rainy and chilly we didn't have a first rate time yet we met with no disturbance from the Rebels, though five thousand men of our Division lay on their arms all night Sunday night to guard against surprise. All passed very quietly. The Rebels have been so roughly handled every time they have tried to surprise the Piquets of our Division that they are getting more peaceable on this end of the lines. I think that Gen. Porter is number one for this business and I guess the Rebs will begin to think so to for on every occasion of their attacking our Piquets they have been forced back with heavy loss while we in a picked position have scarcely suffered at all. Gen. Porter attends to the posting of the Piquets himself and visits them often to see that all is going right with them and I believe that for dilligence in business Gen. Fitz John Porter has no superior in our Army. He is a very quiet and unpretentious man talking pleasantly with any soldier he comes in contact with and with his keen black eye always observant of every thing worthy of notice. He has gained the confidence of his Division so that every man believes in him and trusts him implicitly. The Soldiers call him Old Black Hawk and we expect to do our country some good service under his command when the proper time for action arrives. Mr. Van Pelten Chaplain of the 34th was here to see us this week. He reports that the 34th are to the left of us (toward James River) and that they are having plenty to do. George Morse has been distinguishing himself as a sharpshooter but he found himself treed (sic) one day and has since had to be a little more cautious. It appears that he crept up to within forty rods of the Rebel works got behind a tree and commenced operations. But the Rebels soon found out where he was and the result was that every time he showed head hand or foot a bullet would whistle close by and in one of his jerks to save his head he lost his cap which rolled slightly to one side and he was obliged to leave his cap and creep off back under cover of the tree till out of the range of the Rebel marksman. So much was rather down on the A_____ Hunter but on another occasion he crept out and at a short range fired shot after shot untill he knocked over eighteen of *them* or at least as another man says who was where he could watch the effect of Morses shots and one of the Berdan Sharpshooters attached to our Division has kept the Rebels from using one of their largest guns nearly all the time since we came here. He has a small pit dug at comfortable range and whener a Reb. tries to load the gun he pops him over and so keeps a gun entirely silent which could do much damage if the Rebels were allowed to use it. We were paid off yesterday and I am going to send the greater portion of the money home. I have procured a draft on the U.S. Treasurer at New York as being the safest way I could manage to send it and you can easily exchange the Draft or send and draw the money on it at New York. I wish you to make use of it in any way you wish that is use it as your own. I will give you a description of the draft, and if it does not reach you within a reasonable time you can Telegraph or send word in some other way to the Assistant Treasurer of the United States at New York, that payment may be stopped in case the Draft is lost in the mail. Or if you do or do not receive it let me know as soon as possible and you ought to get it in a week (or ten days at most) from this time. I would not wait at any rate more than ten days from the date of this as a letter or Dispatch in time would stop payment on the Draft in case it is lost and save me another. I will send the Draft in another letter differently directed and thus not awaken suspicion by making the letter too large. Inquire for a letter for Mother which will give you more particulars. I have no more time to write at present so I will close. Write soon and write as often as you can spare time

Your son

J.B. Satterlee

Description of Draft. (Amount $55.00)
No. 581 (drawn at Washington April 25th 1862)
Payable to Lieutenant C.E. Royce or order and signed by Wm.
Richardson, Paymaster, U.S. Army.
Also indorsed on the back payable to the order of Beriah W.
Satterlee, Salisbury Centre, N.Y and signed

C.E. Royce 1st Lieut.

Camp Winfield Scott
April 29th 1862

Dear Parents—

I sit down to write a letter to you. I received Martha's letter yesterday and was most happy to hear from home. Indeed I was getting quite anxious for I had been without direct news from home longer than at any time since I left and when I don't get my regular letter from you I am almost lost. I am well and hope you may be enjoying the same blessing. We don't have much to do now or nothing, just enough to make hard work of it a little drill and now and then a day of Piqueting or work on the road being about all we have to do. Yet you must not suppose that matters are dragging because we don't have to work very hard for there is a large force here to work and many hands make light work and when directed by as skillful brains as those who are directing the siege of York Town many hands make the work move. The Rebel works are skillfully made and there is a ~~wide~~ very stream runs between their works and our Army so we must have a number of bridges built for the transportation of Artillery and that our forces may pass over with the necessary expedition when the time comes and this is part of the work we are now doing so when you consider that these bridges are from twenty to thirty rods in length you can see at once that a safe bridge of that length costs some labor. Then we have roads to make around the hills so that we can get quite close to the Enemy's works without being seen and being seen of course exposed to their fire. Day before yesterday our Regt. worked on the road and I think I did more real work than I have done in eight months before. We worked under the supervision of an Engineer and did a splendid job and one too that will be of great use even after the close of the war. Five hundred men well directed can do a good deal of work in a day and I am informed by one of our Lieutenants that eighteen thousand of our troops are at work every day and night before the Rebel works at this place. Last sunday we were on Piquet and as the day was somewhat rainy and chilly we didn't have a first rate time yet we met with no disturbance from the Rebels though five thousand men of our Division lay on their arms all night Sunday night to guard against surprise all passed very quietly. The Rebels have been so roughly handled every time they have tried to surprise the Piquets of our Division that they are getting more peaceable on this end of the lines. I think that Gen. Porter is number one for this business and I guess the Rebs will begin to think so too for on every occasion of their attacking our Piquets they have been forced back with heavy loss while we in a picket position have scarcely suffered at all. Gen. Porter attends to the posting of the Piquets himself and visits them often to see that all is going right with them and I believe that for dilligence in business Gen. Fitz John Porter has no superior in our Army. He is a very quiet and unpretentious man talking pleasantly with any soldier he comes in contact with and with his keen black eye always observant of every thing worthy of notice he has gained the confidence of his Division so that every man believes in him and trusts him implicitly. The Soldiers call him Old Black Hawk and we expect to do our country some good service under his command when the proper time for action arrives. Mr. VanPetten Chaplein of the 34th was here to see us this week. He reports that the 34th. are to the left of us (toward James River) and that they are having plenty to do. George Morse has been distinguishing himself as a sharpshooter but he found himself treed one day and has since had to be a little more cautious. It appears that he crept up to within forty rods of the Rebel works, got behind a tree and commenced operations. But the Rebels soon found out where he was and the result was that every time he showed head hand or foot a bullet would whistle close by and in one of his jerks to save his head he lost his cap which rolled slightly to one side and he was obliged to leave his cap and creep off back under cover of the tree till out of the range of the Rebel marksman. So much was rather blown on the Ariette Hunter but on another occasion he crept out and at a short range fired shot after shot untill he knocked over eighteen of them or at least so another man says who was where he could watch the effect of Morse's shots and one of the Borden Sharp-shooters attached to our Division has kept the Rebels from using one of their largest guns nearly all the time since we came here. He has a small pit dug at comfortable range and whenever a Reb tries to load the gun he pops him over and so keeps the a gun entirely silent which could do much damage if the Rebels were allowed to use it. We were paid off yesterday and I am going to send the greater portion of the money home. I have procured a draft on the U.S. Treasury at New York as being the safest way I could means to send it and you can easily exchange the draft or send and draw the money on it at New York. I wish you to make use of it in any way you wish that is use it as your own. I will give you a description of the draft and if it does not reach you within a reasonable time you can Telegraph or send word in some other way to of the Assistant Treasurer of the United States at New York, that payment may be stopped in case the Draft is lost in the mail. Or if you do or do not receive it let me know as soon as possible and you ought to get it in a week (or ten days at most) from this time. I would not wait at any rate more than ten days from the date of this as a letter or Dispatch in time would stop payment on the Draft in case it is lost and save one another. I will send the Draft in another letter differently directed and thus not awaken suspicion by making the letter too large. Inquire for a letter for Martha which will give you more particulars. I have no more time to write at present so I will close. Write soon and write as often as you can spare time   Your Son

J. B. Setterlee

Description of Draft (Amount $55.00
No. 581. (drawn at Washington April 25th 1862)
and Payable to Lieutenant C. E. Royce or order
and signed by Wm Richardson

also indorsed on the back   Paymaster
Payable to the order of Beriah W Setterlee ——   U. S. Army
Salisbury Centre N. Y. and signed
C. E. Royce 1st Lieut

Yorktown Va. May 5th (18)62

Dear Parents, Brother & Sister

  I have just got in from standing guard over a lot of Rebel provision taken by our Army and as I have a resting spell now will spend the time in writing home. I am comfortable as to health and hope this letter may find you the same. You will of course expect some explanation about the matter of the taking of this place and I will try to do my best to gratify you with a plain narrative of facts. We had been very busily engaged in the business of planting Batteries &c. up to yesterday all the time under a terrible fire from the Rebel works. Our Gunboats & finished batteries in the mean time playing on them at intervals and doing them much damage when we learned that the Rebels had left or were leaving their fortifications. The 44th was on the way out for a day of digging when the news met them and after marching up near enough to see plenty of our men on the rebel works and to see the old "star spangled banner" once more floating over the hills of Yorktown we took our way back to headquarters left our picks & shovels and bade farewell to trenching for the present.

  We then packed up and about eleven o'clock May 4th 1862 found us within the Rebel works. We found Yorktown much like other Southern towns a small dilapidated looking place boasting of a Court House Jail and not much else of importance. The Rebel works are strong but not impregnable or they would not have left them in so much haste when they thought that we were pretty near ready to pitch in for good. They left in so much haste as to leave their Cannon and large quantities ammunition provision spts. Turpentine Resin Tents medicines &c. which of course Uncle Sam can readily find use for. What should make the Rebels leave just at this time some of us are much inclined wonder but I believe now as I did all the time that they were not half as strong as they were represented and after waiting as long as they dared they must of course run or do worse. Our Batteries damaged the Rascals much or at least so say the Negroes left behind and turn which way they would a shell from the Yankees was ready to scatter them at any time of day or night and so vexed that they could not stop us digging up to them and tormented day and night by our Gunboats & Batteries they took their safest course and got off in the night the best they could. In looking back I find much to wonder at much of narrow escape and imminent peril so much indeed that it seems miraculous that but one man of our Regt. has been killed in the siege. Through all or almost all kinds of exposures incident to a siege of a month in length we have gone and though under the guns of the Rebels or in reach of them all the time night and day for the past month and frequently obliged to listen to music made by the whistling of Rifle bullets past our ears and to the crash of the murderous shell. We have enjoyed ourselves pretty well generally & have never flinched in the hour of danger or duty. It has been my lot to get some pretty good marksmen to shoot their best at me on picquet but though they did make some pretty good shots I escaped untouched and though the matter was really a serious one I felt no worse than I have often felt before in a less dangerous position and the coolness of all our men has been really surprising. We have done much work but may think we have taken the best way to get possession of this noted Rebel stronghold and I am among the number for we could not flank them or get in their rear on account of their works resting by the right and left flanks on the James & York Rivers. So we had no resource but to attack them in front which must have cost us an immense loss of life and if we could drive them out of such a stronghold (confessedly) the key of Virginia without loss of life they were of course as badly defeated except perhaps a loss of life as they would have been had we stormed them three weeks ago but in that case we are even for if we have killed but few of them they have not injured us and the guns, provisions &c. left by them in their stampede from here cannot be replaced to them readily. As soon as possible after it was ascertained that they had gone a large force of cavalry, light artillery & infantry started in pursuit and they (the Rebs) were overtaken yesterday afternoon but the result I don't know yet. They must now fight in the open field if we can catch them which I think we can. At present the 44th is engaged in guarding the forts & property left here by the Rebels but how long we shall remain I am unable to say. Our Col. wants to get the position of garrisoning Yorktown but whether he will succeed or not I do not know. I think it would be better for us to have some such duty to do for a short time on account of the sickness which is so hard on the Regt. at present but whether we get it or not is doubtful. I have reason to think that this is a healthy place for the breeze from the Chesapeake sweeps it and the water of York River is quite salte (sic) as high up as here and our Regt. has had so much of sickness that it seems necessary for us to have a change of duty. I have been unusually healthy all the time notwithstanding the general bad health of the boys and I hope I have seen my worst times as to health. In fact I believe that I have only to be prudent to enjoy good health in the future.

I received that medicine safe and sound and it would take more than ten dollars in gold to buy it (so much I think of it). I was not a little puzzled at the account of that noted doctor but I hope he may do you all some good.

May 6th

I again find myself seated writing home. I have been out this forenoon viewing the works of the Rebels and I was surprised for I thought Centreville strong but set along side the fortifications of Yorktown Centreville was but a plaything and if the Rebels don't defend such places I don't know when they expect to make anything of a fight. The guns are nearly all of large size being most of them old U.S. guns and the supply of ammunition is almost endless to these add fortifications perfect in their kind and a position naturally Gibralter like and you have the Rebel Fort at Yorktown. Yet with all these advantages they ran away in so much of a hurry as to leave tents standing, bedding lying around loose, trunks, baggage and provisions (raw and cooked) ditto and other things much in a corresponding order. From prisoners, contrabands and deserters we gather that they thought that we were digging under their works to blow them up and so thoroughly alarmed they cut stick to fight only when driven to do so. Cannonading was heard yesterday afternoon in the direction taken by the retreating Rebels and I presume we shall soon hear of sharp fighting in that direction. Our Army is hurrying forward and if the Rebels are not pretty good at running they will have to suffer soon. We found some cannon of the Rebels own manufacture on the Fort, but judging from the action of three of them on the side next to our works they will be nearly as fatal to *friend* as for the three refused to have burst during the siege and the remaining ones seem to be worthless being made of poor material and roughed off any way at that so that this first service collapsed them costing the Rebels several men in each case. The remains of the Old Forts held by Cornwallis in Revolutionary times are distinctly visible and though on a smaller scale than the present works they must have been very strong.

May 7th.

I will now try to finish my long letter. The 34th N.Y. has just gone on board boat here to follow the Rebels by steam as far as possible. They all seem healthy and sickness is a stranger to them. Steph. Bowen requested me to put in that he is well and hearty and wants some of you who happen to see any of his folks to tell them that such is the case. M. H. Bliss was somewhat unwell when we marched from our camp and as he was unfit for duty he with about a dozen others of Co. B. have gone north to some Hospital probably at Philadelphia. If you see any of his folks before they happen to hear from him dont alarm them needlessly for all will probably be right with him soon. It has been settled that the 44th is to remain here for a short time perhaps two weeks perhaps more our duty being to guard the Fort and public property here. News came in yesterday that our advanced guard had overtaken the baggage train of the Rebels had a serious fight and taken a large quantity of the baggage among the rest, Gen. Magruder's and though the report may be exaggerated there has probably been a serious fight ending in the total rout of the Rebel rear guard. But I must close this long letter. I received Marthas letter last night and as usual was very glad to hear from home. Give me a letter from home as often as possible for I dont have much to read and news from home is always most acceptable.

Your son & brother
J.B. Satterlee

Yorktown Va. May 8th /62

Dear Parents, Brother & Sister

I have just got
in from standing guard over a lot of
Rebel provision taken by our Army and
as I have a resting spell now will spend
this time in writing home. I am comfortable as to health and hope this letter may
find you the same. You will of course
expect some explanation about the
matter of the taking of this place and
I will try to do my best to gratify you
with a plain narration of facts. We
had been very busily engaged in the
business of planting Batteries &c. up
to yesterday all the time under a terrible fire from the Rebel works our
Gunboats & finished Batteries in the

mean time blazing on them at intervals
and doing them much damage when
we learned that the Rebels had left
or were leaving their fortifications.
The 44th. was on the way out for a day
of digging when the news met them and
after marching up near enough to see
plenty of our men on the Rebel works
and to see the old "Star Spangled banner"
once more floating over the hills of
Yorktown we took our way back to head
quarters left our picks & shovels and bade
farewell to trenching for the present.
We then packed up and about eleven
O'clock May 4th. 1862 found us within
the Rebel works. We found Yorktown
much like other southern towns a small
dilapidated looking place boasting of
a Court House Jail and not much

else of importance. The Rebel works are strong but not impregnable or they would not have left them in so much haste when they thought that we were pretty near ready to pitch in for good. They left in so much haste as to leave their Cannon and large quantities ammunition provisions Salt Turpentine Rosin, Tents medicines &c. which of course Uncle Sam can readily find use for. What should make the Rebels leave just at this time some of us are much inclined wonder but I believe now as I did all the time that they were not half as strong as they were represented and after waiting as long as they dared they must of course run or do worse. Our Batteries damaged the Rascals much or at least so say they who were left behind and from which way they would a shell from the Yankees was

...ready to scatter them at any time of day or night and so fixed that they could not stop us digging up to them and tormented day and night by our Gunboats & Batteries. They took their safest course and got off in the night the best they could. In looking back I find much to wonder at; such narrow escapes and imminent peril so much indeed that it seems miraculous that but one man of our Regt has been killed in the siege. Through all, or almost all kinds of exposures incident to a siege of six months in length we have gone and though under the guns of the Rebels or in reach of them all the time night and day for the past month and frequently obliged to listen to music made by the whistling of Rifle bullets past our ears and to the crash of the murderous shell we have enjoyed ourselves pretty well generally & have never flinched in the hour of danger or duty. It has been my lot to get some pretty good marksmen to shoot their best at me on picquet but though they did make some pretty good shots I escaped untouched and though the matter was really a serious one I felt no worse than I have often felt before in a less dangerous position and the coolness of all our men has been really surprising. We have done much work but many think we have taken the best way to get possession of this note[d] Rebel stronghold and I am among the number for we could not flank them or get in their rear on account of their works resting by the right and left flanks on the James & York River so we had no resource but to attack them in front which must have cost us an im- -mense loss of life and if we could drive them out of such a stronghold (confessed- -ly) the Key of Virginia without loss of life they were of course as badly defeated except perhaps a loss of life as they would have been had we stormed them three weeks ago but in that case we are even for if we have killed but few of them they have not injured us and the guns Provisions &c left by them in their stampede from here cannot be replaced to them readily. As soon as possible after it was ascertained that they had gone a large force of cavalry light artillery & infantry started in pursuit and they (the Rebs) were overtaken yesterday afternoon but the result I don't know yet. They must now fight in the open field if we can catch them which I think we can. At present the 44th is engaged in guarding the forts & property left here by the Rebels but how long we shall remain I am unable to say. Our Col. wants to get the position of garrisoning this town but whether he will succeed or not I do not know. I think it would be better for us to have some such duty to do for a short time on account of the sickness which is so much on the rise at present but whether

we get it or not is doubtful. I have reason to think
that this is a healthy place for the breese from the
Chesapeake sweeps it and the water of York River
is quite Salt as high up as here and our
Regt has had so much of sickness that it seems
necessary for us to have a change of duty.
I have been unusually healthy all the time
notwithstanding the general bad health of the
boys and I hope I have seen the worst times as to
                                        my
health in fact I believe that I have only to be
prudent to enjoy good health in the future
I received that medicine safe and sound and
it would take more than ten dollars in gold to
buy it so much I think of it. I was not a little
puzzled at the account of that curled doctor
but I hope he may do you all some good.
                        May 6th
I again find myself seated writing home
I have been out this forenoon viewing

the works of the Rebels and I was surprised for I thought Centreville strong but set along side the fortifications of Yorktown Centreville was but a plaything and if the Rebels don't defend such places I don't know when they expect to make anything of a fight The guns are nearly all of large size being most of them old N.S. guns and the supply of ammunition is almost endless. So these old fortifications perfect in their kind and a position naturally Gibraltar like and you have the Rebel Fort at Yorktown yet with all these advantages they ran away in so much of a hurry as to have tents standing building lying around loose Trunks baggage and provisions raw and cooked &c. Ditto and other things much in a corresponding order From prisoners contrabands and deserters we gather that they expected a Gunboat attack soon and also that they thought that we were digging under their works to blow them up and so thoroughly alarmed they cut stick to fight only when driven to do so. Cannonading was heard yesterday afternoon in the direction taken by the retreating Rebels and I presume we shall soon hear of sharp fighting in that direction. Our army is hurrying forward and if the Rebels are not pretty good at running they will have to suffer soon. We found some cannon of the Rebels own manufacture on the Fort but judging from the action of three of them on the side next to our works they will be nearly as fatal to friend as foe the three refused to have burst during the siege and the remaining ones seem to be worthless being made of poor material and roughed off any way at that so that this first service collapsed them costing the Rebels several men in each case. The remains of the old Forts held by Cornwallis in Revolutionary times are distinctly visible and though on a smaller scale than the present works they must have

...are very strong. May 9th. I will now try to finish my long letter. The 34th N.Y. has just gone on board boat here to follow the Rebels by steam as far as possible. They all seem healthy and sickness is a stranger to them. Steph. Bowin requested me to put in that he is well and hearty and wants some of you who happen to see any of his folks to tell them that such is this case. M.H. Bliss was somewhat unwell when we marched from our camp and as he was unfit for duty he with about a dozen others of Co. B. have gone north to some Hospital probably at Philadelphia. If you see any of his folks before they happen to hear from him don't alarm them needlessly for all will probably be right with him soon. It has been stated that this 30th is to remain here for a short time perhaps two weeks perhaps more our duty being to guard the Fort and public property here. News came in yesterday that our Advanced guard had overtaken the baggage train of the Rebels had a serious fight and taken a large quantity of the baggage among the rest Gen. Magruders and though the report may be exaggerated there has probably been a serious fight ending in the total rout of the Rebel rear guard.

But I must close this long letter. I received Marthas letter last night and as usual was very glad to hear from home. Give me a letter from home as often as possible for I dont have much to read and news from home is always most acceptable

Yours brother
J. B. Satterlee

Dear Parents

I now sit down to commence another letter to you. I am enjoying very good health at present and hope this letter may find you also well. As you will at once see our Regt. is yet at Yorktown with no immediate prospect of a move. I believe though Col. Stryker seems to think (?) that we shall soon move. The health of our men is somewhat better than it has been *I think* probably owing to the fact that we have good quarters and much less exposure than usual. About all the work we have to do now is to stand guard four hours out of twenty four which is but a small matter comparatively and not much like work. I have got pretty well seasoned to sleeping on the ground and also on brush, floors, &c., so that I now sleep as well on a floor as I ever did on a bed and begin to believe that there is more truth than fiction in the saying that a person can get used to anything. At any rate it seems so in my case for I now manage to get along first rate where I would once have thought it very hard to live at all. Thanks to the Secesh or rather to Gen. McClellan who drove them out in such a hurry we found plenty of meal and flour among their stores left here and as it was good in quality why should we not make use of it. No sooner said than done and after a vigorous thinking to determine what were the proper ingredients for a Jenny Cake I find a deficiency of milk but what can't be cured must be endured so I went to work and in a short space of time I had a Jenny fit for eating baked as I have seen them of old before the fire and rivalling in sweetness anything of the kind I ever saw in more civilised lands. In short the thing was good and so acknowledged by all partakers and from that time to this (for you know I like Jenny cold or hot) Uncle Sam's crackers have been neglected for too much of a good thing is not so good and after eating nothing but crackers for more than two calendar months I for one was willing to rest my jaws for a while by adopting some softer and more tasty food. Yesterday we had fresh bread dealt out to us for the first time since we left Fairfax C.H. and if I had had some butter I could have made one pretty good meal but of course being a soldier I could get along without. Now I think of it I will give you a short list of Yorktown prices current that you may see how hard a face some beings can put on when they get the opportunity. Butter sells at 50 cents pr. pound, cheese at 30 cents, eggs 40 cents pr. dozen, oranges 10 cents apiece and other things much in the same way. In short the most scandalous prices are asked and given for anything fit to eat and whiskey dearest of all has sold for $3.00 pr. quart (I wish it were $1.00) and finds plenty of fools to purchase it even at that monstrous price. I learn from the papers that Moses has arrived in New York and I think from what he told me he will try to get home if he is well enough to stand the journey. I visited him on the Hospital ship before it sailed and wrote to his father afterwards to let him know how I found him and his probable destination. If matters continue to look as favorable as they do at present I think more of the sick will ever come back to the Army but will be discharged when cured. Since I last wrote I have got some information as to what caused the Rebels to leave in such haste and as I consider the source good I will explain it to you. When our Army entered Yorktown the first man met by them was an orderly sergeant in the Artillery of the Rebels who being a native of New York and having been impressed into their service of course owed them no good will and took the first opportunity to give them the slip. He showed our Genls. where the Torpedos were that had been laid for our men and gave them much other valuable information. He was placed in charge of our Captain till after the rush should be over and I had many opportunities of hearing him converse. The account given by him is nearly as follows: the Rebels burst all their new style (long range guns) and after repeated trials found that they had nothing of the kind that would reach our Gunboats or our heavy battery (No. 1) at the mouth of Wormley's Creek and both the Battery and Boats could not only reach them but throw clear over them if necessary thus proving to them the great superiority of our Guns and leaving them only the choice of hopeless resistance or flight which latter being much the safest of the two was the one adopted. Our Artillery is clearly superior to that of the Rebels for *all* the reliable guns they have are old U.S. guns and they though good for the kind are not to be compared to our new Rifled Parrot Cannon any more than a common smooth bore Rifle is to be compared to a good cut Rifle and no one knows this better than Jeff Davis who if report is true ordered the evacuation of Yorktown himself. How true the remark made by Capt. Griffin of our army was we could not at that time see but begin to now. He remarked that the guns in a certain Rebel Battery were aimed by a Union man for they uniformly fell short or went over our men who were at work clearly in range of their guns and it turned out that the above mentioned Sergeant was the very man who aimed the guns in question thus making Capt. Griffin's prediction true and accounting for some very wild shooting (as we thought it was at the time). I have seen quite a number of Rebel prisoners since we came here but they are some of them disinclined to say much of their prospects. Some of them are very ignorant and intensely Secesh but most of them are pretty well satisfied to get under the folds of the "Old Flag" over more and manifest no disposition to return to the dominion of Jeff again.

(from J.B. Satterlee but unsigned)

Yorktown. May 14th 1862

Dear Parents

I now sit down to commence another letter to you. I am enjoying very good health at present and hope this letter may find you also well. As you will at once see Our Regt. is yet at Yorktown with no immediate prospect of a move. I believe though Col. Stryker seems to think (?) that we shall soon move. The health of our men is somewhat better than it has been I think probably owing to the fact that we have good quarters and much less exposure than usual. About all the work we have to do now is to stand guard four hours out of twenty four which is but a small matter comparatively and not much like work. I have got pretty well seasoned to sleeping on the ground and also on brush, floors &c. so that I now sleep as well on a floor as I ever did on a bed and begin to believe that there is more truth than fiction in the saying that a person can get used to anything, at any rate it seems so in my case for I now manage to get along first rate where I would once have thought it very hard to live at all. Thanks to the Secesh or rather to Gen. McClellan who drove them out in such a hurry. we found plenty of meal and flour among the stores left here and so it was good in quality why should we not make use of it. No sooner said than done and after a vigorous thinking to determine what were the proper ingredients for a Johnny Cake I find a deficiency of milk but what cant be cured must be endured so I went to work and in a short space of time I had a Johnny fit for eating baked as I have seen them of old before the fire and rivalling in sweetness anything of the kind I ever saw in more civilized lands. In short the thing was good and so acknowledged by all partakers and from that time to this (for you know I like Johnny cold or hot) Uncle Sam's crackers have been neglected for too much of a good thing is not so good and after eating nothing but crackers for more than two calendar months I for one was willing to rest my jaws for a while by adopting some softer and more tasty food. Yesterday we had fresh bread dealt out to us for the first time since we left Fairfax C.H. and if I had had some butter I could have made one pretty good meal but of course being a Soldier I could get along without. Now I think of it I will give you a short list of Yorktown prices current that you may see how hard a face some beings can put on when they get the opportunity. Butter sells at 50 cents per pound, Cheese at 30 cents, Eggs 40 cents per dozen, Oranges 10 cents apiece and other things much in the same way in short the most

scandalous prices are asked and given for
anything fit to eat and Whiskey dearest of all has
sold for $3.00 pr. quart (I wish it were $1.00) and
finds plenty of fools to purchase it even at that
monstrous price. I learn from the papers that
Moses has arrived in New York and I think from
what he told me he will try to get home if he is
well enough to stand the journey. I visited him on
the Hospital ship before it sailed and wrote to
his father afterward to let him know how I found
him and his probable destination. If matters continue to look as favorable as they do at present I think
none of the sick will ever come back to the Army but
will be discharged when cured. Since I last wrote
I have got some information as to what caused the
Rebels to leave in such haste and as I consider the
source good I will explain it to you. When our
Army entered Yorktown the first man met by
them was an Orderly Sergeant in the Artillery
of the Rebels who being a native of New York and
having been impressed into their service of course
owed them no good will and took the first opportunity to give them the slip. He showed our Genls
where the Torpedoes were that had been laid for our
Men and gave them much other valuable information. He was placed in charge of our Captain
till after the rush should be over, and I had
many opportunities of hearing him converse.
The account given by him is nearly as follows:
the Rebels boast all their new style (long range) guns
and after repeated trials found that they had
nothing of the kind that would reach our
Gunboats or our heavy battery (No. 1) at the mouth
of Wormley's creek and both the Battery and Boats
could not only reach them but throw clear
over them if necessary thus proving to them the
great superiority of our Guns and leaving them

only the choice of hopeless resistance or flight which latter being much the safest of the two was the one adopted. Our Artillery is clearly superior to that of the Rebels for all the reliable guns they have are all U.S. guns and they though good for the kind are not to be compared to our new Rifled Parrot Cannon any more than a common smooth bore Rifle is to be compared to a good cut Rifle and no one knows this better than Jeff Davis who if report is true ordered the evacuation of York town himself. How true the remark made by Capt. Griffin of our army was we could not at that time see but begin to now. He remarked that the guns in a certain Rebel Battery were aimed by a Union men for they uniformly fell short or went over our men who went at work clearly in range of their guns and it turned out that the above mentioned Sergeant was the very man who aimed the guns in question thus making Capt. Griffin's prediction true and accounting for some very wild shooting (as we thought it was the time). I have seen quite a number of Rebel prisoners since we came here but they are some of them disinclined to say much of their prospects. Some of them are very ignorant and intensely Secesh but most of them are pretty well satisfied to get under the folds of the Old Flag once more and manifest no disposition to return to the dominion of Jeff again.

Camp No. 14 "en route" to Richmond
May 24th 1862

Dear Parents Brother & Sister

I have just read your letter and as it is rainy and I have nothing else to do I will write a return. We left Yorktown last Monday afternoon and after a tolerably pleasant Steamboat trip landed at White House Landing on the Pamunkey River on Tuesday and as soon as we could form started to join our Brigade which we effected about sundown. We were glad to get back with the Army for our position at Yorktown was not pleasant and we had staid long enough. The health of our boys improved a great deal however while we were there and it was to many just the thing though for my own part I enjoy activity much better than anything as dull as garrison duty. Our position in the Army is different now from what it was before Yorktown—then we were in the advance and continually exposed. Now we are in the Grand Reserve and so with most of the troops who had the hardest of it in the former operation of the campaign and it seems to be the plan of Gen. McClellan to change round so as not to put all the hardship and danger upon one Corps but to make all share alike. We are too far in the rear to know much of what is going on ahead of us but as we are within twelve miles of Richmond and consequently within hearing and hear no roar of strife the silence tells us plainly that the struggle has not yet commenced and some say that the Town has been or surely will be evacuated or surrendered. However I can of course say nothing certain of the truth or falsity of the reports so freely circulated among us and we don't believe anything untill we have some proof of its truth. So you see I can tell you nothing of our prospects except that the Rebels have got plenty to do if they persist in trying to fight it through, which they probably will do if they can get any advantage which we dont mean they shall do. The old story of the ill look of country holds good here as well as in all other parts of Virginia that I have yet seen though the natural features are good and such things as stones are seldom in fact hardly ever seen so free and easy in the soil. You would hardly expect to hear me say that oats are heading out and that clover is nearly fit to mow but such is the fact and corn in some cases is nearly or quite six inches in height. Blackberry bushes are in bloom and potatoes are fit to hoe so you see there is quite a difference between this state and New York in this respect as well as in many others. The people along the road seem very willing to renounce their allegiance to Jeff and quite anxious to gain the favor of Uncle Sam and which flags were flying from nearly every house making the aspect of the country quite different from anything we had seen before and indicating that the chivalric sons of the South feel the power if they don't love the Government of the United States and I hope the lesson may be salutary in its effects. There is some appearance of suffering for something to eat among the poor class of the people here and I fear they will suffer much before anything can be grown or otherwise obtained to feed them. Some might say that it is good enough for them but I feel sorry for them for if they are Secesh which some of them are they are the most ignorant set that I ever saw in my life—they scarcely know enough to keep out of the fire and are about as ignorant of matters and things outside of their own poor shanties as horses or any other dumb beasts—so much for the chivalry of the Sunny South. It don't seem as if this part of the country so fair by nature should be so weighed down as to be fifty years behind States far less favored by nature but so it is and though Slavery may be good I don't see it and I am five thousand fold more anti Slavery than I ever was before I saw with my own eyes the working of this accursed system. I know now by actual sight and hearing what I only knew by hearsay before namely that the condition of the poor whites of the South is worse in many respects than that of the slaves and they are lower in the moral scale than the very lowest slave on the plantations. Their huts for I won't call them houses are poorer generally speaking than the slave cabins and I believe they know less of what is going on in the world than the slaves. Their clothing and general appearance is certainly much worse. Such is the state of Virginia one of the oldest of the original thirteen and who could be sorry if the foul blot that has covered her face so long were at once and forever removed & she free from what has so long kept her behind other states enjoying far less of natural advantage in the shape of climate soil &c. advancing to take her proper place among her sister states. But I shall tire you so hoping that this may find you as well as it leaves me I will close for the present.

Your son & Brother
J.B. Satterlee

(P.S. Dont fail to write because you hear some rumor but write
often as you can spare time.)

J.B.S.

Amos.

   I was very glad to get your part of the letter for it was all interesting to me. You must write as often as you can make up your mind to take time. Don't fear but that I shall always be glad to read your letter for news of all kinds (home news I mean) comes good.

Good bye
Your Brother
Jerome

Amos

Camp No. 14 en route to Richmond

May 24th 1862

Dear Parents Brother & Sister

I have just read your
letter and as it is raining and I have nothing else to
do I will write a return. We left Yorktown last Monday
afternoon and after a tolerably pleasant Steamboat trip
landed at White house landing on the Pamunky River
on Tuesday and as soon as we could form started to join our
Brigade which we effected about sundown. We were glad to
get back with the Army for our position at Yorktown
was not pleasant and we had staid long enough. The
health of our boys improved a great deal however
while we were there and it was to many just the thing
though for my own part I enjoy activity much better
than any thing as dull as Garrison duty. Our position in
the Army is different now from what it was before Yorktown — then we were in the advance and continually exposed
now we are in the Grand Reserve and so with most of
the troops who had the hardest of it in the former operations
of the campaign and it seems to be the Plan of Gen
McClellan to change round so as not to put all the
hardship and danger upon one Corps but to make
all share alike. We are too far in the rear to know
much of what is going on ahead of us but as we are
within twelve miles of Richmond and consequently within
hearing and hear no roar of strife the silence tells us
plainly that the struggle has not yet commenced and some
say that the Town has been or surely will be evacuated
or surrendered however I can of course say nothing
certain of the truth or falsity of the reports so freely
circulated among us and we don't believe anything

untill we have some proof of its truth. So you see I can tell you nothing of our prospects except that the Rebels have got plenty to do if they persist in trying to fight it through, which they probably will do if they can get any advantage which we dont mean they shall do. The old story of the ill look of country holds good here as well as in all other parts of Virginia that I have yet seen through the natural features are good and such things as stones are seldom in fact hardly ever seen so free and easy is the soil. You would hardly expect to hear me say that oats are heading out and that clover is nearly fit to mow but such is the fact and corn in some cases is nearly or quite six inches in heighth. Blackberry bushes are in bloom and potatoes are fit to hoe so you see there is quite a difference between this state and New York in this respect as well as in many others. The people along the road seem very willing to renounce their allegiance to Jeff and quite anxious to gain the favor of Uncle Sam and white flags were flying from nearly every house making the aspect of the country quite different from anything we had seen before and indicating that the Chivalric sons of the South feel the power if they dont love the Government of the United States and I hope this lesson may be salutary in its effects. There is some appearance of suffering for something to eat among the poor class of the people here and I fear they will suffer much before anything can be grown or otherwise obtained to feed them. Some might say that it is good enough for them but I feel sorry for them for if they are deceish which some of them are they are the most ignorant set that I ever saw in my life they scarcely know enough to keep out of the fire and are about as ignorant of matters and things outside of their own poor shanties as horses or any other dumb beasts — so much for the Chivalry of the sunny South.

It dont seem as if this part of the country so fair by

nature should be so weighed down as to be fifty years behind States far less favored by nature but so it is and though Slavery may be good I don't see it and I am five thousand fold more Anti Slavery then I ever was before I saw with my own eyes the working of this accursed System. I know now by actual sight and hearing what I only knew by hearsay before namely that the condition of the poor whites at the South is worse in many respects that that of the slaves and they are lower in the moral scale then the very lowest slave on the plantations. Their huts for I won't call them houses are poorer generally speaking then the slave cabins and I believe they know less of what is going on in the world then the slaves their clothing and general appearance is certainly much worse. Such is the State of Virginia one of the oldest of the original thirteen and who could be sorry if the foul blot that has covered her face so long were at once and forever removed & she free from what has so long kept her behind other States enjoying for less of natural advantage in the shape of climate soil &c advancing to take her proper place among her sister States. But I shall tire you so hoping that this may find you as well as it leaves me I will close for the present.

Your Son & Brother

J. B. Satterlee

P S Dont fail to write because you hear some rumor but write often as you can

Spare time.

J. B. S.

Amos I was very glad to get your part of the letter for it was all interesting to one. You must write as often as you can make up your mind to let the time. Don't fear but that I shall always be glad to read your letter for news of all kinds (home news I mean) comes good

Good bye
Your Brother
Jerome

Amos

Camp near Hanover C.H. May 28th, 1862

Dear Parents

I take the first opportunity to let you know that I am well and sound though much tired out with the exertion of the last twenty four hours. We have had a severe battle and the 44th has suffered severely but through the mercy of God I am safe when alas too many of my comrades are laid low. We have routed the Rebels but about 1/5 of our men (the 44th) are killed, wounded & missing. We have taken plenty of prisoners and the victory is most complete though dearly purchased. Our Cavalry is in pursuit and they are almost constantly engaged in bringing in prisoners. Our Regt. was for (I think) nearly two hours engaged with a force much superior to our own and at the arrival of reinforcements we were terribly exhausted but we held our ground during all that terrible storm losing not an inch though exposed to the most terrible crossfire that I ever expect to witness. Prisoners tell us that through all that terrible time we held in check seven Regts. of Rebels but of the of this (sic) I am not entirely convinced. Our fire was most deadly to the foe nearly all the men hit being hit in the head or breast and of course killed. The 44th lost 22 killed 60 and odd wounded many of them it is feared fatally and 40 odd missing (supposed wounded and crawled off or stragglers). Our Major & Adjutant are both among the wounded and our officers have most of them proved themselves brave soldiers. Those of Co. B. are all I could wish. Co. B. has 3 killed & 3 wounded two of them quite seriously. Eleazer Stoddard was killed fighting as bravely as a soldier ever fought. He was loading his gun when he fell. If I can get time I shall write to his folks soon all about the matter

You will see that we have left the direct advance on Richmond (our Division) and for the purpose of cutting of the Rebels communication which object we have most handsomely effected. I hope we shall soon give them satisfaction. I will write more particulars as soon as I get time. Till then Good bye be of good cheer for all will yet be right. Write as soon as you can

Your son
J.B. Satterlee

1862

Camp near Hanover C. H. May 28th.

Dear Parents

I take the first opportunity to let you know that I am well and sound though much tired out with the exertion of the last twenty four hours. We have had a severe battle and the 44th has suffered severely but through the mercy of God I am safe when alas too many of my comrades are laid low. We have routed the Rebels but about 15 of our men (the 44th) are killed wounded & missing. We have taken plenty of prisoners and the victory is most complete though dearly purchased. Our Cavalry is in pursuit and they are almost constantly engaged in bringing in prisoners. Our Reg. was for (I think) nearly two hours engaged with a force much superior to our own and at the arrival of reenforcements we were terribly exhausted but we held our ground during all that terrible storm losing not an inch though exposed to the most terrible crossfire that I ever expect to witness. Prisoners tell us that through all that terrible storm we held in check seven Regts of Rebels but of this I am not entirely convinced. Our fire was most deadly to the foe nearly all the men hit being hit in the head or breast and of course killed. The 44th lost 22 killed 60 and odd wounded many of them it is feared fatally and 40 odd missing (supposed wounded and crawled off or straggler. Our Major & Adjutant are both among the wounded and our officers have most of them proved themselves brave Soldiers those of Co. B are all I could wish. Co. B. has 3 killed & 3 wounded two of them quite seriously. Eleazar Stoddard was killed fighting as bravely as a Soldier ever fought. He was loading his gun when he fell. If I can get time I shall write to his folks soon all about the matter. You will see that we have left the direct advance on Richmond (our Division) and for the purpose of cutting off the Rebels Communication which object we have most handsomely effected. I hope we shall soon give them satisfaction. I will write more particulars as soon as I get time till then Good Bye be of good cheer for all will yet be right. Write as soon as you can

Your Son

J. B. Satterlee.

Camp No. 17. (near Cold Harbor Virginia
June 13th, 1862)

Dear Parents Brother and Sister

I have just received and read your letter. It found me in good health and enjoying myself as well as could be expected. There is but little stirring here now and consequently I have very little news to write. Our Regt. was called out to day on an alarm but it was false and they soon came back. I was on guard and did not go with them. All is now quiet but how long it will remain so I can not of course tell. We are camped but a short distance from the house where the Rebel Gen. Pettigrew wounded and taken prisoner at the Battle of Fair Oaks, is lying. Dr. Gaines the owner of the house and of the land we are camped on is a notorious Secesh and is in Ft. Monroe for his evil behavior he having made many threats of what he was going to do &c. I wrote a letter home so lately that I have but little to write. You wanted me to write the particulars of the Battle of Hanover—I have already done so and if you dont get the letter I will write again. Eleazar Stoddard was not near me when he was shot he being so much shorter was at the lower end of the Company. He was instantly killed the ball striking him under the eye and going through his head. I don't think he suffered any pain or was concious of what hit him. I have written a letter to his folks giving them the particulars of his death burial &c. I am sorry to hear that you are not enjoying any better health but I hope now that the time of Spring's work is past you will recruit up some. I hope you will not worry about me any more than you can help. I am well and tough and I would not have any of you concern yourselves any more than you can help. Remember that God ruleth and that He in His infinite mercy ever doeth all things well. If it is His will I hope to come home safe soon but otherwise I want to be resigned to His will and I hope You will be also. Our Regt. may never be in an other engagement—Not half the Regts. that went with us to Hanover got near enough to be in the least danger and in any event you would I am sure wish me to be at my post in the hour of Battle as at other times. I have no disposition to shirk and I know you would despise me if I should fail to do my duty so then cheer up and be hopeful now is no time for despair but the time for cheerful effort backed by love of Country and a perfect trust in God and victory is certain (I believe). The delay in the operations of our Army before Richmond has been unavoidable on account of high water. The Chickahominy flats have been flowed more or less for some time but they are clearing up some now and if we have no more rain soon I think there will be a chance to do something. Many of the Troops are across but the heavy Guns are not yet over. We are on the reserve and are yet on the north bank. I have not seen Edgar nor heard from him since we left Yorktown. I expect he is acting as orderly to some of the Generals. He was at McClellans head Quarters the last I knew of him. But it is getting dark and I must close for this time. Write soon and as often as you can spare time.

Your Son
J.B. Satterlee

(1862
Camp No. 17. (near
Cold Harbor Virginia
June 18th

Dear Parents Brother and Sister

I have just
received and read your letter. It found
me in good health and enjoying myself
as well as could be expected. There is but
little stirring here now and consequently
I have very little news to write. Our Regt.
was called out to day on an alarm but
it was false and they soon came back.
I was on guard and did not go with
them. All is now quiet but how long it
will remain so I can not of course tell.
We are camped but a short distance from
the house where the Rebel Gn. Pettigrew
wounded and taken prisoner at the Battle
of Fair Oaks, is lying. Dr Gaines the owner
of the house and of the land we are encamped on is a notorious Suesh and is
in Ft Monroe for his evil behavior
he having made many threats of what
he was going to do &c. I wrote a letter
home so lately that I have but little to write
you wanted me to write the particulars of
the Battle of Hanover — I have already done

so and if you dont get this letter I will write again. Eleazer Stoddard was not near me when he was shot he being so much shorter was at the lower end of the Company. He was instantly killed the ball striking him under the eye and going through his head. I dont think he suffered any pain or was conscious of what hit him. I have written a letter to his folks giving them the particulars of his death burial &c. I am sorry to hear that you are not enjoying any better health but I hope now that the time of Springs work is past you will recruit up some. I hope you will not worry about me any more than you can help I am well and tough and I would not have any of you concern your -selves any more then you can help. Remember that God ruleth and that He in His infinite Mercy ever doeth all things well. If it is His will I hope to come home safe soon but otherwise I want to be resigned to His will and I hope You will be so also. Our Regt may ouver be in an other engagement Not half the Regts that went with us to Henover got over enough to be in the least danger and in any event you would I am sure wish me to be at my post in the hour of

Battle as at other times — I have no disposition to shirk and I know you would despise me if I should fail to do my duty so then cheer up and be hopeful now is no time for despair but the time for Cheerful effort backed by love of Country and a perfect trust in God and victory is certain (I believe) The delay in the operations of our Army before Richmond has been unavoidable on account of high water. The Chickahominy flats have been flowed more or less for some time but they are clearing up some now and if we have no more rain soon I think there will be a chance to do something. Many of the Troops are across but the heavy Lines are not yet over. We are in the reserve and are yet on the north bank. I have not seen Edgar nor heard from him since we left Yorktown. I expect he is acting as orderly to some of the Generals. He was at McClellans head Quarters the last I knew of him. But it is getting dark and I must close for this time. Write soon and as often as you can spare time.

Your Son

J. B. Setterlee

Camp near Cold Harbor Va.
June 20th, 1862.

Dear Parents Brother & Sister

With pleasure I now sit down to write another letter to you. I am well and hope this letter may find you all well also. We are still encamped in the same old place and for aught that I know we may stay here for some time yet. However as there is so much uncertainty about military movements in general I don't think I should wonder much at a call any time being pretty well used to them by this time. There is nothing of much importance going on on our part of the line now occassional cannonading being the most exciting events that we have to deal with and with the exception of a days piqueting about once a week and two hours (daily) drill we spend our time in laying around waiting for the time to come. There is more excitement with those who being in the front are already across the Chickahominy and severe skirmishes are not unfrequent the Rebels generally getting very much the worst of the bargain and retiring discomfited to await the next opportunity for mischief. Day before yesterday we were on piques just across the Chickahominy. We had a very good time. The Rebel piquets do not shoot at us as they used to and of course we wont begin any such thing. We are quite close to their piquets all day and some of our boys talked to some of them in as friendly a manner as if they were friends instead of foes. They seem very tired of the war and plainly say they wish things were back again to the good old times but still some of them express a determination to to (sic) fight to the death rather than give up. The Rebel piquets on that day were from the 8th Georgia Regt. and so of course much more likely to be open hearted Secesh than the border state men but I think more of the principle they exhibit and I think them a much more honorable for than the troops of N. Carolina or Virginia. You will probably see an account of a conversation between Sergt. Galpin of Co. B. and a Sergeant of the 8th Georgia and as he can tell his own story better than I can I won't attempt it. Our troops of Smiths Division had a pretty smart fight with the Rebels on the afternoon of Wednesday caused by the Rebs. trying to drive in Smiths piquets and the Chivalry got very roughly handled so much so that they had to run leaving dead and wounded on the field to be cared for by our troops. Our general seems to make things very sure as he goes so that our troops are ready for them in almost every spot where they try to effect anything and the result is they don't make much of trying to surprise the Yankee troops. Dr. Bushnell was at our Camp yesterday. I saw shook hands and had a short talk with him. He is going home soon I expect if nothing of importance turns up within a short time. Lieut. Perkins (aid de Camp to Gen. Butterfield) who was taken from the hospital on the field of Hanover by the Rebels and taken thence to Richmond has been exchanged and is back to his post. He gives quite an interesting account of what he saw heard &c. during his stay with the Rebs. He was left sick in the Hospital on the left of our position and when the Rebs swept down trying to turn our left flank (which they would certainly have accomplished had not the 44th been there to treat them back) a company of them made a dash at the Hospital contrary to all usages of war that make the Hospital a sacred place and carried Lieut. Perkins and a Surgeon or two off as prisoners. Perkins was so sick that he could hardly sit on a horse yet the brute of a Rebel Capt. who had him in charge repeatedly threatened to shoot him if he did not ride faster untill at length desperate the poor fellow mustered up and dared him to shoot when he put up his pistol and leaving Perkins in charge of a Dragoon he hurried on ahead. Perkins says the panic of the Rebs was complete and they did'nt stop till they were in Richmond. After he got to Richmond he was pretty fairly treated. He was there when the Battle of Fair Oaks took place. The Reb Surgeon who attended him told him that thirty thousand of our troops were across the River and that the bridges were all gone so they were bagged sure. They felt big on the Saturday night after the first days fight but were terribly disappointed when Sunday night found them so defeated in this their cherished plan for Gen. Sumner did get across and that too in season to turn the scale on the Rebels in a most terrible manner costing them by their own admission nearly ten thousand of their best troops. They evidently did not like to say much about the matter after the terrible fight on Sunday and Richmond mourned instead of rejoicing as they had fondly anticipated. Lieut. Perkins seems to be of the opinion that the Rebels are removing a part of their valuables south since the Battle of Fair Oaks preparatory probably to another stampede if necessary to save their bacon and this is about all the information obtained by Lieut. Perkins. You will doubtless wonder as many do why it was that the troops across the Chickahominy were not supported sooner on the Saturday of the Battle of Fair Oaks but I can explain it in a satisfactory manner (I think). Man was not to blame. All was done that could be but the terrible flood tearing away the causeways & bridges kept back our hurrying troops and it was only by an almost miraculous chance that they did finally get across the turbid stream in time to save the field to Uncle Sam on the next day (Sunday) and for a number of days after the Battle the men suffered for food so little sight was there for any getting across the River. The Rebels claim Fair Oaks as a victory but if it was it gave our troops a firmer foothold on the South side of the Chickahominy than they had before at least ten fold and to day there is hardly a possibility of our returning other than a victorious army. The Rebels will hold on hard but I believe they will be defeated in the end and so terribly too that they will never recover from the blow. We have had some quite warm weather lately but it is very temperate now and I don't think it is much warmer here than at home. I think the health of our Regt. is some better now than it has been and I believe all our troops are pretty generally healthy. I have nothing more to write at present so I will close.

Your son & Brother
J.B. Satterlee

(Amos I want to hear from you in the next letter if you will please to write to your Brother

J.B.S.)

Camp near Cold Harbor Va
June 20th, 1862.

Dear Parents Brother & Sister

With pleasure I now sit down to write another letter to you I am well and hope this letter may find you all well also. We are still encamped in the same old place and for aught that I know we may stay here for some time yet. However as there is so much uncertainty about Military movements in general I don't think I should wonder much at a call any time being pretty well used to them by this time. There is nothing of much importance going on on our part of the line now occasional cannonading being the most exciting events that we have to deal with and with the exception of a days picqueting about once a week and two hours (daily) drill we spend ourtime in lazing around waiting for the time to come. There is more excitement with those who being in the front are already across the Chickahoming and severe skirmishes are not infrequent the Rebels generally getting very much the worst of the bargain and retiring discomfited to await the next opportunity for mischief. Day before yesterday we were on picquet just across the Chickahominy. We had a very good time. The Rebel picquets do not shoot at us as they used to and of course we wont begin any such thing. We are quite close to their picquets all day and some of our boys talked to some of them in as friendly a manner as if they were friends instead of foes. They seem very tired of the war and plainly say they wish things were back again to the good old times but still some of them express a determination to fight to the death rather than give up. The Rebel picquets on that day were from the 8th. Georgia Regt. and so of course much more likely to be open hearted Rebels than the border state men but I think more of the principle they exhibit and I think them a much more honorable foe than the troops of N. Carolina or Virginia. You will probably see an account of a conversation between Lieut. Galpin of Co. B. and a Sergeant of the 8th. Georgia and as he can tell his own story better than I can I wont attempt it. Our troops of Smiths Division had a pretty smart fight with the Rebels on the afternoon of Wednesday caused by the Rebs. trying to drive in Smiths picquets and the Chivalry got very roughly handled so much so that they had to run leaving dead and wounded on the field to be cared for by our troops. Our general seems to make things very sure as he goes so that our troops are ready for them in almost every spot when they try to effect anything and the result is they dont make much by trying to surprise the Yankee troops. Dr. Bushnell was at our camp yesterday, I saw shook hands and had a short talk with him. He is going home soon I expect if nothing of importance turns up within a short time. Lieut. Perkins (Aid de Camp to Gen Butterfield) who was taken from the hospital on the field of Hanover by the Rebels and taken thence to Richmond has been exchanged and is back to his post. He gives quite an interesting account of what he saw heard &c. during his stay with the Rebs. He was left sick in the Hospital on the left of our position and when the Rebs. swept down trying to turn our left flank which they would certainly have accomplished had not the 44th. been there to beat them back a company of them made a dash at the Hospital contrary to all usages of war that make the Hospital a sacred place and carried Lieut. Perkins and a surgeon or two off as prisoners. Perkins was so

THE CAMP LETTERS OF JEROME B. SETTERLEE 273

sick that he could hardly sit on a horse yet the brute of a Rebel Capt. who had him in charge repeatedly threatened to shoot him if he did not ride faster untill at length desperate the poor fellow mustered up and dared him to shoot when he put up his pistol and leaving Perkins in charge of a Dragoon he hurried on ahead. Perkins says the panic of the Rebs was complete and they did not stop till they were in Richmond. After he got to Richmond he was pretty fairly treated. He was there when the Battle of Fair Oaks took place. The Reb surgeon who attended him told him that thirty thousand of our troops were across the River and that the bridges were all gone so they were bagged sure. They felt big on the Saturday night after the first days fight but were terribly disappointed when Sunday night found them so defeated in this their cherished plan for Gen. Sumner did get across and that too in season to turn the scale on the Rebels in a most terrible manner costing them by their own admission nearly ten thousand of their best troops. They evidently did not like to say much about the matter after the terrible fight on Sunday and Richmond mourned instead of rejoicing as they had fondly anticipated. Lieut. Perkins seems to be of the opinion that the Rebels are removing a part of their valuables south since the Battle of Fair Oaks preparatory probably to an other stampede if necessary to save their bacon and this is about all the information obtained by Lieut. Perkins. You will doubtless wonder as many do why it was that the troops across the Chickahoming were not supported sooner on the Saturday of the Battle of Fair Oaks but I can explain it in a satisfactory manner (I think) Man was not to blame all was done that could be but the terrible flood tearing away the causeways & bridges kept back our hurrying troops and it was only by an almost miraculous chance that they did finally get across the turbid Stream in time to save the field to Uncle Sam on the next day (Sunday) and for a number of days after the Battle the men suffered for food so little sight was there for any getting across the River. The Rebels claim Fair Oaks as a victory but if it was it gave our troops a firmer foothold on the south side of the Chickahoming then they had before at least ten fold and to day there is hardly a posability of our retaining other than a victorious army. The Rebels will hold on hard but I believe they will be defeated in the end and so terribly too that they will never recover from the blow

We have had some quite warm weather lately but it is very temperate now and I don't think it is much warmer here then at home. I think the health of our Regt is some better now then it has been and I believe all our troops are pretty generally healthy. I have nothing more to write at present so I will close.

Your Loving Brother
J. B. Satterter

(Amos I want to hear from you in the next letter if you will please to write to your Brother
J. B. S.)

The Tobacco Factory, Richmond Va.   July 1st 1862

Dear Parents. I take the first opportunity to write a few lines to you. I am a prisoner of war in this place. I was taken in the fight of June 27th near Gaines Mill and not far from our place of encampment. I am enjoying tolerable health and have no reason to complain of the treatment I have received at the hands of the Confederates. They give us enough to eat and that very good so we manage to get along. News is of course inadmissable which is just as well for I have none. I am in hopes not to have to stay here long but God only knows. In any event I hope you will not worry about me for I think I shall get along very well and I would not have you uneasy on my account for thank God my health is good and I am not wounded. You must not expect to hear from me as often as if I were in another place for it is only a matter of courtesy in the Authorities here allowing us to write and we can't write very often. I should be very glad to hear from home and know how you are all getting along but that is impossible at present so I must content myself as best I can. Keep up good courage and don't allow yourselves to worry for me for I am a soldier and used to almost all kinds so that there is little fear that I shall find much worse than I have already seen in my soldier experience. There is a small number of 44th boys here with me so I am not among entire strangers. I will give a list of them and if it proves to be contraband I can tear it off again. I must close. Hope for the best and all will be well at last.

Affectionately your son & brother
J.B. Satterlee

(Martha & Amos I want to see you and I hope at some day not very far distant to do so. Good bye,

Jerome)

Prisoners of the 44th in this building

S.H. Hickok,	Co. C.
J.H. Champline	" A
J. Nolton	" "
L.C. Crain	" D
" Roe	" E
V.Z. Bradt	" F
R.A. Teeling	" G
Frank Persons	" H
L.P. Gilbert	" "

July 7th.

Dear Parents. Today is the first chance to send this letter. I am well and hopeful so don't get uneasy. Good bye for this time hoping soon to see you, I remain now as ever

J.B.S.

In Tobacco Factory, Richmond Va
July 1st 1862

Dear Parents I take the first op
portunity to write a few lines to you. I
am a prisoner of war in this place
I was taken in the fight of June
27th near Gaines mill and not far
from our place of encampment.
I am enjoying tolerable health and
have no reason to complain of the
treatment I have received at the
hands of the Confederates. They give
us enough to eat and that a very good
so we manage to get along. News of
course are miserable which is not
as well for I have none. I am in
hopes not to have to stay here long
God only knows. In any event I hope
you will not worry about me for
I think I shall get along very well
and I would not have you uneasy

Belle Island   Aug. 27th 1862 (Near Richmond)

Dear Parents, Brother, & Sister. I write to inform you that I am tolerably well and in very good spirits for a prisoner. I hope for a release soon but don't know when. I want you to keep yourselves as easy as possible on my account for I think all will be right soon. I can't complain of treatment and if I knew you were all well and hopeful I could be happy even here. Write to me as soon as you get this. Write all "in small compass" and direct to me as 'Prisoner of War' Belle Island Va. 'care of Capt. Montgomery,' and I think it will come to me. Mother keep up good heart. Your son thinks often of you and daily asks God to protect and sustain you.

Your Affectionate
J.B. Satterlee

Bulkland Aug 29th 1862 Dear Richmond

Dear Bro – Brother Richm. I will be informed

you that I am totally well and in my good spirit

for a prisoner. I hope for a release soon but don't

know when. I want you to keep yourselves as easy

as possible on my account for I think all will

be right soon. I can't complain of treatment

and if I knew you were all well and hopeful

I could be happy even here. Will-B are as am

as you sh. Pts. Will-Pell in small company and

drink me as Prisoner of war Bells Island will

care of Capt. Montgomery, and I think it shall some

to ask. Neither shall your Brothers am think

often if you and child ask God to will stand us in

this. Your Affectionate

B. B. Slater

Dear Parents, Brother & Sister

    I again seat myself to try to write a letter to you. I wish I could write something of encouragement but so far as health is concerned I can't say that I feel any real improvement. I have been feeling a little better for two or three days back but today I hardly feel so well and so it goes one day I feel tolerable smart and cheerful and the next I am sometimes too unwell to enjoy anything. So too with my appetite. One day it is good and food don't seem to hurt me the next I can't bear the sight of food and if I force down anything have to throw up so I make very slow progress at all. Under such circumstances you can readily imagine that I would be most happy to obtain a discharge but as I have told you before tis a hard matter and though some are getting discharged now along they are those who have been disabled by wounds and the intention is to keep the sick till they get well that is if there is after a trial any hope of their getting well within any reasonable time. I have spoken to the Doctor who attends me a couple of times on the subject and though he has plainly said that in his opinion twas barely possible that I should get fit for service again yet he tells me tis next to impossible for a sick man to get a discharge now and so I like others similarly situated must wait and see if there is not a possibility of our getting fit for soldiers again. I hate to stay in the hospital so long as it seems as if I might have to but what cant be cured must be endured and I am able as many others so I try to be hopeful to do the best I can hoping for the best. As near as I can learn none of the men who came from prison when I did are yet exchanged. At any rate we have had no notice of the exchange and although all may be right I hardly think the Rebels mean to exchange us from what I heard from their own officers and also from the tone of their papers. They think they have the advantage of our Government in the matter of prisoners (and so they have) and they mean to keep it. This may of course turn out to be only one of their scares but they have generally used every advantage and they may do so again if our agents are not up to them.

Sunday 26th.

    I will now try to finish this letter and first as Ma wished I will try to give something near the form of the oath of parole administered to me by the Rebels. As near as I recollect the words they are as follows. "I do solemnly swear that I will not during the continuance of the present war between the Confederate States and the United States aid or abet the enemy of the Confederate States by bearing arms or giving information against them unless regularly exchanged or released by the proper authorities of the Confederate States so help me God!" You will see at once that the oath is a strong one and we all had to swear by the uplifted hand that oath then our names, age, height,

---

complexion, color of eyes and hair also our occupation before enlistment were carefully taken down as if they had no idea whatever that we should ever be exchanged and meant to make sure of us if we should be caught violating the parole. They have us fast enough and though they may exchange they also may not or if they do so at all only do it after our Government has been subjected to a large amt. of unnecessary expense. The weather has been very nice here since I cam here and the trees are yet quite green as there has been no hard frost. There has been considerable chilly weather much like fall at home and to day it rains but nearly all the time the sky is clear and the Sunny South appears in all splendor as yet. I feel a longing to see you all but I can only wait and hope. I believe I shall see you though some time may elapse and I wish you would all try to worry just as little about me as you possibly can for I am in good quarters and thanks be to God hopeful though not strong. I feel very little like Complaining of my lot even though I am not where or as I should like to be for I am among human beings and friends and tis never difficult for me to get along comfortably under such circumstances. I have a kind and noble brother soldier to attend to me (if I need it) one who has been sick himself and knows what it is to need help, so I can't feel to complain any but rather to thank God that I am so much better off than many others. Ma I could hardly help but laugh to think that the prospect of a Draft had so injured the health of the hired man but I hope he may recover for of all things a mean sneak of a coward is least to be considered. Soldiering is not pleasant but if every man had done his duty the Rebel Army would have been scattered to the four winds. Not every one has the pluck to face the music and work when it comes to the battle or McClellan would have had Richmond long ago instead of being where he now is and I've seen enough of cowards to hate the name as every true man or woman should. I know of course that twill cost considerable to send the box of things to me but things are very high here and I thought they would cost much less according to what they would be worth than they would purchased here so I think twill pay very well. I expect to get paid off soon and shall probably get five perhaps six months pay when I do get paid as the six months is nearly due. It has been said that we would get pay for our rations while we were prisoners but although I don't expect it I think we ought to get something to pay us for going without, but in any event if nothing happens I shall have quite a sum to send home I hope. But my sheet is full and I must close another long letter. I get to writing and find so much to write that I make terrible long letters but perhaps you can worry through them or perhaps you may feel as I do that letters from those near and dear can hardly be too long. Good bye for this time.

Your Son & Brother
Jerome

Annapolis Hospital Oct 25th 862

Dear Parents, Brother & Sister

I again seat myself to try to write a letter to you. I wish I could write something of encouragement but so far as health is concerned I can't say that I feel any real improvement. I have been feeling a little better for two or three days back but to day I hardly feel so well and so it goes one day I feel tolerable smart and cheerful and the next I am sometimes too unwell to enjoy anything. So too with my appetite one day it is good and food dont seem to hurt me the next I can't bear the sight of food and if I force down anything have to throw up so I make very slow progress if indeed I can be said to make any progress at all. Under such circumstances you can readily imagine that I would be most happy to obtain a discharge but as I have told you before tis a hard matter and though some are getting discharged now along, they are those who have been disabled by wounds and the intention is to keep the sick till they get well that is if there is after a trial any hope of their getting well within any reasonable time. I have spoken to the Doctor who attends me a couple of times on the subject and though he has plainly said that in his opinion twas barely possible that I should get fit for service again yet he tells me tis next to impossible for a sick man to get a discharge now and so I like others similarly situated must wait and see if there is not a possibility of our getting fit for Soldiers again. I hate to stay in the hospital so long as it seems as if I might have to but what cant be cured must be endured and I am able as many others so I try to be hopeful to do the best I can hoping for the best. As near as I can learn none of the men who came from prison when I did are yet exchanged at any rate we have had no notice of the exchange and although all may be right I hardly think the Rebels mean to exchange us from what I heard from their own Officers and also from the tone of their papers they think they have the advantage of our Government in the matter of prisoners (and so they have) and they mean to keep it. This may of course turn out to be only one of their scares but they have generally used every advantage and they may do so again if our Agents are not up to them. Sunday 26th. I will now try to finish this letter and first as Ma wished I will try to give something near the form of the oath of parole administered to me by the Rebels. As near as I recollect the words they are as follows. "I do solemnly swear that I will not during the continuance of the present war between the Confederate States and the United States aid or abet the enemy of the

Confederate States by bearing arms or giving inform- ation against them unless regularly exchanged or released by the proper authorities of the Confederate States so help me God!" You will see at once that the oath is a strong one and we all had to swear by the uplifted hand that oath then our names, age, hight complexion, color of eyes and hair also our occupation before enlistment were carefully taken down as if they had no idea whatever that we should ever be exchanged and meant to make sure of us if we should be caught violating the parole. They have us fast enough and though they may exchange they also may not or if they do so at all only do it after our Government has been subjected to a large amt of unnecessary expense. The weather has been very nice here since I came here and the trees are get quite green as there has been no hard frost. There has been considerable chilly weather much like fall at home and to day it rains but nearly all the time the sky is clear and the Sunny South appears in all splendor as yet. I feel a longing to see You all but I can only wait and hope. I believe I shall see you though some time may elapse and I wish you would all try to worry just as little about me as you possibly can for I am in good quarters and thanks be to God hopeful though not strong. I feel very little like complaining of my lot even though I am not where or as I should like to be for I am among human beings and friends and 'tis never difficult for one to get along comfortably under such circumstances. I have a kind and noble brother Soldier to attend to me (if I need it) one who has been sick himself and knows what it is to need help. so I can't feel to complain any but rather to thank God that I am so much better off than so many others. I could hardly help but laugh to think that the prospect of a Draft had so injured the health of the hired man but I hope he may recover for of all things a mean sneak of a coward is least to be considered. Soldiering is not pleasant but if every man had done his duty the Rebel army would have been scattered to the four winds. Not every one has the pluck to face the music and work when it comes to the battle or McClellan would have had Richmond long ago instead of being where he now is and I've seen enough of coward to hate the name as every true man or woman should.

I know of course that 'twill cost considerable to send the box of things to me but things are very high here and I thought they would cost much less according to what they would be worth then they would purchased here so I think 'twill pay very well. I expect to get paid off soon and shall probably get five perhaps six months pay when I do get paid as this six months is nearly due. It has been said that we would get pay for our rations while we were prisoners but although I don't expect it I think we ought to get something to pay us for going without but in any event if nothing happens I shall have quite a sum to send home I hope. But my sheet is full and I must close another long letter. I get to writing and find so much to write that I make terrible long letters but perhaps you can worry through them or perhaps you may feel as I do that letters from those near and dear can hardly be too long. Good Bye for this time. Your Son & brother

Jerome

Wellsboro   Tioga Co. Pa.
November the 2. 1862.

Cousin Jerome,

By the request of my father and your mother, I now endeavor to write you a few lines, though strangers. I presume you will excuse the impropriety of my commencing the correspondence as you are a soldier and I your cousin.

I think a soldier likes to get letters. I know I should if I was in their (sic) situation and a word from home and friends would do much to make me contented. It is warm and pleasant today, but one week ago to day we had a very hard storm. It rained and froze until it broke many trees down. Hurt the orchards badly.

Fruit is quite plenty about here. My father had a nice lot of peaches, but you know I never lived at home so they didnt do me any good.

My brother Herman is in the army. I wish you could see him he would like so well to see you and get acquainted.

I see by your mother's letter that you are a paroled prisoner and sick too, so I presume you were one of the unfortunate ones that suffered such cruel treatment in Richmond prison. Oh! when will this war be over, and the inocent (sic) cease to suffer for others crimes? Not till the noble and good men are all dead. I fear.

We have rather quiet times here. The boys are nearly all gone to war and what are left are just as good as nobody. Girls dont fancy cowards you know, so they dont stand a very good chance. I tell you it looks dubious to us girls that are out of our teens. We put on sober faces occasionly (sic) but dont know as we grow poor any.

I presumed you have learned that J. Jennings a cousin of ours was kild (sic) at the Battle of Antetiem (sic) and George wounded. Herman was slightly wounded at the Battle of South Mountain.

They have a Rebel captain here in jail. He was from Lawrenceville forily (sic) and came home to visit his relatives and wore his rebel suit used some languaged (sic) not very becoming for a man in a northern state. So they have got him in safe keeping.

If you are discharged, we would be very glad to have you come this way home and make us a visit. I dont think it would be very far out of your way. I must stop for it is time for Sunday School.

Louisa Jennings.

Wellsboro. Tioga Co. Pa.

November. Nye 2. 1862.

Cousin Jerome

By the request of
my father and your mother. I now endeav
vor to write you a few lines. though
strange. I presume you will excuse the
impropriety of my commencing the corresp
ondance as you are a soldier. and
I your cousin.

I think a soldier likes to get letters
I know I should if I was in their situa
tion and a word from home and friends
would do much to make me contented.

Camp near Falmouth
Jan. 25th 1863

Dear Parents, Brother & Sister

I received your letter (long looked for) this morning and hasten to write one in return. We have just returned from a toilsome and muddy attempt to move on Richmond which has failed not because it was not well planned but because on account of rains the roads became impassible and stuck us fast before we were fairly outside of the Piquet lines. We left Camp last Wednesday afternoon and on the same night rain begun to fall and after wading through mud such as none but soldiers see we found that the Artillery must stop for twelve horses could not budge a twelve pound Howitzer one inch and as twas a move of the whole Army we had to stop. The roads only grew worse and as the Rebs had by this time found out the point of attack contemplated and were prepared we returned to our old camp after building roads for the Guns, Wagons &c. to pass over. We only got about 5 miles from camp but I tell you it has cost the Army horses enough to frighten even G.W. Barnes if he could see their carcasses lying in the almost bottomless mud of these Virginia Roads. Of the objects and expectations of our Commander I know nothing but the papers probably do and from them you will learn more than I could possibly tell you so I will leave the task to them only remarking that a winter campaign is by no means so funny a thing as some are trying to make you believe. As for myself I am doing pretty well. I get plenty to eat and I have stood the fare first rate so far much better than I expected. I think too that I never had a better appetite or was in better spirits than at present and of the three Hospital, Camp Perole or Camp near Falmouth I prefer the latter on more than one account. I have done very little duty for we don't have much to do and Cap. Larrabee don't allow me to do any heavy duty—Captain is one of the best of men and has always been a friend to me. It seems to me that there is something rather curious in the fact that a strong Universalist like Mr. Hyatt should marry a zealous Methodist like Lucinda but so it seems and truth stranger than fiction as usual is stronger than usual here—however stranger things do happen even in old Stratford. I am sorry to hear of so much sickness but I am in hopes that you will be spared from farther visitations. Martha I will answer your questions in order. I was taken prisoner at the Battle of Gaines Mills not by the two men whom I had in charge who were South Carolineans but by the 42nd Va. Regt. who came down upon us with other Regts. whose numbers and states I do not know. A few others of the 44th were taken at the same time or at least at nearly the same though none of them were with me and those two were the only prisoners there at that time though a small squad had been sent to the rear a little before we retreated. I stopped not to drink myself but solely to let the prisoners do so and at their request and by this means lost the Regt. and was cut off from the rest of our retreating troops. I dont know as I have any more to write just at present so I will close this letter hoping that it may find you all well and enjoying yourselves as well as possible.

Write soon
Jerome

Camp near Falmouth
Jan 28th 1863

Dear Parents, Brother & Sister
I received your letter long looked
for) this morning and hasten
to write one in return. We
have just returned from a
toilsome and muddy attempt
to move on Richmond which
has failed not because it
was not well planned but
because on account of rains
the roads became impassible
and stuck as fast before
we were fairly outside of the
Piquet lines. We left camp
last wednesday afternoon
and on the same night rain
begun to fall and after wading
through mud such as none
but soldiers see we found

of the best of men and has always been a friend to me. It seems to me that there is something rather curious in the fact that a strong Universalist like Mr. Hyatt would marry a zealous Methodist like Lucinda but so it seems and truth stranger than fiction as usual is stranger than usual here however strange things do happen even in old Stratford. I am sorry to hear of so much sickness but I am in hopes that you will be spared from farther visitations. Martha I will answer your questions in order I was taken prisoner at the Battle of Gaines Mills not by the two men whom I had in charge who were South Carolineans but by the 2d or 3d Regt. who came down upon us with other Regts. whose numbers and states I do not know. A few others of the 44th. were taken at the same time or at least at nearly

the same though none of them
were with one and those two
were the only prisoners there at
that time though a small squad
had been sent to the rear a little
before we retreated. I stopped
not to drink myself but solely
to let the prisoners do so and
at their request and by this means
lost the Regt, and was cut off
from the rest of our retreating
troops. I dont know as I have
any more to write just at present
so I will close this letter hoping
that it may find you all well
and enjoying yourselves as
well as possible. Write soon

Jerome

Camp near Falmouth

Feb. 6th. 1863.

Dear Parents, Brother & Sister.

I don't know as I can write much to day but I felt that I wanted to do something and as it is raining I will try to write. I am getting along well at present and hope this letter may find you well also. I received Marthas letter of Jan. 25th just after writing my last one and though I had learned most of the news I was shocked to find that Ma had been so bad as I learned by the letter. She had I felt as if I would give all I have to be allowed to go home for a short time but as I know twould be almost impossible to obtain permission to do so. I had to do the next best thing that is worry as little as possible trusting that all might be well at last. We are having a great deal of stormy weather now cold one day enough to freeze a fellows ears. The next brings a snow storm generally ending with rain and slush slush is the consequence. The Winter Campaign seems a failure and there is very little prospect that we shall do much before March at least. In the mean time we are quite comfortable in our huts and like any other soldier taking it as easy as possible. We get plenty to eat more than we can make way with in fact and though some might think our Biscuit hard we manage to make them do very well. I don't know how people in general like the last change in the command here but I for one had much rather had Burnside remain for though Hooker is a fighter I have not that confidence in him that I had in Burnside. However I suppose Burnside understood to his satisfaction that the leading Generals of the Army were hostile to him and that he stood no chance of success and I honor him for declining to lead an Army so clearly hostile to his plans. Hooker seems more popular and though no other man can ever command the confidence of the Army as McClellan does I hope something may be done under Hooker (fighting Joe) to humble the haughty chins of the Sunny South.
There is a move being made now to furnish soft bread for the Army and the boys are feeling pretty well over it but for my part I would sooner have the Crackers than Bake Bread so I don't rejoice very much. I can't think of much more to write now and that little don't amount to anything so I will close for the present hoping soon to hear that you are better at home and that the sickness now so prevalent in Salisbury may soon cease entirely.

Good Bye for the present
Jerome

Camp near Falmouth
Feb. 6th. 1863.

Dear Parents, Brother, Sister,

I don't know as I can write
much to day but I felt that
I wanted to do something
and as it is raining I will
try to write. I am getting along
well at present and hope
this letter may find you well
also. I received Martha's letter
of Jan 23th just after writing
my last one and though I
had learned most of the
news I was shocked to find
that Ma had been so bad as
I learned by the letter She had
I felt as if I would give all I
have to be allowed to go home
for a short time but as I know
it would be almost impossible

Chins of the Sunny South.

There is a move being made now to furnish soft Bread for the Army and the boys are feeling pretty well over it but for my part I would sooner have the Crackers than Baked Bread so I don't rejoice very much I cant think of much more to write now and that little dont amount to anything so I will close for the present hoping soon to hear that you are better at home and that the sickness now so prevalent in Salisbury may soon cease entirely. Good bye for the present

    Jerome

Camp near Falmouth Va.
Feb. 13th. 1863

Dear Parents, Brother & Sister

I am doing nothing this afternoon so I will write to you. I came off guard this morning having been down at the railroad looking after U.S. property for the last three days and this forenoon I have been washing my clothes which by the way is a kind of business that I don't like to do. I escaped going on piques by being on guard and a three days piqueting at this time of year is no joke so I don't feel sorry that I was not here to go for we dont go more than once a month and seems likely to be better weather before the next time comes.

I am well as usual but though comfortable as to health I cant help feeling uneasy about home when I know that any of you are unwell as at present and I want to hear from you just as often as you can write without too much trouble. I received a letter a few days ago and I felt much easier to learn that Ma was so much better. Ma don't allow any thought of me to keep you from getting along for I am doing first rate and I want to hear that you are as well as ever next time I hear from home. Amos write to me wont you for you don't know how lonesome I get sometimes. Write something about what you are doing how large you have grown how many Rabbits you kill and how you are getting along at school or almost anything you can think of. There is very little here to write about but I expect you would find something to laugh about if you should see the little huts we have to live in down here on the Rappahannock. Mine is just long enough for me to lay in and high enough to stand in without stooping but tis a pretty good house after all so you see we learn to live in a small house when we can't get a large one. I saw Nate Wood a few days ago. He is fat and I guess he has a pretty good thing of it but he is homesick as a dog and wants to get to Old Stratford badly which I hope he may do at the end of the war. He is acting as Darkey for the Major of the 121st and has never done any duty as a soldier so Manheim paid a pretty good price for a man to curry horses &c. We get soft bread, now and then now which makes the boys feel much better and of Potatoes we get quite plenty so we fare very well for soldiers. But you are getting tired and I must go and chop a little wood so I will bid you a good bye for this time

Jerome

Camp near Falmouth
March 7th. 1863

Dear Parents, Brother & Sister

I am going to try to write another line to you though I hardly know how to commence what to write of. I am enjoying myself pretty well and my health is tolerable good better indeed than I thought it would get by this time but I am uneasy as a fish out of water for I have not had a letter from you since the 16th of last month. I know it must be you have written one or two letters before this time but they have miscarried and it seems a very long time since I heard from you. Amos I did not forget that yesterday was your birthday that you are now sixteen years old old enough to be a man in size and action and i hope you are one in strength and principle. I should like very well indeed to see you to day for I presume you have grown almost out of my recollection and you must be nearly as large as I am now. I don't forget how you used to say that you were going to get big enough to tumble me around and I don't know but you will for you have the advantage of me now. Do you ever think when you sit down at the table to plenty of good bread and butter meat and potatoes and almost all else that you could wish for that Jerome is far off in desert Virginia in a little tent and making his breakfast or dinner on crackers or bread and meat with a cup of coffee or for change perhaps a few beans rice or some little Potatoes if you never did think of this when something on the table happened not to suit you exactly think of it next time you feel dainty and as often as you would complain remember that many a soldier is living on poorer fare to day than is usually dealt out to old Bear and sleeping on a bed poorer than the naked floor along side of the stove you are sitting by this winter morning. But there is another thing to think of are you growing manly as you grow large. Are you trying to learn are you trying to be all the help you can at home. You know size don't make the man if it did some people known to you who live close to you would be very great men but they are instead great boobies so you see that action makes the man and if you would do well you must see how much knowledge you can gain how kind pleasant and good you can be so that you may while growing to mans size grow also into the qualities that make such men as you like to see not men so savage and cross that their jaw is heard as far as their voice can reach not men who living from hand to mouth make the bunch of Shingles to day that must buy their bread for tomorrow not men who steal crows from your traps and let the cattle run on their neighbors land not men so cross and disagreeable that they are dreaded at home and abroad but men of the kind who careful attend to their business and intelligent enough to do it in the right manner are loved at home and well thought of by their neighbors and al] else who know them I hardly know anything about how you are getting along now day. Amos because you don't write to me—what you do or anything of the kind and I sometimes think you have almost forgotten that you ever had a brother. I think often of you and love you just as well as if I could see you every day and I do want you to write to me. If you are doing well and trying to be a man it will make me feel glad to hear about it if you don't get along well perhaps I can help you to do better even if I am far away for I have seen more of the world and I will do anything for you that I possibly can. You don't know what a pleasure it is to get a few lines from you it almost makes me feel at home and I think you might write once in two or three weeks at least and let me know all about your work your school or anything else you can think to write. Dont hesitate because tis hard work for you to make up a letter for practice will make it easier and I can always understand what you write without any trouble besides twill make it easier for me to eat hard crackers and sleep on the ground this summer and perhaps I can fight better if I can know that Amos is at home doing all he can to help Pa and Ma and trying to be a man and that he thinks sometimes of Jerome. Do you go hunting occassionally. I have not been since last spring at Yorktown and then I only killed one little Rabbit with my revolver for Soldiers are not allowed to do much hunting unless they can do it on the sly and there is hardly anything here worth going after. I don't know as I can close my letter better than by giving you a list of the price asked by Sutlers here for some of the things you probably have at home common enough. Butter sells at sixty cts. a lb. Cheese at thirty eggs five cts. each Apples also five cents and a decent pair of coarse boots can not be had for less than eight dollars. Nearly everything else in proportion so you see Soldiers need piles of money or else they must do without which is generally the best plan. Most of the stuff Sutlers bring being of but little account and some of it worse than nothing. May I hope that this letter will find you all well and if so or not that you will remember me with a good long letter is the wish of

Jerome

Camp near Falmouth
March 7th, 1862

Dear Parents, Brother & Sister

I am
going to try to write another line
to you though I hardly know how
to commence or what to write of.
I am enjoying myself pretty
well and my health is tolerable
good better indeed than I thought
it would get by this time but I
am uneasy as a fish out of
water for I have not had a
letter from you since the 15th of
last month. I know it must be
you have written one or two the
before this time but they have
miscarried and it seems a
very long time since I heard
from you. Amos I did not
forget that yesterday was your

to you who live close to you
would be very great men but
they are indeed great boobies
so you see that action makes
the men and if you would
do well you must see how
much knowledge you can gain
how kind pleasant and good
you can be so that you may
while growing to mans size
grow also into the qualities that
make such men as you like
to see not men so savage and
cross that their jaw is heard as
far as their voice can reach not
men who living from hand to
mouth make the truth of the
lie to day that must to them
bread for tomorrow not men
who steal crops from your
trees and let the cattle run
on their neighbors land not
men so cross and disagreeable
that they are dreaded at home
and abroad but men of the
kind who careful & attentive &

attend to their business and
intelligent enough to do it
in the right manner are
looked at home and will
thought of by their neighbors
and all else who know them
I hardly know anything about
how you are getting along now
days Amos because you don't
write to me about what you do
anything of the kind and I
sometimes think you have
almost forgotten that you
ever had a brother. I think
often of you and love you
just as well as if I could
see you every day and I do
want you to write to me. If
you are doing well and trying
to be a man it will make
me feel glad to hear about

Butter sells at sixty cts a lb.
Cheese at Thirty Eggs five cts
each Apples also five cents ane
a decent pair of coarse boots
can not be had for less than
eight dollars nearly everything
else in proportion so you see
Soldiers need piles of money
or else they must do without
most of the stuff sutlers bring
being of but little account and
some of it worse than nothing
May I hope that this letter will
find you all well and I ...
... that you will ...
... with a ...
to the ... of ...

Camp near Falmouth Va.
May 7th 1863

Dear Parents, Brother & Sister

I hasten to inform you that I am yet alive and tolerably well though much tired out with toilsome and muddy marching and that the Army of the Potomac is once more north of the Rappahannock. Why this is so I cant for the life of me give a reason though it is said there is a good one it being that as usual a screw was loose some where and the machinery failed in some point. Last Saturday and Sunday the Army fought one of the most fiercely contested battles of this or any other war and we gave Lee and Co. a good whipping as need be holding our ground and taking several thousand prisoners (this was at Chancellorsville) when the Reb thinking he could make more somewhere else managed to switch off in such shape as to endanger our suppllies (sic) and Gen. Hooker after making one of the most brilliant movements of this or any other war was obliged (through the defection of some one else) to retire to the north side of the River which he has done without loss. We got in here yesterday muddy (for it rained all day), and tired with a march of fifteen or sixteen miles. I know you will expect some particulars of the Battle but I cant give any at present except that it was obstinate and on the side of the Rebs most bloody for they fought us on ground of our own choosing and our loss is comparatively small. Our Regt. lost a few men skirmishing and on picket but we were not in the ugliest of the scrape and have suffered little. Whose fault we attribute this lack of success to will come out in time. I am ignorant as any of causes. The mail will go soon. I must close. Write soon and let me know all the news.

Jerome

Camp near Falmouth Va.
May 7th 1863.

Dear Parents, Brothers & Sisters.

I heisten to inform you that I am yet alive and tolerably well though much tired out with toilsome and muddy marching and that the Army of the Potomac is once more north of the Rappahannock. Why this is so I can't for the life of me give a reason though it is said there is a good one it being that as usual a screw was loose somewhere and the machinery failed in some point Last Saturday and Sunday the Army fought one of the most fiercely contested battles of this or any other war and we gave

Chancellorsville Va.　　　　　May 12, 1863

Dear Parents

I take the opportunity by this mail to let you know that i am well. We are encamped in the woods south of the Rapidan River near the place above named. We have captured some Rebs but do not know whether they are in much force in our immediate front. We got the start of them and got across the Rappahannock and Rapidan before they knew that we were on the move. Thus far all looks promising. We had to march hard but I have stood it first rate so far and hope to go through well. Affairs are taking shape and we hope for complete victory. We crossed the Rappahannock on Pontoons and forded the Rapidan both on Wednesday and it is said we marched 21 miles that day. The 44th was the first of our Division (Infantry) across the Rapidan and we waded about fifteen rods in a rapid current two and a half or three but deep which though not as funny was quite novel and was done in style under the eye of Gens. Meade & Griffin who complimented the steadiness of the men. All is well at present and hope is in the ascendant. I must bid you good bye for the present for the mail goes soon. Moses is here and well. Hoping this may find you in good heath I am

Jerome

Chancellorville Va May 12th 63

Dear Parents

I take the opportunity offered by this mail to let you know that I am well. We are encamped in the woods south of the Rapidan River near the place above named. We have captured some Rebs but do not know whether they are in much force in our immediate front. We got the start of them and got across the Rappahanock and Rapidan before they knew that we were on the move. Thus far all looks promising. We had to march hard but I have stood it first rate so far

and hope to go through well.
Affairs are taking shape and
my hope for complete victory.
We crossed the Rappahannock
on Pontoons and forded the
Rapidan both on Wednesday
and it is said we marched
21 miles that day. The 14th
was the first of our Division
(Infantry) across the Rapidan
and we waded about fifteen
rods in a rapid current two
and a half or three feet
deep which though not as fun
was quite novel and was
done in style under the
eye of Genl. Meade & Griffin
who complimented the
steadiness of the men.
All is well at present and
hope is in the ascendant.
I must bid you good bye

for the present for the
mail goes soon. Moses
is here and well. Hoping
this may find you in good
health I am

Jerome

Camp near Falmouth Va.   May 23rd. 1863.

Dear Parents, Brother, and Sister

I am going to try to write a letter to you though for the life of me I can scarcely tell what I shall make out to write. I am well as usual and comfortable with nothing to do of any importance. We have moved camp within the last three days moving back from the R.R. a distance of about two miles and we are now in the prettiest camp we ever occupied a (little nearer Falmouth Station than we were before). Here water is good and it seems as if we might pass a few days here quite comfortably that is if we were allowed. I received your letter of May 17th yesterday and was glad to hear that you were getting along as comfortably as you are. Pa it is but little I can tell you about the movement and fight across the River. A private soldier can tell but little about the movement of the Army especially in a country so woody that he can hardly see the length of his own Regt. The movement took the Rebs by surprise and we were south of the Rapidan before they knew we were out of camp and we think the reason why the movement was not a perfect success was the failure of Sigels old Corps (who wont fight without him to lead) and the natural difficulties in the way in the shape of woods swamps and underbrush. The failure of the 11th Corps took the 2nd from Sedgwick thus crippling him and causing his defeat thus endangering our communications and rendering it unsafe for us to operate on the line then held by us and the country was so difficult as to render it a move without any good prospect of success so twas deemed expedient to abandon the undertaking. However we were not whipped as some will have it but quite to the contrary we came away at our leisure without any interruption from the Rebels. The 1st. Division of the 5th Corps (of which the 44th forms a part) under command of Gen. Griffin covered the retreat and we were last across suffering no inconvenience at the hands of the Chivs, who never once came up in sight of the rear of our Army. So you see the Rebs. much as they want to boast failed to drive us though they made the most desperate attempts and lost their best bravest and most noble General Stonewall Jackson, and probably 20,000 men in the attempts of the 2nd. and 3d. of May. I never in my life heard more terrible fighting than on Sunday May 3d, and I know the Rebs. got it terribly for besides all the killed and wounded I saw no less than 3,000 prisoners pass to the rear and after fighting with awful desperation for about seven hours they drew off glad to let the matter end as it was. Of course they will brag but I guess when they come to count the cost they will find a balance against them. Jackson alone was worth 50,000 men and they can never replace him for his equal they have not South and I like to have said his superior does not live in the world. He was a good man if he was a Rebel and we have to regret the mistake that made an enemy instead of an ally of Thomas F. Jackson. Ever kind and humane to those who fell into his hands through the chances of war strictly religious and earnestly zealous in the cause of the South he never stooped to illtreat a prisoner or do any mean action but ever the same consistent active enemy to us he was the most dangerous foe the Union ever had. He has gone but we can't rejoice as we should if Davis, Lee, Tombs or others of that crew had suffered death at the hands of our Army for we feel that he was worthy of a better fate that we had rather have taken him and had him live than that he should die in such a bad cause. I have not been able to learn much about the 121st. for they are some distance from us. Merton Tanner is in a hospital near here and though somewhat badly hurt is smart and is doing first rate or was two or three days ago. The rest of the boys I don't know much about. It seems to be the impression that Alphonso Casler is killed but no one seems to know that such is the case so perhaps he may have been taken prisoner. I would not try to have his folks think but that there might be some prospect of his turning up all right nor would I try to encourage hopes that might end in disappointment still there may be a hope and tis better that they never despair, while it is uncertain. The Young's boys seem to be among the missing too and it may be that they are taken for they were so closely engaged as to render such a conclusion quite reasonable. Some of the Papers seem to be trying hard to make the people think that Gen. Hooker has lost the confidence of the Army and all such trash but they either lie willfully (which is the most natural conclusion) or else they know nothing about it for I believe the Army has as much confidence in Hooker as before and we are just as willing to do under his command now as we ever were before the late movement. I was attacked with Diptheria Ma while I was on "Belle Island," and was bad enough so that the medicine the Dr. put in my throat loosened large chunks of putrid matter but the Doctor (who though a Southerner was a good man) did his best for me and I soon got better. I can say in praise of the Doctors of the Richmond Prisons that they did all they could for me when I was in need of their help and I shall always remember the kindness of one of them who attended me as faithfully as if I had been other than a Yankee prisoner. Amos I am glad you remembered you can hardly know how much pleasure it gives me to hear direct from you. You must write oftener if you can. I don't know as I have any more to write so I will close for the present.

Good bye for this time
Jerome

Camp near Bank's Ford Va.   May 29th 1863.

Dear Parents, Brother and sister

I am seated in the open air close by the Rappahannock River at the place above named (about four miles above Fredricksburgh). At present it seems rather uncertain whether we shall remain here long though we were told when we came that we were coming to remain for some time. We came here yesterday afternoon and spent the night on the outpost in picket duty having withal a very easy time for none of the Rebs seem inclined to be hostile and all went well with us. This morning when we had light enough to see we found that we were within a stones throw of the Rebel pickets just across the Ford but no one seemed scared though of course both parties were a little shy at first but this soon wore off and after a little some of the Rebs came to the River and went in swimming—some of our boys soon followed and though orders prevented them from getting together they got near enough to talk with each other and parted in good humor when we were relieved. After we came off picket I went fishing for a while but did not have much luck. I only caught one Bullhead one Chub and one Shiner just enough to taste not much more. After I gave up fishing I found a nice lot of Strawberries and filled myself nicely for twas the first time since I left home that I had tasted such a thing as a Strawberry. However they are quite plenty here and perhaps I may get another chance at them if we remain here long enough. All the Rebs we have come across yet seemed to be inclined to act in a civilized manner and we don't anticipate any trouble if we have to do picket duty here for some time as we rather expect we may. The River here is quite broad and deep except at the Ford where though the current is strong tis easy enough to wade it so this is the place we have to watch and a few senties posted at rare intervals answer very well for the rest of the way up and down. The country here looks wild but the land seems good and the situation is most pleasant. We have some novelties here too for instance I helped kill a black snake today that measured six feet in length being much the largest of the snake kind I ever saw and of the identical kind (I believe) that gave our friends Sneak and Joe (of Wild Western Scenes, memory) so much fun and finally so much trouble. I dont like the critters but they are harmless and rare for this is the first one of the kind I have ever seen alive so they cause no trouble. I don't think of anything else to write at present except telling you that I am well as usual and a little more so feeling in fact first rate and with the hope that this letter may find you well I will bid you good bye for the present

Jerome

Camp near Bank's Ford Va. May. 29th 1863.

Dear Parents, Brother and Sister

I am seated in the open air close by the Rappahannock River at the place above named (about four miles above Fredricksburgh). At present it seems rather uncertain whether we shall remain here long though we were told when we came that we were coming to remain for some time. We came here yesterday afternoon and spent the night on the outpost in picket duty having withal a very easy time for none of the Rebs seem inclined to be hostile and all went well with us. This morning when we had light enough to see we found that we were within a stones throw of the Rebel Pickets just across the Ford but no one seemed scared though of course both parties were a little shy at first but this soon wore off and after a little some of the Rebs. came to the River and went in swimming. some of our boys soon followed and though orders prevented them from getting together they got near enough to talk with each other and parted in good humor when we were relieved. After we came off picket I went fishing for a while but did not have much luck I only caught one Bullhead one Chub and one shiner just enough to taste not much more. After I gave up fishing I found a nice lot of Strawberries and filled myself nicely for the first time since I left home that I had tasted such a thing as a Strawberry however they are quite plenty here and perhaps I may get another chance at them if we remain here long enough. All the Rebs we have come across yet seem to be inclined to act in a civilized manner and we don't anticipate any trouble if we have to do picket duty here for some time as we rather expect we may. The River here is quite broad and deep except at the Ford where though the current is strong t' tis easy enough to wade it so this is the place we have to watch and a few sentries posted at rare intervals answer very well for the rest of the way up and down The country here looks wild but the land seems good and the situation is most pleasant. We have some novelties here too for instance I helped kill a black Snake today that measured six feet in length being much the largest of the snake kind I ever saw and of the identical kind (I believe) that gave our friends Sneak and Joe (of Wild Western Scenes, memory) so much fun and finally so much trouble. I don't like the critters but they are harmless and rare for this is the first one of the kind I have ever seen alive so they cause no trouble. I don't think of anything else to write at present except telling you that I am well as usual and a little more so feeling in fact first rate and with the hope that this letter may find you well I will bid you good bye for the present

Jerome

Camp near Crittendens Mills Va.
June 5th 1863

Dear Parents

I have but little to write about but I will try to do as much as to let you know
that I am very well and in fact better than I have been before in a great while. We left
Bank's Ford yesterday morning and marched in the direction of Warrenton Junction till
night when we encamped (after marching about sixteen miles or more) for the night.
This morning the order came for us to come to this place which is off the Warrenton
Road and on the road to Kelly's Ford on the upper waters of the Rappahanock and is
the place where we crossed when we went to Chancellorsville. We are some distance
from the River and in a pleasant situation but tis hard telling how long we'll be able to
stay here. I think not very long though we may of course remain some time. The weather
is very pleasant and warm almost too warm for marching but all things considered quite
fine and the men are in good condition (generally speaking). The place where we are
laying now is rather ahead of the average of Virginia villes for besides a grist mill, with
two run of stone it has an old broken down sawmill and Tannery with a pretty decent
looking dwelling and some Negro cabins. We happened to be in season to day to see
quite a crowd of the Chivs who had come to mill, and it may be interesting to you to
hear something of the appearance of these F.F.Vs. First was rather an ancient looking
man with a profusion of black hair and beard and sporting an awful bony and shoeless
old Horse. This old Covey was dressed in a suit of brown linen with the cape of some
soldiers coat over his shoulders and he looked suspicious and cross at us. Next was a
youngerly looking man with Sorrell top, and dressed in a seedy ragged butternut
Kentucky Jean suit and carrying a treacherous smile on his not beautiful phiz that was
enough to destroy all confidence in him at once and he too had a most seedy looking
nag to carry his bag of corn. Next comes a Va. matron dressed in the style of fifteen
years ago and looking ill pleased with the appearance of the Yanks taking care too to
stand well aside and to hold on well to a worse looking old Plug, than either of the before
mentioned. The said Plug being accountered with a Side Saddle (probably a hundred
years old). This Lady was accompanied by a son probably about fifteen years of age and
he did manage to strut round and look very important at us though he was the hardest
most ragged and patched looking specimen of a juvenile twas ever my fortune to see.
However he was clean withall and this spoke well for his mother suspicious as she
seemed towards Yanks. Next was quite a well dressed young woman also attended by
a (in this case fair) looking horse and not seeming to possess the same hostile feeling
towards us so plainly shown by most of the others. And lastly came an old Lady (near
as large as Old Mrs. Bloodough) riding in a wagon drawn by a yoke of oxen (one of

them without horns) driven by a youthful son of Ham who seemed to be a servant to the Old Lady. This wagon was loaded with a pretty good grist of corn and wheat and the appearance of the Lady was that of a person in good circumstances. She wore mourning and seemed quite friendly with some of our officers who conversed with her a little. The Miller a pale good natured looking man with a miserable look completed the group odd enough looking to a man born in N.Y. yet full of interest to me as showing so much of the manners and customs of these F.F.Vs. I don't know as I have much more to write and probably you will think tis poor business to be making sport of these miserable people but the scene was so odd that a smile would start and though tis something I seldom do I could not resist the temptation to waste a little ink a the expense of these proud beggars the First Families (self styled) of Virginia, who of course feel themselves as much above us Yankees as the stars are above the Earth. But you are weary and so hoping that you are enjoying good health and are doing well I will bid you good bye for the present

Jerome

Va.

Camp near Kittendews Mills.
June 8th. 1863.

Dear Parents

        I have but little
to write about but I will try
to do as much as to let you
know that I am well and
in fact better than I have
been before in a great while.
We left Banks' Ford yesterday
morning and marched in
the direction of Warrenton June
tion til night when we encamped
(after marching about six teen
miles or more) for the night.
This morning the order came
for us to come to this place which
is off the Warrenton road and
on the road to Keily's Ford on
the upper waters of the Rappahan

a treacherous smile on his not
beautiful phiz that was enough
to destroy all confidence in him
at once and he too had a most
sorry looking nag to carry his
bag of corn, Next comes a
Va. Matron dressed in the style
of fifteen years ago and looking
ill pleased with the appearance
of the Yanks taking care too to
stand well aside and to
hold on well to a worse look
ing old Plug than either of the
before mentioned the said Plug
being accoutred with a Side
Saddle (probably a hundred
years old) This Lady was accompanied by a son probably about
fifteen years of age and he did
manage to strut around and look
very important at us Thought he
was the hardest most ragged
and patched looking specimen
of a juvenile I was ever of
fortune to see however he was

clean withall and this spoke
well for his mother suspicions
as she seemed towards Yanks.
Next was quite a well dressed
young woman also attended
by a (in this case fair) looking
horse and not seeming to
possess the same hostitful
-ing towards us so plainly
shown by most of the others.
And lastly came an "old
Lady" (near as large as Old
Mrs. Bloodbough) riding in
a wagon drawn by a yoke
of oxen (one of them without
horns) driven by a youthful son
of Ham who seemed to be a
servant to the Old Lady. This
wagon was loaded with a
pretty good grist of Comand

McVeigh Hospital
Alexandria Va. June 28th. 1863

Dear Parents

    I have waited a little longer than usual about writing, to you in hopes to get some news from you. I have heard nothing from home since I left the Regt. and I begin to get a little puzzled for a reason. I wrote to you as soon as I could after I cam here and also to Capt. Larrabee requesting him to send on any letters that might come for me but I hear nothing from him as yet so I have had no means of knowing whether you were well or ill for some time. I am pretty well myself—my leg is about as well as ever and has been for several days. I expected to be sent away two or three days ago but when they sent all away (in obedience to an order to clean out the Hospital) I was left. I don't know why for I was certainly as well able to go as many that went. Don't think that I was in a hurry to go for I had rather stay here till perfectly well then go to Convalescent Camp but I rather wondered that I should be left however I think 'twas because the Dr. took a fancy to be friendly to me because I belonged to a Regt. in which he had many friends. I think this is much the best conducted Hospital I was ever in. Both the Surgeon in Charge Dr. Crafts and the Medical Director Dr. Bently seem to take an interest and both of them are very fine men. News of any importance is a scarce article here and people here know very little what is going on in the Army. None of us can even make a good guess where the Army of the Potomac is. Be sure however that it is not idle that Fighting Joe is busy and that he will do the best he can to work the destruction of the Rebel host. I will send you today's Washington Chronicle which is the best paper for news we have and the most reliable and there is not much in it at that. People here are not enthusiastic as they once were but there is much of confidence in regard to present military operations based principally I think, on the fact that Hooker seems to possess the ability to fool the Rebs most beautifully as to his whereabouts and to keep a good eye upon them. God grant that victory may crown his efforts for I believe if any man ever worked earnestly and faithfully that one was and is Fighting Joe Hooker. I don't know as I've anything more now. I expect there is a letter from home somewhere on the road and I am waiting patiently.
    Good bye for this time

                Jerome

McVeigh Hospital
Alexandria Va June 28th 1863
Dear Parents—

I have waited a
little longer than usual about
writing, to you in hopes to get
some news from you. I have heard
nothing from home since I left
the Regt. and I begin to get a
little uneasied for a reason
I wrote to you as soon as I
could after I came here and
also to Capt. Larrabee requesting
him to send on any letters that
might come for one but I hear
nothing from him as yet so
I have had no means of know-
-ing whether you were well or
ill for some time. I am pretty
well myself— my leg is about
as well as ever and has

I think, on the fact that Hooker
seems to possess the ability to fool
the Rebs, most beautifully as to his
whereabouts and to keep a good
eye upon them. God grant that
victory may crown his efforts for
I believe if any man ever worked
earnestly and faithfully that man
was and is Fighting Joe Hooker,.
I dont know as I see anything more
now. I expect there is a letter from
home somewhere on the road
and I am waiting patiently.
Good by for this time

Jerome

McVeigh House Hospital
Alexandria Va.   July 9th. 1863

Dear Parents

       I dont know that I have much to write but I will at least write enough to let you know that I am tolerably well and enjoying myself as well as possible. The morning is very pleasant and I am sitting where I can see the Capitol when I look up for eight miles is not a long distance and the Capitol is magnificently large. The muddy Potomac covered with sails and looking grand enough is in sight nearly all the way from Washington and as it is much more muddy than usual I hope tis owing to its being so much higher so that the traitorous Lee with his rebel host may find in its waters the grave they ought long ago to have occupied.

       The news from the Army is very good now but you will probably get all before this letter can reach you so I will not write any. Alexandria is to take a 'Puke' today that is the Secesh are to be sent South at the expense of Uncle Sam that they may have a chance to try the 'Realities of Jeffdom' and no longer plot and act treason here in our midst. Many of them go off with long faces for they fear the conscription but go they must and the day of their banishment already too long delayed has come at last. Somewhere about four hundred of them are to go to day I believe mostly able men who too cowardly to fight could furnish information to Jeff and shoot down our Soldiers on duty in the streets so that the only thing I sorrow for in their case is that they are not shut up or hung instead of being sent off. A cell in some prison and plenty of work with coarse diet would cool the chivalry of their nature and make them wiser (perhaps better) men. There is much outcry about 'arbitrary arrests' &c. but I would state prison twenty where the Government banishes one and (hang too if that did not answer) that's my doctrine beaten into me by the pelting storm while I have kept guard or marched for the defence of the Government these traitors are attempting to ruin wrought into my nature by toil such as none but the Soldier knows. I believe in showing mercy but to be merciful here is to destroy ourselves and charity begins at home. The Rebel soldier who meets me in the field I can respect for though ignorant he is earnest and brave but the sneak who on our midst seeks and sends information to our foe and in the darkness of the night shoots the sentry on his post I would hang high as the tallest tree would make a gallows or chain in the lowest dungeon as a thing to mean to contaminate the Earth. And those too at the North like so many I could name (is it possible I have a relative who belongs to that contemptible crew) who have so much fault to find with the Government and not one word to condemn the Traitors. Oh what do they deserve the blood of hundreds and thousands of our soldiers lies at their door and yet they tell us they are Union men. They oppose the Government as much as possible they plead for free speech (the Devils plea) they block every wheel of war Chariot by their senseless and base cries of incompetence Niggerism and arbitrary power and Jeff. Davis looks on and smiles. Blow most noble Democrats of the north illustrious Copperheads below and spout do your best for free speech free press &c. and bye and bye I will give you a chance to do what you so much long to do yes yes Horatio and Fernando and your most noble followers you shall have the coveted privilege you shall kiss the feet of the Darkey who blacks my illustrious boots you never shall regret never that you worshipped at the shrine of Slavery while my name is Jeff. Oh I tell you I am down on the treason mongers of the North. It is perhaps best that I am not where I can reach them or some of them would feel Union blows if they talked any of their foul deviltry to me and perhaps I should get hurt. Our Rulers are not perfect God knows but we must sustain the Government or bow to Slavery and God forbid that I should ever put one straw in the way of those who honest and faithful though they are are (sic) not free from faults and therefore need all our best endeavors to assist them in this our Country's need. The day will come "I believe as sure as there is a God" that those who now counsel resistance to the draft and encourage desertions those who oppose the Government now when to oppose it is to aid and comfort its foes will be a Byeword and a hissing (more contemptible than was Arnold the great Copperhead of our first great struggle for a nationality), may it not be far distant. But I've said enough twice more than I intended to when I commenced and you will tire of such. I have just recd. and read your letter of the 5th. I was happy to hear from you all again. Ma don't give yourself any uneasiness on my account. I am doing very well. You see the Rebel Army that was to capture Philadelphia and overrun the North is on the back track. The people of the North once awake no Rebel Army lives on our soil. The Army of the Potomac you see can do something yet. With the help of God let us hope that the dawn is at hand. Vicksburg taken and Lee defeated—glorious victories both may they begin the ending of this fearful struggle. Keep up good courage all of you assured and awaiting Gods own time.

Good bye for the present

Jerome

McVeigh House Hospital
Alexandria Va. July 9th 1863

Dear Parents

I dont know that
I have much to write but I
will at least write enough
to let you know that I am
tolerably well and enjoying
myself as well as possible.
The morning is very pleasant
and I am sitting where I can
see the Capitol when I look
up for eight miles is not a
long distance and the Capitol
is magnificiently large. The
muddy Potomac covered with
sails and looking grand
enough is in sight nearly all
the way from Washington and
as it is much more muddy
than usual I hope tis owing to

the Government these traitors are attempting to ruin wrought into my nature by toil such as none but the soldier knows. I believe in showing mercy but to be merciful here is to destroy ourselves and cherish behind at home. The Rebel Soldier who meets me in the field I can respect for though ignorant he is earnest and brave but the sneak who in our midst lurks and sends information to our foe and in the darkness of the night shoots the sentry on his post I would hang high as the tallest tree would make a gallows or chain in the lowest dungeon as a thing too mean to contaminate the Earth. And those too at the North like so many I could name (is it possible I have a relative who belongs to that contemptible crew) who have so much fault to find with the Government and not one word to condemn the Traitors oh what do they deserve the blood of hundreds and thousands

of our Soldiers lies at their door
and yet they tell us they are
Union Men. They oppose the
Government as much as possible
they plead for free speech (the
Devil plea) they block every
wheel of the war Chariot by their
senseless and base cries of
incompetence Niggerism and
arbitrary power and Jeff.
Davis looks on and smiles.
Blow most noble Democrats
of the north illustrious Cop-
-perheads bellow and spout do
your best for free Speech free
Press &c. and bye and bye I
will give you a chance to do
what you so much long to do
ye ye Horatio and Fernando
and your most noble followers
you shall have the coveted

again. So don't give yourself
any uneasiness on my account
I am doing very well. Don't
the Rebel Army that was to capture
Philadelphia and overrun the
North is on the back track. The
people of the North once awake
no Rebel army lives on our
soil. The Army of the Potomac
you see can do something yet.
With the help of God let us hope
that the dawn is at hand. Vicksburg
taken and Lee defeated glorious
victories both may they begin the
ending of this fearful struggle.
Keep up good courage all of you
assured and awaiting Gods own
time—good bye for the present
                              Jerome

McVeigh House Hospital
Alexandria Va.   July 17th 1863

Dear Parents

I am going to try to write something though to tell the truth I have very little to write. I am tolerably well and nothing much to do so I get along as well as can be expected. I have just recd. a letter from M.U. Bliss (mailed at Frederick) which contained some sad news. Capt. Larrabee was killed at Gettysburgh and we are a hero and a patriot less in the 44th. Tis sad for me for I loved that man and was closely bound to him by the ties of friendship but so it is. He has gone and I hope to a better land for he was a Christian if there is one on earth. He died as he had lived in the front of the battle where duty called and he has gone from this world of strife to a more peaceful land above. New York City is showing the effect of Copperhead teachings it seems but there is a hope that they will come to reason soon not probably however till many of them (some innocent) perhaps are killed. I hope the President will not allow the Draft to be postponed at all on account of this but push forward and show Feronando and Co. that we yet have a Government. News by way of Vicksburg, Port Hudson and Charleston is good—prisoners enough taken all around to make a mighty army and the Rebs are getting hard pressed. I think the dawn is at hand. Pay day has not come to me for I stay hardly long enough in a place to give it time and I shall soon be out of money. I have spent considerable it seems but much of the time my appetite has been poor and I humored it some for I can't see it my duty to do otherwise. Bread without butter is dry when a person is not very sharp and all these little things cost very high down here yet I don't feel that I ought to deny myself and so I don't do it. I could have got my pay a few days ago but I had no Descriptive List, here so I must wait till I can get one from the Regt. Pa you may enclose five dollars if you please in the next letter you write and I think I'll be able to make out. Send Greenback by all means if you have or can get it for that is the currency here. I don't know as I've anything more to write so hoping that this letter may find you all well I will close for the present

Jerome

Mrs Leigh House Hospital,
Alexandria Va July 17th 1863
Dear Parents
            I am going to try
to write some thing though to
tell the truth I have very little
to write. I am tolerably well
and nothing much to do so
I get along as well as can be
expected. I have just rec d
a letter from M U. Bliss (mailed
at Fredrick) which contained
some sad news. Capt. Larrabee
was killed at Gettysburg and
we are a hero and a patriot
less in the 44th. Tis sad for
one for I loved that man and
was closely bound to him by
the ties of friendship but as it
is he has gone and I hope to a
better land for he was a

write and I think I'll be able
to make out. Send Greenback
by all means if you have or
can get it for that is the currency
here. I don't know as I've anything
more to write so hoping that this
letter may find you all well
I will Close for the present

Jerome

PART IV

THE CAMP LETTERS OF
ROBERT H. DEPRIEST
2ND VIRGINIA REGIMENT, C.S.A.

"Excuse my mistakes my head is a little out of fix this morning i have bin thinking a bout comeing home..."

—*Robert H. Depriest*

INTRODUCTION

From March 16, 1862 to September 12, 1864 and from Mount Jackson to Winchester, Robert H. Depriest of the 2nd Va. Regiment Company, C.S.A. fought the Yankees, fought for courage amid the deprivation, and struggled to keep in touch with his family and guide them through his absence. He was one of many soldiers to go off to war with dreams of Southern Independence and by the fall of 1863 realize the war was a horrific experiment in savagery that had no end in sight. These letters present a wonderfully personal and human account of those lonely camp nights, long forced marches, the death of close friends, and the worries of how a wife and family were coping back on the family farm.

The authors have chosen to include these letters exactly as they were written with all of the words misspelled, the virtual absence of punctuation, and the curious phrases and idioms so that the historian would have this magnificent collection exactly as it was written over a century ago. The authors are likewise indebted to Mr. Paul Gibson of Blountville, Tennessee for lending this collection for inclusion herein. If it were not for lovers and preservers of history like Paul, so much of America's past would be lost and so many of the thoughts, words and deeds of its unsung heroes forever denied to historians.

LAST LETTER HOME

By the flickering campfire the lonely Reb sat
Digesting a dinner of salt pork and back fat
With whittled pencil he wrote on paper of rag
A few thoughts home to counsel and brag

Of heroics by neighbors in distant fights
Tempered by countless unspoken horrific sights
As words came slowly for what he had seen
So as to shelter loved ones from duties so unclean

Attention turned instead to fields and crops to start
Children's school and advice not to depart
The sale of hogs, cows, corn and feed
The health of relatives prayerfully not in need

As he stares at dimming embers and coffee pot cold
Folding tonight's letter for the eyes of family to behold
His tent will be his only refuge this night
From the horrors of war and loneliness of fight

—*Wayne L. Wolf*

March the 16 (1862)

If you have the chance send me a shirt and all the tobacco that is thare and one pare of socks try to get the ground proud and the corn planted if you can

    Direct yore leter
    2nd Va Regt Company
    Col Alen

I in tend to come home as soon as i can i can not tel when that wil be.

                    Unsigned (but R. Depriest)

March the 26: 1862
Mount Jackson

Deer wife I take the oppertunity of wrighting to you a gene to let you know that I am well and hope this may finde you all well there is a greateal of con fusion her over sence we have bin her we marcht on sunday from a buve Mount Jackson one mile be low on sunday thare was a fife, fore miles a bove Wincheter

Mch the 27 i commest wrighting yesterday and we was orded to march we marcht 10 mils down the road to the narrow parage on monday we was down ten miles be low her where we met the Jackson on retreat we was orded back her that knight the next day up to Mount Jackson the have bin fifing with th_____ for three weeks wright to me son and let me know all the neuse some thinks the wil fite her and some think we wil fall back to Staunton we hear meny reports and dont know what to beleav the report our loss at Winchester five hunda th loss on the other side 15 hun

When you wright me lit me know hoo got in the naberhood i have bin well ever sense left home i have to go and drill now nothing at this time yore affectionate

husband
R H Depriest

Direct yore letter
major paque buttalion
in care of cap tullermans

April the 4: 1862

Deer wife I take the oppertunity of wrighting to you to let you know that i am well and hope this may finde you and the children well i received yore leter yesterday by bily guilbert and was glad to hear that you was well you seed you had got one letter i had sent too one by lankford we are 2 miles be low Newman 45 miles from home we have teen 25 miles be low her we march narle evryday. We dont know what will be done with us yet tho i think thare will be a draft in a few days the pickets has teen fiteing ever sence we have bin her i think we will fall back to Staunton you seed you wanted to know about flower. I think you had better by abarl or too if you can get them handy try to get somebody to bring them to you.

Morgan got her yesterday we get orders evry day to get redy to march and some times in the nite tel bily gave me a drum and shoud me her like ness soon as he got here. Wright to me soon tell me all the nues the letter i got wase great sadisfacsion i hav my helth and a good appitite. We have 8 in our mes and draw for ten and we eat it all i can hear the cannon evry day the are about ten miles from us now i dont think thare will be aregler battle befor we get to Staunton we can draw cloaths the same as the colinteers some has droud i bout rob whit backs overcoat for 8 dollars. Try to get the ground plowd if you can and the corn planted if i dont get home in time give my respect to and all my frends

yore husband
Robert H. Depriest

May the 18 (1862)

Deer wife i take this oppertunity of wrighting to you to let you know that i am well and hope this may finde you and the childern well i got up with the regtment that day i started from home the batle was young on when i got thare but the second was not gon the got orders about dark to go to the battle. I did not go when they got that th fite wase ove and the yanks gon we went with in 12 miles of where the stops and forma line of battle and wated for un til we got in half mile of them and the left and went on to frankline we went on and was form in lin of battle but cold not get to them they had thare canon fores so they cold throw shels evry corse the fel all round us none fel nurder than 80 yards of me but that is neurder than i want them we went out agane the next day but cold not get to them and we turnd back. the report is that we are going don to harisonburg they did not doo eny thing with me for going home the put glass and leash under guard for too weeks they braught about one hundard from Staunton yesterday and poot them in thare will cleavin had my bankkets so i got them I have not saw John nor Jo nor peet tho I heur from them near by evryday. Tha are well i beleve they ar be fore us we have ent teen getting much to eat i am as harty as every i wore in my life i can eat eny thing that i can get holt of that is to eat i think if you had better get anethe barl of flower for i think it will get her be shore to wrigh to me son and let me know wither you have hourd from bily guilbert.

I have nothing more of importance to wright when you wright to me let me know evry thing that is going on.

Noting mor

yore husbun
R.H. Depriest

man the 18 Dagus tidings

Der ... take this oppier
tunity of ... you
to let you ... this ...
well and ... this ... wroten
you and the children ware
I got up with the regtment
that day got ... from home
the ... in ... on ...
got thare but ... was no
you one got orders ... that
to go to the batle ... not
g when than got ... I tell
... and that you is ...
we went with in ... miles of fronk
whare the stopt and form line
of batle and wated for until
we got in half mile of th...

billy guilbert

I have nothing nomay,
im portence to wright
when you wright to me
let me know every thing
that is going on
nothing mor
you dis banting no

Winchester May the 26: 1862

Dear wife i tak my seat to wright to you to you that i am well and hope this may finde you well. We have had a hard time of it tho i think we will have some rest now. We hav teen fifing for three days but the second redgement did not get in to it til sunday morning about sun up about 10 clock we charged on them and the run we run them 6 miles and left the cafelry after them we was sent back to winchester forguard we have got about 3000 three thousand prisners her and at frountrayl th was 2 men kild in our compny and 4 worded. I dont think we had more than one hundard kild in the three days tho thare is ageat meny wonded i have jus bin berring won that was kild by my side we was so close that i filt shel burn me when it struk him it was don th mines we got in th field it kild too and wonded too. I have just herd the was runing yet i expect to send my coat and blanket home by jentry he will send them to haraser be shore to wright soon direct yore let to as you did to the second regt compny's let me know all the nues

R H Depriest

July the 3: 1862

Dear wife i take this oppertunity of wrighting to you to let you know how i am i am not verry well i am a bout like i wase when i wase at home. We are a bout 30 miles be low richmond they have teen fifing for a week we have drove the yanks a bout 25 miles i think the have as fur as we can get them the has teen a bout five or six thousand kild on each side i think the reson i did not wright sooner i have not had time we have teen marching or fiteing evry day tho i have not done much of the fifing my self i am sick or of this wore now then ever i was be fore we are don her in th swomp and pines no budy lives in this naberhood evry house is a hospittle i never got to se a docter while i was in Staunton. I dont think it is wort while to try to get a discarg her i ha no budy when i will get home agune i have not saw morgan nor peet for a few days they was both well when i seen them i have no mure of importance to write you can hear more a bout the battle then i can wright soon and let me hear from you

nothing   R.H. Depriest

July the 6 i had rote this and nocana to send it i received yore leter this morning i was glad to hear from you and hear you was well. I am not verry well i went to the docter last sunday he gave me sum pill and told me to kep up if i cold the ridgement started munday and i Sunday never teen with it send i stay back with the wagon our docter ters name is straff but i dont think it wold doo eny good to wright to him he thinks he knss much as enny buddy i wold like to be detailed for enything a tall i think if daddy had seen the docter while i was thare he wold got me of i dont think th is much chance of geting of her morgan is well i seen peet thursday he was well doo the best you can wright to me son as you get this yore husband

Robert H Depriest

July the 23: 1862
Cap 5 miles from gordins vill.

Wife i take this opper of writing for the forth time to let you know that i am still a live an talorbel well i hope this may finde you in good health i heard the nues hud thare that i was deaf i wont you to wright to me and let me know how that nues come thare was one kild in the company th colnel was kild and the major wonded an died in a few days the 1st letter i received from you was dated July the 2 i sent one by Davis Bell and too by mail i did not pay the postage let me know wether you got them or not. I have no nues of _____ to wright we are in _____ not much to doo thar geting of over 35 and som wagners i askt the cap to let me go and be detailed for wagner but he wold not concent to it. John Harman is not her if he wore i wold go to him he has the powr to detail hoo he peses i think he is at home if he is tel daddy to see him and i think he will have me detailed. Wright to me soon i have bin looking for to for too weeks let me know what John is doing nothing more

Robert H. Depriest

August the 5: 1862

Dear wife i received yore letter to day of the 3 and was glad to hear from you and to hear that you was well but sor to hear the baby was sick i received yore letter of the 27 of July on the 3 of August and ancerd it on the same day this is the 6 i have sent to you and have received fore we are stil in camp 5 miles from gordinvill. I have no nues of importance to wright i am well and hope this may finde you and the children well we hear all kind of nues her some days they think thre will be peas son and the next seem like the never will be thare is about 60 thousand her some of the cmpnses has bin paid we have not tho i suspect we will be paid soon it wont be much morgan got 7 dollars if you have good luck with the calf sel it for as much as you can get sheep sels her for 15 dolar her bacon cts 75 a pound milk for 25 cts a quart corn meal for 2 dolar a bushel tobacco 75 cts such as you sent me if you have the send me som more tobaco and dont let eny budy have eny of it wright soon and let know wether add is cold out a game i wold like mity well to come home but thare will be nocance now tell the ror is over if i keep my helth they are geting stricter evry day i askt the caton to let me go and try to get a wagon to drive when the concrips was getting of but he wold not a gettact i think i cold have got one then the wagon master tuck my name for to drive a amelance but i dont think i will get it i have not seen morgan for a few days i am on guard at them generuls tent i have to stand 2 hours at a time and off 8 salt sent hard duty one set has to stay 7 or 8 days at a time when you wright let me know wether you have to pay the postag on the letter i send if you doo send me some stamps nothing mor at present

yore kinde husband
R H Depriest

Febuary the 7: 1863

Dear wife i take this opertunity of writing to let you know that i got to camp last eavning when i got to orange i heard the yankes was crosing the river and expected a fight this brigade was down thare on they did fight some yesterday i have heard too cannons this morning the capton and three of the ions that was left her went down this morning i think thare will be a fight but if thare is i will not be in it the capton told me to stay in camp to colk roshens and go on guard if enny was cold for the brigade wil not come back til wendsday if thar is no fight the trops hur all gon down it is twelve miles from her i am very lonsom her in my shanty by my self thare is a few barfooted men in camp i feel so bad and lonsom i can hardly wright John Huffman stade with me last night be shore to wright as soon as you get this for the time will seme long to me i will sonto hear from you i hope it will not be so long be fore we se each other agane this leavs me will and hope it may reach and finde you all well i have nothing more of at this time yore affectionate husband un til death from

R H Depriest to Mary I Depriest

Wily you must be a good by and Annah must be a good girl and doo evrything that ma tiels you.

May the 8: 1863

Dear wife i take this oppertunity of wright to you to let you know that i am well and hope this may finde you all well we have bin marching and fightting for 8 days we got in to camp last night. I feel verry tired i have bin in some very hard places but was lucy a nuf not to be hurt i seen John yesterday he was not in the fight he was on guard. I have not heard from Jo they was ten wonded in my compny will cleavland and tom myres was worded. The Yankeys is gon back to the side of the river i have bin looking for a letter for too weekes be shore to wright soon i sespect to draw my mony soon i was to draw my detail mony the day we started as soon as i get it i will send some home i have no more nues of importance to wright

from R H Depriest
to Mary I Depriest

May the 16: 1863
Camp Paxton

Dear wife i received yore letter this morning and was glad to hear from you and to hear that you was well this leaves me well i started a letter to you the 8 and received one that eavning dated the 23 of Aprile. I was in the battle the third but i come out safe thare was ten wonded let me know wither they have got home i drew twenty too dolors pay i will send 20 to you by mrs yunt i have not got my detail mony yet i expect to get it it is therteen 75. John was not in th fight he was on guard i was with him all day last sunday we are in camp now nothing to do but i am afraid it will not last long. Bob Whitlock was shot in the heal of his boot the ball lodged in his boot but did not hurt him much he went to the hospttal a few days be shore to wright as soon as you get this if you have sate the day before and let me know how you are getting a long. Tel daddy i wold like to get a letter from him papr is carce her so i cant to meny but i wold like for them to wright to me. Tel Willy and Anah they must be good i hope the wore will be over som day and i can get home nothing more yore affectionate husband

R H Depriest

May the 26: 1863
Camp Paxton Near Hamil

Dear Wife i tak this oppertunty of wrightting to you a gene with _____ the too last ones i received yore letter you sent by croft and ancerd it i sent the letter by yunt and twenty dolors in mony i have no nues of importance to wright i think you have for got yore promis you said you wold wright to me once a week wether you got one or not but in stid of that it is too and three weeks i can tel by the letter i get all that you wright i se John evry few days and peet and Jo they are all well and i am well i hope this will finde you all well let me know wither you have got the corn planted and wether they can be eny hay made or not and evry thing elce you can think of be shore to wright as son as you get this when you direct yore letter in the place of saing Jackson command poot Stonewall Brigade i have drew 13 and 75 cts detail wages if i have the chance i will send ten home when you wright let me know wether Tom Myrs and Will Cleavland has got home or not one of the lutements and and ordly sargent has dide from thare wonds since the battle. Robert Whitlock is well and sends his respect to all it is very dry her and has bin very hot but is a clowdy and cool to day and yesterday that is a graft meny Dosserting this army and going to the yankes besides them that gose home i and tierd staying her but dont wont to doo Bather i am afraid peace will not be maid soon but we will have to put up with it you doo the best you can meby all well be wright some day finde out wether morgan got a letter from me and Rob Whitlock we rote one to him and Rob has rote to him since but gets no ancer i put one dolor in the letter i sent to Morgan for him to send me some stamps i have plenty of stamps now nothing more at this time

yore husband
R H Depriest

Dear sone i will wright a few liens to you i wont you to be a good boy and keep the hogos and cattle out of the fields and tel annah she must keep the chickens out of the garden and not go close to the well.

May the 30: 1863
Camp Paxton   Spotcilvany co va

Dear wife i received yore letter yesterday eavning and was glad to hear from you and to hear that you was all well this leavs me well you said you had started a letter to me the wek before i did not get it the last one i got was the one croft brought before this. I wold like for you to wright oftener and a little more at a time you said you had soald the cow and baught a nether i wold like to know hoo you sold too and hoo you baught of you said you got too hundrd and twenty dolars and bought for on hundred i thought meby you made mistake wright soon and let me know a little more a bout it let me know wether you have got eny corn planted and wether thare can be eny hay made thar to feed the cow next winter. We have a talorbel eagy time at this time we are in a nise cams we have to drill twise a day i expect to go to se John an peet to mor i like to go to se peet to get somthing good to eat. We get plenty of flower and bacon and shugur the bacon sent fit for a day to eat i can bake as good lite bread as you can i baked six dozen seet cakes to day just as good as eny body can bake i have no nues of importance yore affectionate husband

R H Depriest

June the 15: 1863
fore miles be low Winchester

Dear wife i take this oppertunity of ancering yore letter of the 3 i received yore letter the tenth and i have teen on march and in lin of battle evercence tel now we got to Winchester saderday morning we was scrumishing with the yakes al day sudderday and in line of batle sunday til one oclock in the night they was so well fixt i thought we wold not get the out but we got where we cold shel thare fort sunday eavning and sheld for a bout 3 hours they left thare fort in the night to make thar escape but we started at one oclock and got be low them we met them about sun up and chardged on and took narely all of them the 2 ridgement took too yankey ridgements and the bregde general the officers road up to ours and gave up thare swords and horses i sespect we will go on we are wating for the wagons to come up to cook i recon John has got home he left the first night we started i did not get the leter you wrote the 3 of May i got one dated May the 11 and one my the 26 and one June the 3 and if you wright once a week i think it is time i was getting anether i cant allwais wright i haf to wright when i can but you can and must be shore to wright evry week tel liss i was glad to get a few liens from her and to hear that she was well and cooing well if she is staing at hammers i think they might all to gether wright wright to me if they do i will ancer thare leters with grate peskier wen you wright let me kow hoo you sold the cow too and hoo you bought of and wether dady is able to work or not i seen peet the ether day he is well and Jo is with me now he is well and sends his best respects to you i think you had better keep the calf if you think you can get plenty of feed hay will cost you a goodeal but doo what you think best this leavs me well and hope well finde you well and the childern tell Willy i rote to him and never receivd ancer i wont him to be good boy and wright a few lines in the next letter and mammy a few i have nothing more to wright be shore to wright evry week

from yore husband
R H Depriest to Mary I Depriest

June the 21: 1863
Washington Co Md.

Dear wife i take this of wrightting to you to let yu know that i am wel and hope this may finde you all well the last letter i got was wrote the third of June i got it the 10 and ancerd it the 13th when i was neer Winchester we have bin in marland three days the peple seem very cever and not meny yanks a bout the caveldry brings a few evry one and a wile they get them a bout frulrick sitty we are at Sharpsburg i dont know what they in tend to do but i think we will go to Harpersfery i dont know how it is that i cant get no more leters the ballance of the compny gets letters evry male and i get one a bout once a month i in tent to ancer the letters i get and no more so if you wont to hear from me ofton you will wright tel lis to wright i wold like to hear from you all i seen Jo and peet a few days ago they was both welt Bob Whitlock is well and sends his respects to all i must close i was on picket last night on the out side post i feel sorter drowsy nothing more til i hear from you

R H Depriest

July the 11: 1863
Washington Co: Md.

Dear wife i received too leters to day and was glad to hear from you one was dated the 23 of June and one the 27 the last one i got be fore was dated the 3 of June i have wrote too sence i have had hard times sence we have bin fifty of sixty miles in Pecisivany and had a hard fight for three days. Bob Whitlock was takin prisner Bob Ramyay was kild at Gettersburg the 3 of July. I was not in the main batle our compny was on picket and srumishing all the works it was bad a nuf i havens time to wright much i exspect to move evry mines i think we are going a cros the river wright as soon as you get this i wold lik to se you but i dont think it is worth while for you to try to come down becas thare is no teling when we will stop marching th Yankes is going round evry was they can i am sorrow to hear the you are not well and have to carry yore wood you to try to get some body to holl wod as soon as you can and as much as you

Robert H Depriest

July the 18: 1863
Camp neer Darkevill   Berkly Co Va.

Dear wife I received yore letter this morning of the 5 and was glad to hear from you i received too when i was in Marland neer Hagerstown i ancerd them the same day i said in that we was expectton to march i dident have time to wright as much as i wontted til we had to go we went a mile and laid in line of battle three days and nites the yanks woldent come up our ridgement was out scrumishing with them the last day til a 11 oclock in the night we left to cross the river we marcht all night and got to the river at day light and had to ward it up to my armes and too hundred yards wide we had the hardest time that we have ever had coming out of pencilvany marcht day and night and not half a nuf to eat some times nothing for too days you say you cold live on brad and if i was at home i wold be wel of to what i am if i cold get a nuf of that her one third of the men is barefeeted and thare close tore all to peces i havens had cleen shirt for a month

nor drawers for too months my pants is wore out i have mended them as often as i can if the dont gave me some close soo i am coming home the drm is beting now for inspection but i havens clend my gun and dont intend to go you said somthing a bout coming down i dont think it wold be worth while i dont think we will stay in camp long and if we do thare is no plase for you to stay i dident by

enny thing while i was over the river the mony wold not pas thare and cant pas it her for
nthing but tobacco at too dollars a plug you had teeter spend all yore money for somthing
to eat and feed with if you have plenty you are well of with i hope you have and allwais
will have i know what it is to be hungerry if i ever get home i wonto eat let me know
wether you have lout hay or had eny maid let me know what redgement grayham is in
and how he went in and where he lives and how they get a long i havens seen Jo nor
peet sence i left Winchister Joes compny wasent in the fight they was garding prisners.
Bob Whitlock was taken prisner. Bob Ramyy was kild wright as soon as get this and let
me know wthe you got the ether you had teeter by hay soon and wait til winter let me
know how dady is getting along and wether they have got penty tel Wily he must be
earful when he gos upstars to smel my jacket and not fall don tel Annah i am glad to
hear that she is a good girl let me now whether marryely can talk i wold like to be home
to se you and the childern and i am in hopes i can be before long i think the war will haf
to be ended some way i have no more nues to wright gave my respects to all my finds
nothing more

       I remain yore affectionate husband until death
       Robert H Depriest to Mary I Depriest

July the 22: 1863

Dear wife i received yore letter to day and was glad to hear from you and hear that you was well but sorow to hear yore mah is so porly i have bin in good health for some time i am harty as i ever was in my life and get plenty to eat now i am worse of for cloths now than i ever have bin sence i have bin in the army but i expect to draw some soon th wagons has bin a way from us ever sence we went in to pencilvania they will come to us to night we are three miles be low Winchester we come her to day i think we are going back fords Frederinburg i received yore letter of the 5 and ancered it the 18 let me know wether Betsy went with John i seen peet a few days ago he is well let me know ware Graham lives and how he wint in the army and what redgement he belongs to i have no nues of importance to wright you be shore to wright as soon as you get this nothing more at this time

yore Husband
Robert H Depriest

Orange Co Va.   August the 7: 1863

Dear wife i this oppertunity of ancering yore letter witch i received to day i was glad to hear from you and to hear that you was well but very sorrow to hear o the Death of yor mother and to hear that daddy was not well yet this leavs me well i have not dun eny duty for too weeks i have had a bile on my ne it is about well now i was sick yesterday i took a blew mar pil i am well to day i get plenty to eat now and have got a new sute of close i received Grahams letter on the 4 and ancered it and rote one to you the same day when we started from Fredericsburg we had 55 men in our compny now we have 18 they was nun kild nor wonded some stade in Pencilviny and the balance at home we foned camp yesterday about a mile and are fixing like they expected to stay her some time i am in hopes they are doing sumthing fords making pece i it will have to be made soon and i dont care what way so they make it they wont be eny more prisners exchanged i think that will help to stop the war if they dont make _____ thay will be all _____ we havent drwd myny for three moths i early out i have to pay too dollars a plug for tobacco and 25 cts a sheat for paper and 25 for envellope and evrything els in perpasion wright soon and let me know all the nues nothing more

                              yore husband
                              Robert H Depriest

August the 15: 1863
Orange Co Va.

    Dear wife i received yore letter this eavning and was glad to hear from you but sorow to hear that you dont get my letters i wrote to the 4 and 7 i get yore the letter you wrote the 2 and ancerd it the 7 and was wating for an ancer the one i got to day was rote the 9 and maild the 13 i have got plity of cloths now i droad 22 $ this week i wold send ten home if i had a cance i dont know wen i will get home but i hope i will get home some day i dont know what you will do if you cant by hay i expect pork will be so hy that you cant eny you had teeter try to ceep the cow if you can and if you cant sel her any by pork with mony i think you cold do better with out meat than you can with out the cow if you can keep her you have to do the best you can the officers is strictter with us now than they ever was since so meny run of half of our compny has gon the cornal is going to the valy hunt then i expect he will be in Agusta we have bin in camp for teeter than too weeks i dont know how long we will stay her i dont think we will stay much longger i have no nues of importance to wright to you this leavs me well and hope will finde you and the childern well be shore to wright son as you get this nothing more but kinde Husband until death

                Robert H Depriest to Mary I Depriest

August the 18: 1863

Dear wife i received yore letter to day and was glad to that you was all well you diad not send me eny paper or envelopes i can get them now narle as cheap as you can now the sutlers has come in to camp when the was to hy the suttlers had not come to camp i haf crowd twenty too dolors and if we stay in camp til the first September i will crow a gene and will send some home if i can get acance i cant tel when i will get home but sil live hops of getting home some day i wold like to get thare onoruble and free so i cold se some plesher thare i wold like to hear from John and know how he is getting a long and where he is they was an order red this eavning on ares perraid to gave furlows to out of evre hundred for fiften days but i dont expect to get one soon if ever the officers will get them i am in hops they will make peace soon it some times sems like the will be peace soon and some times like they never wold we get tolabel plenty to eat and can by rocinyear for one dollar a dosen i some times get clare out of hart and some times in tolabel good perets you must wright often as you can and let me know the dates of the letters you get and ancer i ancerd gahams letter the forth nothing more at this time

Robert H Depriest

August the 21: 1863
Orange Co Va.

Dear wife i take this oppertunity of ancering yore letter witch i received on yesterday eavning yore letter found me well and was glad to hear that you was all well you spoke of coming down i wold like very well to se you but i wold much rather se you at home i think it wold be pore saisfaction to come her it wold be hard to get a house for you to stay at thare is peple bording at evry house and i cant get a pase to go out of camp with getting a pase from the capt and cornal and general the report is that we are going to the valy to swift run gap if we oto i will come home if i can we will crow pay the first of September 22 $ and the first of November we will crow clothing mony i think i will crow a hundred dollors clothing mony we are a loud one hunderd and thirty for clothing i dont think i have crowd more than thirty if i dont get home before November i will try to come then let me know wether you have herd what was in Johns letter i wold like to know what he has to say tel yore paw i wold like for him to come down he can stay in camp and if we are moving he can move too if he wold come down i cold tel him more than i can wright i have nothing more to wright of importance excuse my mistakes my head is a little out of fix this morning i have bin thinking a bout comeing home

Robert H Depriest

August the 29: 1863
Camp near Orange Cort House

Dear wife i take this oppertunity of ancering yore letter witch i received yesterday eavning i was glad to hear you i no nues of importance to wright we are stil

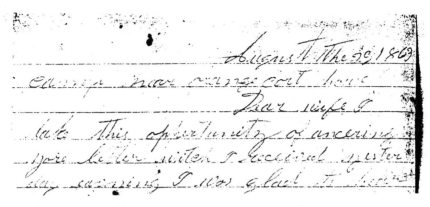

in the same camp i am in good health and get plenty to eat now i dont know how long it will it willwill be so nor how long we will stay her we hear all kins of reports sometimes like the wold be peace soon and some times like we wold be fifing soon i still live in hops of being peace some day i wil have to stay her and wate for time to decide it i am verry tired of this way living but it must be so thare is some runing of narly evry night

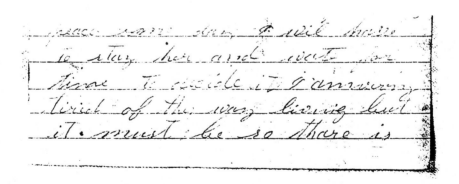

they have more guard round the camp than ever was to keep them in and stricter orders too left thare post night before last and run of and too get out of the guard house a few nites a go and got a way John Dugles was one of them tut wiles from Springhil the ether i expect they wold bin shot if thay hadent got away the orders is to chane the deyerters

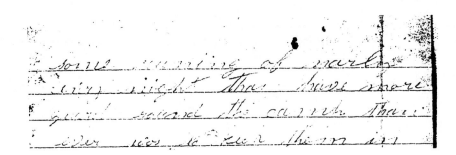

in th gard house evry night tel hannah that i havens seen peet sence we left the valy he was well then they are a bout ten miles from us let me know how traner stays at tom so long nothing more

R H Depriest to Mary I Depriest

Sept the 17: 1863

Dear wife i take this opertunity of ancering yore leter of the 11 i was glad to hear from you but sorow to hear of so much sickness they has bin some excitement her this week the yankes advanst Sunday and Monday we was marcht out Monday and have teen laing a round Orange cort house ever sence the cavelry was fifing some Sunday and Monday evry thing has bin quiet sence i think we wil go back to camp to day the yankeys captued a bout fifteen hundred of our cavelry i got yore letter on the 14 i was wating to se what wold be dun before i wold ancer it i have no more nues of imoortance to wright let me know wether wily is going to scool yet and how he likes to go i am very uneasy for fear the childern wil get the dipthery you must wotch them to docter in time if the get it this leavs me well and hope will finde you all well nothing more but remain yore husband

R H Depriest
to Mary I Depriest

Sept the 25: 1863   Orang Co Va

Dear wife i take this opertunity of wrightting to you to let you know that i am well and hope this may finde you all well yore pa was down her but he went back so soon that i coldent think of eny thing i wanted to tel him he come at night and went a way next morning at nine oclock it tuck me all the time to ask him about things thare we have moved bout half mile from where we was we can se thare pigets i dont think thare wil be a fight soon some of our men is stil going over nearly very night glass come down he said he seen John at the hospital wright to me soon and let me know wether it is so and how he gut thare and where he has bin he sais Sam Rees come down with him and add and Morgan is comin they brought in sevin deserters last night i expect one of them wil be shot tel Willy i heard a good report on him i heard that the scoll teacher said he was the smartest boy that come to scool and lernt fast i wont to know how much he has lernt i wil send you some mony when we draw clothing mony that wil be due next month i dont know wether we will get it or not you must do the best you can and hope for a better day to come nothing at this time

yore husband
R H Depriest

October the 1: 1863

Dear wife i take this oopertunity of ancering yore letter of the 25 witch came to

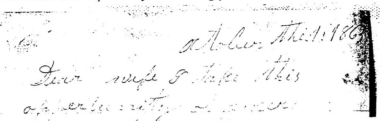

hand the 30 i was glad to hear from vou and hear that you was all well it found me well we are in camp close bv the yank and have orders to keep too days rashions on had to be redy to fove at eny time glass told me t,hat he seen dohn at the hospittal i have heard sence that he is at the redgment in the guardhouse let me know wether you know eny thing about him i cant til when i wil get home they have quit givin3 furloes it will be a good while before i get one they onely gave one in this comDny sank soeck and three ethers went to the yankes night before last some is going neariv evry night we have bin exoecting to crow mony for a month i heard to day that we wold not crow it for 60 days i recon i can send som hom when i get it i have no nues of eny importance this leavs me

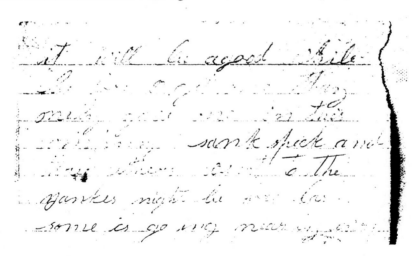

well and hope it will finde you all well when you se Jery Graham ask him why he dident ancer my letter nothing more but remain yore affectionate husband

Robert H Depriest

October the 19 1863
Culpeper Co Va

Dear wife i take this oppertunity of wrightting to you i received yore letter to day by mr kilderbran i was glad to that you was al well i have received too letters sense i have bin on this march but had not an oppertunity of ancering them we started on this march the 8 and have bin marching ever sence they has bin some fifing but our brigad was not in it i seen Jo and Robert to day they are well i seen Sam Rees and Curt Coffmen a few days ago the are well. Sam expects to get a furlow when he gets of ov this march to go home to get a hors he has bin in too or three little fifes i havens seen peet sence we left the valy i was glad to hear from John let me know where he is and how he is goin and where she is to meets him i wold be very glad to be wihhim i dont expect to get a furlow much be fore crismus i am agoing to keep triing til i get one then i can tel you all about it i dont think th wil be much fiting her do the best you can

R H D

November the 18: 1863

Dear wife i take this opertunity to ancer yore letter witch i received this morning i was glad to hear from you and to hear that you was well yore letter found me well i am on guard to day the regment is birding brest works neer where we was when yore pa was down her i havens seen peet yet nor Jo and Robert sence i wrote before we have teen marching up and down the line evry day or too the yankes has bin making severer attemps to cross the Rapidan tho hav teen drove back i dont think they will give it up til they have fight it is reported that they have one hunderd thousen men i think we have a bout thirty five thousand i think from the way evrything is going on now the war will have to come to a close soon try to doo the best you can til spring i think they will be a chang by that tim if thare is not i will try to make a cange ov sum kind when you wright let me know how much mony you have i sent twenty dollars by Bily Fisher let me know wether you got it thare is one man to get a furlow before i get one his has bin sent in but some times they are a month before they get them after they sent in i recon mine wil come some time this winter keep the cow if you can and if you cant doo the best you can withhe Virginia trisher nots is no better the confederates noth more

R H Depriest

December the 3 1863   Orange Co Va

Dear wife i take this oppertunity of ancering yore too letters witch i received this morning i was glad to hear from you and to hear that you was all well we have jest

got back to camp we was cold out last Thursday the yankes was advancing we met them fryday about twelve oclock and fought til dark and each party held thare side of the field til about twelve in the night when both moved to the right and we bilt brist works and lade thare fore fays and they moved to the left and we moved with them last night they went back over the river and we come to camp we had twenty six men in our compoy and thre was kild and eight wonded i had a ball shot in my napsack i was laing don shuting thru the crack of the fins with it on my back it went threw my crowers and it made twelve holes in them and lodged i think the fifing is over for a while her i will try to get a furlow as son as i can i dont think it wil be before Chrismas i havens heard from Jo nor Robert nor Grayham sence he come down i sent ads discriptive list to him let me

know wether he gets it or not i dont think he wil wright i rote to him and he put the same letter in anether envelope and sent it back to me tel him if he dont wonto wright to me he need not send me the old letters that i wright my sef they are pore sadisfation to me i can read them before send them and i think you might think of a nuff to fill one side of a small sheat if you cant try to get somebody elce to fil it out most eny thing you cold think you cold think of wold be som sadisfaction i dont think it is worth while to send wily to scool eny more this winter it wil be too cold for him to go you or ter fern him att so he wold not for get what he lernt at scool tho i recon you havens much time to spare i wold like to get home mity well to se you all i am stil in hope that i will soon i dont see much more chance for the wor to be over than i did at first i have bin very lucky not get hurt and hope i never wil be. George Dull was kild out of my mes he was from Agusta and semd like a brother to me he lived five miles a bove Staunton i have nothing more of importance this leaves me well and hope will finde you all well nothing but remain yore affectionate husband

R H Depriest

January the 1 1864   Orange Co Va.

      Dear wife i take my ceat to wright to you a gane to let you know that i am well and hope tis may finde you and the childern well i have o nues of importance to wright i have bin looking for a leter for a week i started a leter to you too weeks a go and havens got an ancer yet we have moved camp sence i rote before and we bild nether shanty we have just it don i am afraid i will not get a furlow this winter if you cold send me a box i wold be verry glad if you get the chance to send it send too or three cabish and a few potatoes some lite bread and buter and pies some unions dont put yore self to too much torobel to send it if you send it thare is a car comes down evry fryday with boxes and oficer in carge of them you orter send it to town on thursday thare is somebody thare to take care of it wright to me soon and if you send the box let me know when it wil come so i can go to the cort house to get it have it directed lik you wold a leter i exspet to crow mony next wek i wil get one hunderd and twenty eight dollars i wil send some home the first chance nothing more

      R H Depriest to Mary

January the 5 1864   Orange Co Va.

Dear wife i received yore letter last night i was sorow to hear that you was not well and that dady and ad was so porly you said that you hadent got a leter from me for three weecks i rote too weecks a go and on the first of January i said in my last leter that i did not expect to get a furlow as thare is too to get before me but i have heard sence thare is more to get furlows in a compny than thare has bin and i think now i wil get one towords spring it snode her yesterday too inches deep it is the first we have had it is very purty day i think it wil be gon by night i heard the snow was a foot deep thare last week i rote to you to try to send me a box if you do be shore to wright to long anuf for me to get the letter before the box comes so i can go to get it send fore or five cabish send as much butter as you can the ether boys in myer is getting bockser and i eat with them and i wold like to get one too if it wont be too much troble to you. If you send one send it to town on Thursday and put it in care of luetinent rows and it wil come safe i know that you have a hard time and a heap of troble but you must put up with it the best you can i hope this troblesome time will _____ some day i am a going to try my best to get a furlow betwn this and spring i wold lik to se you all mity well but i dont wont to se you down her for it wold be pore plesher for you to come her you wold work you never had a come let me know wether you have got we will draw mony in a few day i will send a hunderd dollors home the first chance wright soon and let me know how you are getting along take good care of our lisle childern i hope i will be at home with you all som day good by

R H Depriest to Mary I Depriest

January the 18: 1864   Orange Co Va.

Dear wife i take my ceat to wright to you to let you know that i got the box and was very well pleast with it it was a goodeal better than i exspected and more in it i was in orang when it come i was on piqet when i got the first letter you said you exspected to come down and i got a pass to go to meet you and stay three days we was twelve miles below camp the lutenent let me go to camp when i got to camp and had my pass i got the next letter that you was not coming i felt verry much disapointted i met yore pa thare he went with me and stead all night i went with him down to se Robert and Jo we found them both in the guard house yore pa staid with them last night i exept him her to day i think i will get a furlow in a bout three weecks then i can tel you more than i can wright i am well and harty and have plenty to eat this is the fifth box that has come to my mess in the last fore weeks i dont think we will get out this winter with what we crow we live bitter than eny ether mess in the compny this is a rany day i wil send fifty dolars by yore pa i will bring the ballance when i come i wold like for you to make a hut for me i have no hut and cant by one wright as soon as you git this so i can no how dady is thare is someny in my shanty they bother me so i dont knw what i wonto wright i wil wright a gane soon tel mammy i wold like for her to hook a pare of gloves aganst i come home

R H Depriest

February the 16: 1864   Orang Co. Va.

Dear wife i received yor letter yesterday and was glad to hear from you and to har that you was all well but very to hear that daddy was no better i got her on sadure eavning the compny was on piqet til Wendsday Jah kindly got her Wendsday i was very lonsom her by my self and dont feel much better yet i hate to stay wors than i did be fore i was at home we will go on piqet the 24 we have piety to eat we crow corn meal all the time and have John Kindig got a barl of aplees with a goodeal of peruision in it tom myers come down a sadureday he dont exspect to stay he is lame but none of them is not much compny for me i dont feel sad is fede her and dont think i ever cold i seen John Curry he told me that Jo had bin sent to Richmond to work three month with a ball and chane to his foot and Robert had to work 50 days at the ridgment under guard and stay in the guard house ova night the was a man shot last Thursday i seen him shot John Curry told me that 28 men left the 50 2nd last fryday night and i heard thare was a good meny more left the brigade the same night i wonto se my brothers very bad but i dont recon they wil come to se me be shore to wright soon nothing more but remain yore affectionate husband

R H Depriest

March the 4 1864   Orange Co Va

Dear wife i received yore letter last night and was glad to hear from you but sorow to hear that you have got that old complaint you ort to take better care of yore self when you are well i thang that wold be the way going to bead bare footed an getting up be fore you poot yore cloths on next time mind what i tel you i have no nues to wright i commenst a letter the ether day and did not have time to finish it the was a man going to Staunton and i sent it we are on pitit yet the yankyes has bin making rack in different pises. We hear so meny diferrent reports from them i dont know what to bereave i recon you hear as much from them as i do thare has bin seven men gon a cros the river sence we have bin down her James Wever was one of them Edward Hal has bin exchanged he was with Bob Whitlock all the time he sais he is very ancious to be exchanged but i think he is very sorrow that was we get fore days rashers of of corn bred at a time it is baked at camp and sent down and as much meat as i can eat at one time th balins or the time we eat corn bread and water this leave me well and hope it may find you all well nothing yore affectionate husband

R H Depriest

Orange Co. Va.   Aprile the 10: 1864

Dear wife i received yore letter of the 6 on yesterday i was glad to hear that you was all well i havent much nues to write i wold like to hear from mammy what she is going to do i think that she had teeter keep house if she can but i wont her to do as she thinks she wold be the best sadisfied if she stays at our hous ovanight she ort to move all of the things over thar that eny body cold steal thar is so much stealing that some body mite brake in of anight if i cold get home i wold try to trade thefor flour and whot over she wold need to eat i dont think that she can keep it let her move in with you if she workes as one of the famly if syntha can get eny pise to stay tel mammy not to go to sarahs nor eny plase els from thare for fear she rues it after when it is too late Mr. Arcjin Brigtt is looking evryday for a letter from his girl if it comes rite i will try very hard to come with him tel yore pa to try to git corn planted if posible for it will be hard to by next year tel wily and mary ella that i will make rings for them if i can get enV thing to make them ov i am afraid thare will not be much chance for me to get a furlow with out it is to go with arginbright i have nothing to write this leavs me well and hope when this comes to hand it may find you all well write soon and let me kow mamy is a going to do i feel veary bad and lonsum i wold gave all that i have if cold get home to stay nothing more yore husband affectionately

R H Depriest

Orange Co. Va. Camp Stonewall
Aprile the 17: 1864

Dear wife i received yore letter of the tenth yesterday eavning and was glad to hear from you and to hear that you was ad and that was a getting along as well as you are let me know what kind of a bargin you and yore pa has and wether you have to pay bils for plowing and choping wood you wonted to know wethe i got yore letters of the 27 and 31. I did and ancerd them both to gether when i got the one of the 27 i did not have the chance to ancer it til i got the next when eveer you hear from John or enny of them boys let me know mr. arginbright got a leter from his girl a few days a go she wold hav to se his mother before she cold tel him what she cold do she said that she loved him but she wold like to se him before she wold go too fur as she had never saw him but onst i ancerd his leter and wrote one to her mother asking fore her in the politeest way that i wold and the lovlyest to her i cold i have done trader corting for him than i ever did for my self but i am afraid it will be a failure if she dont give a sadisfacurl ancer the next time i will drop her and write to a nether i am bound to have him mared to somebody you said that mammy had sold the coals at the old prise but you did not say what that wose i think that was the that best that she cold of done he will gave her what it is worth i think i was very to hear that marty whitlock and old Jony Miller was not well i seen peet rees yesterday he is well i went to orange for a boy for Tom Myers and met peet in the road he was driving his wagon and cold not talk much with him Tom got leter from Morgan a few days ago he is well we have bin very csearce of meat for some time Tom got a boild ham and a peace of midling in his box so we will do very well for a while...be shore to ancer the same day you get it so i wil get it be fore i go on pick it we will go Monday week nothing more yore husband

R H Depriest

Let me know how yore pa is fixing the pens i think mamy is rite to keep house she will be beter sadisfide than she wold after break up a whil let me know wetha you got a pig or not if y did not you ort to get one if you can home when can if get thare.

Orange Co Va.   April the 28: 1864

Dear wife i received yesterday of the 21 and was glad to hear from you and to hear that you was all well i saw Jo a few days ago him and Robert is well Jo looks better than he dose for common he sais that he had a good time while he was in Richmond he dident work eny while he was thare i sent my over coat to Mr. Kindigs he will bring it down when he comes to hires it is not the same coat that had at home it is split up the back thare has bin to good meny deserting from hir lately seven started from the 4th the ether night three got away and the ether fore was caught at the river l sopore the wil be shot in a few days. Mr. Arginbright hasent found out yet wether his guirl will hav him or not he is looking for a letter evry day from her he has asked the cereal about the furlow me and him he sade we cold get it as son as the sitificate come i havens eny thing new to wright ondly that saly whitlock is mared she mared a man by the name of hanger you say that Hanah behaved her self while peet was at home that is the way you ort to of don dont blame me for what you done wright soon let me know how much flower you have and wether you hav baughting sens i was at and wether you can get it for goverment price let me know how the cow dose wether you have plenty of milk and buter and what mamy has to eat and she gets wood and wether Wily lerns his book i hope the time wil come when i can be with you all a gane but looks slough to come it seams to be th opinion of evry body that the wor wil end this sumer one way or the ether it dont make much diference to me witch way this leavs me well and hope it my reach you and find you and all well and enjoying yore selves better the i can her nothing for this time from yore kind husband

R H Depriest to Mary I Depriest

Spotcilvany Co. Va.   May the 19:64

Dear wife i take this oppertunity of writing to you once more to let you know that i am well and hope this may find you all well we have bin fifing for fifteen days and i dont think it is half done yet i havens had the chance to write sence we started tho i sopose you hav heard from me i have cent you word by difernt ones a bout 2 thirds of this division has bin takin prisner i havens time to tel you much nues about the fifing I recon you hear as much about it as i can tel you I sen Jo the ether day he was slitly wonde i sopose he is back at his regt by this time i heard of Robert being in the rear i dont think he has bin in much of the fifing we are in the ditches now we have bin run out of them twist by the brigad gaveing way on our right and left the come upin our front yesterday we drove them back nothing more for this time write soon yore husband

R H D

Hanover Co. Va.   May the 24: 1864

Dear wife i take this oppertunity of writing let you know that i am living and in good health i hav had very hard times sence the 4th of this month we have bin fiting prety much all the time we have fel back to Hanover Junction I rote to you a few days ago I havens had the chance to write much we are on picket at this time 4 miles be low Hanover Juntion we have lost 27 hunder out of this division takn prisner beside the kild and wonded thare is about 6 hunderd left i think we will hav a lisle easer time the are fifing all day to day about 4 miles from her near the Jundian. John Kindig was wonded the first days fite Tom Myers got behind the day we fel back from Spotcilvany I think he was taken prisner the last leter i got from you was writen the third of May I wold like for you to writ as son as you get this I cant tel when i will have the chance to write a gene i havens got paper nor eny thing elce write a gene i havens got paper nor eny thing elce to write with i havent dreu eny pay sence i was at _____ wonted to wait til this fite was ove so the be so meny to pan nothing for this time this leavs me well and hope it may reach you and find you all well yore affectionate husband

R H Depriest

June the 5: 1864
Hanover Va Co.

Dear wife i take this oppertunity of writing y for the third time sence i got one from you the last one that i got from you was of the third of May we are nine miles east of Richmond in brest works th scrmishes is fiting in front i sopose that you hear as much about the fits as i can tel you I have bin eight in gage but hav bin luky anuf not to be _____ yet the meny of my has fel and i am afraid meny more wil have to be fore it is over but i think them that _____ this fite over can go home i think the wil end I wont you to be shore to write soon i wold like to hear from home we have bin in line of betel or fifing erve sence the fifth of May very often under hevy under hevy fire when we are not in gageal we charged them th either day and takn thare worke but we hav fel back a gene to our workes thare is not a minis hardly that the fireing is stops sence it first commenst Bather rite or left or in front of us i hope that i may be spard to get throo saf nothing more write soon yor kind husband

R H Depriest to Mary I Depriest

Shanadoar Co. Va.
July the 1: 64

Dear wife i take this oppertunity of writing a few lines to let you know that i am well and where i am we are ner Strasburg 20 miles a bove Winchester we exspect to get thare to morrow we camps at Mount Crafford the day i left home i got to camp at ten oclock that nite it is reported that thare is sixty housen yankes in Martainsburg if we keep on we wil get thare on Monday th ballans of the compny will go home to morrow thare will be no body in the compny but me i have no nues to write you write as soon as you get this and let me know yore pa is and how he gets a long working the corn you neadent to write a short letter becas i did i have nothing more to write at this time yore affectionate husband

R H Depriest to Mary I Depriest

August the 9: 1864   Winchester

Dear wife i take the present opertunity of writing a few lines to let you know that i got her yesterday i was fore days getting down her my compny is at home as i left them the rest of the gedgmint is in Winchester i wil stay her we hav an easy time her the army is at Bunkers Hill they hav bin in merland and fel back on Sunday twelve miles below Winchester i dont think thare wil be eny chance to get a pos to come home for a while some of the ethers her bin trying i was the only one that got home that lived up that way if i hadent bin reported i mite of stade a week or too and it wold a bin all rite when i got back wright as soon as you get this direct yore leters as you did the wil stop her i got the one that you had sent before let me know what done with glass i had a verry lonsom time coming down by my self thare has bin several ranes down her sence i left i can se grate improvement in the corn let me know how the seven is thare when you wright i no nues of importance the are bringing in a few yankes evry once and while it agravats me to be her when i cold of bin at home if evry body wold at tend to thare one bisness nothing more this leave me well and hope it may find you all well yore affectionate husband

Robert H. Depriest to Mary I Depriest

Shanadore Co. Va.   July the 23: 1864

Dear wife i take this opertunity of ancering yore letter witch i received a few days ago the resee that i did not ancer it sooner i had started that day and thant as that had bin so long that i wold get a nether soon we are one mile below Strausburg we havens done eny fifing sence we left Washington thare was a fite on the river and one at Winchester but this division was not in them the yankes folerd us up her we forma lin of batle her yesterday eavning and the hav gon back to Winchester we hav orders to chook too days rashings and move in the morning at day lite i dont know witch way we will go but i think we will go down the valy i havent much nues of importance this leave me well and hope it may find you all well you must _____ and i dont hav the chance to send my leters out it is very dry her the corn is twisted up if it dont rane soon thare be no corn in this part you had better by as much flower as you can if you have enny mony to by with we hav not bin paid yet if they ever pay i wil send it home John Fisher and Tom Brient was kild at Frederick that was all that that you are a quaented with i seen Jery Graham yesterday he is well nothing more at this time yore affectionate husband

R H D

August the 30 1864

Dear husband i seat my self this evening to let you know that we are all well only i have the neuralgia in my head very bad i have no nues of importanc to write i got a letter from you last Thursday and you said that you had not got a letter from me scins you left home and i thought i would write often so you would be sure to get some of them i herd that the men that went to yankedom is coming back and going in the army here i hope that you can come home soon when you write let me know what you think a bout coming wether you think you can come before long or not you must come in October if if you dont be fore i wish that you had a staid when you was here you must excus my short letter i will write a gain you must write as soon as you get this i hope it will reach you and find you well nothing more but remain your affectionate wife

Mary I Depriest

Winchester Fredric Co. Va.
September the 12 1864

Dear wife i tak my ceat this morning to write a few liens to let you know that i am well and hope when these few lines reach you they may find you all in good health. I received a leter frm you a few days ago i thaght it wosent worth while to be in a hury about ancering it as you had got one from me on Wendsday and ancerd it the next Thursday the one i got was dated the 30 of August I hav bin looking for a nether Mr. Fry past through her on Saderday he is coming back to day and going home so i thought i send leter by him I havens much nues to write we hav drew fore months pay I will send twenty dollors to you they say that we wil be paid a gene in a few day if we do i wil send some more I wil send aring for Mary Ella i am afraid it is too small for her but if it is you can save it for some body els. I heard that other grouns hav come back from the yankes and is a going in the army fry told me that Betsy hadent heard of John sens she went out thare let me kno wether ausy has gone out or not if she has not she had better no go I saw Peet Res a few day ago he is well he said that he havens heard from home sence he was at home i think you hannah is both getting of writing you said that you hav the pneuralsy in yore head that was about all that was in the leter I hope that you hav got well by this time next time let me know how the corn and Buck wheat come out or wether it come to enything and wether you have got eny thing to eat or eny wood and wether you got the hoggs home and all of them sort of things I wonto know all that is agoing on and how mamy is a getting along I intend to try to come home about the 20th of Octpber the mager is giving passes to the men for fore or five day if i cant get one for enny longer i will try to get one for five days and take the ballance i am afraid that we wont stay her long some of the officers gets drunk evry day and i expect we wil be moved out on that acount. I saw Jerry Grayham the 9 he is walking he said that he was a going home in a few days but i dont think he will he talks like he can go when he pleses but i dont think he can thare geneal is very strict he stuck up and is for us to take up evry one of his men that come in town and put them in the guard house we put some of them in evry day they get drunk and ride in houses and cut up by one shot a nether day be fore yesterday he was berryed yesterday I cant think of eny thing els to write that wil interrest you you must ancer this the same day that you get it not wate a week Fry says that he is a carring down a fane in a few days if he dose i wold for you to send me a pare of socks the army is five miles be low her not doing much some peple is in gate sperete about peace.

Author's Note: This letter from R. H. Depriest stops abruptly at this point and is unsigned. It is the last letter from Depriest home that is part of this wonderful collection.

PART V

ROGUES OF
RECONSTRUCTION

*"No roar of cannon met us for the sneaks had gone and
taken all their goods with them."*

—*J.B. Setterlee*

INTRODUCTION

At the close of the Civil War the soldiers of both the North and the South returned to their homes (or what was left of them) and began to rebuild their lives, hopes and dreams. As is typical of any war however, many turned to a life of vagrancy, crime and corruption. How much of this attitudinal change resulted from war experiences may never be known but its effects are recorded in the court files they left behind. The authors have acquired the following magnificent collection of Reconstruction Era arrest warrants, commitment papers and court documents which allow the reader to see first hand the crimes they were charged with, the sentences they received, and their fellow conspirators. All of these documents came from our nation's capitol, were filled in by hand, signed by the Justices of the Peace, and have never before been published. They provide a fascinating glimpse into crime in the three years following the war and shed light on the problems facing a nation trying to reconstruct itself from the ravages of a bloody, fratricidal conflict. The clues contained in these court papers only await the thorough analysis of historians to draw the conclusions which may help to foreshadow the problems plaguing American criminal justice today.

U.S. MARSHAL'S OFFICE,
Washington City, D.C., Octo. 5, 1866.

Mr. T.B. Brown

     Warden U.S. Jail, D. C.,

     Release from Jail the following=named Prisoner, to be brought before the Judge
now in session, viz: Geo. Wilder

     by order of Judge Fisher

                  D.S. Gooding
                  U.S. Marshal, D.C.

On verso: 1548

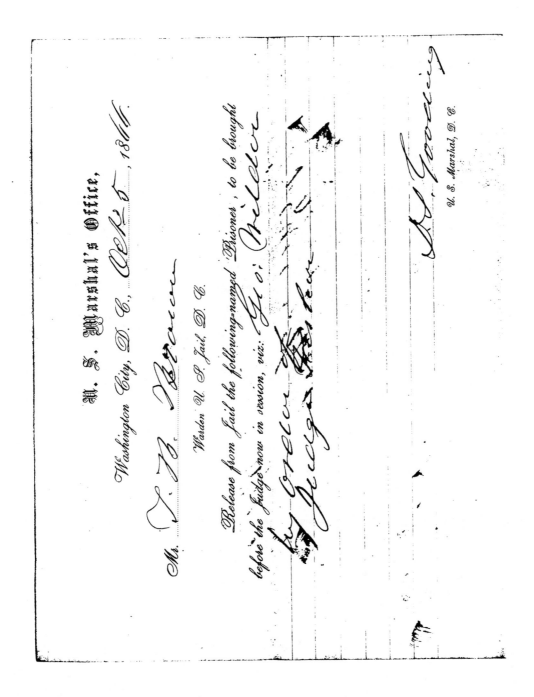

General Commitment.—Printed and Sold by R.A. Waters, Pa. Ave. betw. 11th and 12th streets.

DISTRICT OF COLUMBIA,

COUNTY OF WASHINGTON, To wit:

To the Warden of Jail of the District of Columbia:

RECEIVE into your custody the body of Marshall Tait herewith sent by any qualified officer, Constable of the said County, brought before me, F.A. Boswell, one of the Justices of the Peace in and for the said county, and charged before me upon the oath of Columbus Winkleman with having

on the 10th day of December 1866 in the County aforesaid feloniously stolen taken & carried away, 620 lbs. iron flue frames the property of Thomas Martin value $13

him therefore safely keep in your said custody until he shall be discharged by due course of law; and for so doing this shall be your sufficient warrant.

GIVEN under my hand and seal this 18th day of Dec. in the year of our Lord one thousand eight hundred and sixty-six.

F.A. Boswell   J.P.

On verso:
1928
United States vs. Marshall Tait
Summons for U.S.
Thos. Martin
Columbus Winkleman 11 Wharf
A. Leppard
N st. 4 1/2 & 6 st.
F.A. Boswell   J.P.

General Commitment —Printed and Sold by R. A. Waters, Pa. Ave. bet. 11th and 12th streets.

DISTRICT OF COLUMBIA,

COUNTY OF WASHINGTON, *To wit:*

To the Warden of Jail of the District of Columbia;

RECEIVE into your custody the body of *Marshall Sail*

herewith sent by *Churfsnessus Green* Constable of the said County,

brought before me, *C. A. Barrett* one of the

Justices of the Peace in and for the said County, and charged before me upon the oath of

Columbus Minkerman with having

on the 10th day of December 186 in the county

Afraair Selwing stolen taken Hamre .

Gray, 62st Born this it cene the property of

Thomas Marten value $15 .

him therefore safely keep in your said custody until he shall be discharged by due course
of law; and for so doing this shall be your sufficient warrant

GIVEN under my hand and seal this *10 L* day of *Die*

in the year of our Lord one thousand eight hundred and sixty *six*

[SEAL]

F. A. Barrett

1928

United States
vs
Marshall Tait

Summons for U.S.
Thos. Martin,
Columbus Winkleman
1st Wharf
A Leppard"
No. 4 1/2 & 6 "

J. M. Burnett

General Commitment.—Printed and Sold by R.A. Waters, Pa. Ave.
bet. 11th and 12th streets.

DISTRICT OF COLUMBIA,

COUNTY OF WASHINGTON, To wit:

To the Warden of Jail of the District of Columbia.

RECEIVE into your custody the body of Thomas Sheppard herewith sent by any qualified officer Constable of the said County, brought before me, F.A. Boswell one of the Justices of the Peace in and for the said County, and charged before me upon the oath of Benjamine Gross with having

on the 17th day of December 1866 in the County aforesaid feloniously stolen taken and carried away two shirts the value of $250 $^{c}/$ each $5—his property of the said Gross

him therefore safely keep in your said custody until he shall be discharged by due course of law; and for so doing, this shall be your sufficient warrant.

GIVEN under my hand and seal this 18th day of December in the year of our Lord one thousand eight hundred and sixty-six.

F.A. Boswell   J.P.   SEAL

On verso: 1929
United States vs. Thomas Sheppard
Summons for U.S.
Benj. Gross, 4 1/2 St. bet. E. St. & Va. Ave.
Joseph H. Gunnell
Police Station
F.A. Boswell   J.P.

General Commitment.—Printed and sold by R. A. Waters, Pa. Ave. bet. 11th and 12th streets

DISTRICT OF COLUMBIA,

COUNTY OF WASHINGTON, To wit:

To the Warden of Jail of the District of Columbia:

RECEIVE into your custody the body of *Wm Shepherd James Shepherd*
herewith sent by *Wm Smith* Constable of the said county,
brought before me, *A Ames* one of the
Justices of the Peace in and for the said County, and charged before me upon the oath of
Benjamin Ames with having

*on the 19th day of J.C. under $146 in the Country
a Chancery Petters taken and to take and carried
Carry and hold the said Petter $350; each $3
his property of the Petter take Ames*

him therefore safely keep in your said custody until he shall be discharged by due course
of law; and for so doing, this shall be your sufficient warrant.

GIVEN under my hand and seal this _____ day of *December*
in the year of our Lord one thousand eight hundred and sixty *six*

[SEAL]

U.S. MARSHAL'S OFFICE.
Washington City, D.C.,   Decr. 18, 1866.

Mr. T. B. Brown

Warden U.S. Jail, D.C.

Receive into your custody the following=named Prisoner, for safe=keeping until released, viz:

Francis Christmas
Fanny Wilson
Emma Barnard

D.S. Gooding
U.S. Marshal, D.C.

On verso:
1930 &1931 & 1932

U. S. Marshal's Office,

Washington City, D. C., Dec 19, 1865.

Mr. G. H. Brown

Warden U. S. Jail, D. C.

Receive into your custody the following-named Prisoner, for safe-keeping until released, viz:

U. S. Marshal, D. C.

<u>Chas. Walter, 397 D street, opposite City Hall.</u>

DISTRICT OF COLUMBIA,

    COUNTY OF WASHINGTON,

To the Warden of the Jail in the District of Columbia:

    RECEIVE into your custody the bodys of Robert Sales & James Clark (col) herewith sent by Wm. H. Fuss, Metropolitan Police Officer of the said County, brought before me, Charles Walter, one of the Justices of the Peace in and for the said County, and charged before me upon the oath of O.P. Pitcher with having

stolen about 100 thousand copies of religious & other books valued about $70. in the month of December 1866 in said County

them therefore safely keep in your said custody until they shall be discharged by due course of law, and for so doing this shall be your sufficient warrant.

    GIVEN under my hand and seal, this 18th day of December 1866.

                Chas. Walter   J.P.   SEAL

On verso:
1933 & 1934
Committment of
Robert Sales
<u>James Clark</u>
Witnesses
O.P. Pitcher) 23 South
J. S. Kellogg) A street
Wm. Fuss

District of Columbia,
COUNTY OF WASHINGTON, } to wit:

To the Warden of the Jail in the District of Columbia:

RECEIVE into your custody the body of Robert Sailes frances Clark & (Col)

herewith sent by Wm H. Crus   Metropolitan Police Officer of the said County,

brought before me, Chas Walter   one of the

Justices of the Peace in and for the said County, and charged before me upon the oath of

J. D. Pitcher   with having

Stolen about 100 thousand copies of religious & other books valued about $170 - in the month of December 1866 in said County

him therefore safely keep in your said custody until he shall be discharged by due course of law, and for so doing this shall be your sufficient warrant.

GIVEN under my hand and seal, this 18th day of December 186 6 —

Chas Walter J. P. (SEAL)

CHAS. WALTER, 397 D street, opposite City Hall.

1933 & 1934

Committments
of

Robert Sales
James Clark

Witnesses

S. S. Pitcher   23 South
J. S. Kellogg   A Street
Wm Fuss

U.S. MARSHAL'S OFFICE,
Washington City, D.C.,   Decr. 19, 1866.

Mr. T.B. Brown

    Warden U.S. Jail, D.C.

    Release from Jail the following=named Prisoner, to be brought before the Judge now in session, viz:

            L.L. Cavender   2L
            Marshal(l) Tait   Debt

                      D.S. Gooding
                      U.S. Marshal, D.C.

On verso:
1928&

Washington City, D. C., Dec 19, 1866.

Mr. J. B. Brown

Warden U. S. Jail, D. C.

Release from Jail the following-named Prisones, to be brought before the Judge now in session, viz:

G. E. Carrington O. L.

Acin &c Jack Debt

_____
U. S. Marshal, D. C.

U.S. MARSHAL'S OFFICE,
WASHINGTON CITY. D.C.,   (undated but circa Dec. 1866).

Mr. T.B. Brown

    Warden U.S. Jail, D.C.

    Release from Jail the following=named Prisoner, to be brought before the Judge now in session, viz:

    Michael Clary & Albert Miller

        D.S. Gooding
        U.S. Marshal, D.C.

On verso: 1967.
      1963.

H. S. Marshal's Office,

Washington City, D. C., _____, 18___

Mr. J. B. Brown

Warden U. S. Jail, D. C.

Release from Jail the following-named Prisoner, to be brought

before the Judge now in session, viz:

Albert Miller, Michael Clancy

A. G. Gording,
U. S. Marshal, D. C.

U.S. MARSHAL'S OFFICE,
Washington City, D.C.,   Decr. 19th, 1866

Mr. T.B. Brown

Warden U.S. Jail, D.C.

Release from Jail the following=named Prisoner, to be brought before the Judge now in session, viz:

Francis Christmas   Col. W
Wm. Smith   2R

D.S. Gooding
U.S. Marshal, D.C.

On verso:
1711 & 1930

U. S. Marshal's Office,

Washington City, D. C., Dec 19th, 1866.

Mr. G. B. Brown,

Warden U. S. Jail, D. C.

Release from Jail the following-named Prisoners, to be brought before the Judge now in season, viz:

[illegible name]	1 R
[illegible name]	2 R
[illegible name]	Out

[signature]

U. S. Marshal, D. C.

U.S. MARSHAL'S OFFICE.
Washington City, D.C.,   Decr. 19, 1866.

Mr. T.B. Brown

Warden U.S. Jail, D.C.

Release from Jail the following=named Prisoner, to be brought before the Judge now in session, viz:

Emma Barnard

D.S. Gooding
U.S. Marshal, D.C.

On verso:
1932

DISTRICT OF COLUMBIA.   )
) to wit:
COUNTY OF WASHINGTON,)

To the Warden of the Jail in the District of Columbia:

RECEIVE into your custody the body of Adam Hines (alias Pink Jackson) herewith sent by A. Kelly, Metropolitan Police Officer of the said County, brought before me, Chas. Walter, one of the Justices of the Peace in and for the said County, and charged before me upon the oath of A. Kelly with

Robbery
       (for a hearing)

him therefore safely keep in your said custody until he shall be discharged by due course of law, and for so doing this shall be your sufficient warrant.

GIVEN under my hand and seal, this 19 day of Decber. 1866

                         Chas. Walter   J.P.   SEAL

On verso: 1936
Committment of
Adam Hines alias
Pink Jackson
for a hearing

District of Columbia,

COUNTY OF WASHINGTON, } to wit:

To the Warden of the Jail in the District of Columbia:

RECEIVE into your custody the body of *Adam Hilly alias Smith Sucker*

herewith sent by *A. Lilly* Metropolitan Police Officer of the said County, brought before me, *Adam Miller* one of the Justices of the Peace in and for the said, County, and charged before me upon the oath of ____ with ~~having~~

robbery

for a hearing

him therefore safely keep in your said custody until he shall be discharged by due course of law, and for so doing this shall be your sufficient warrant.

GIVEN under my hand and seal, this *19* day of *October* 1866

W. B. Webb J.P. (SEAL)

430

PART V

1936

Committment
of

Adam Hines
alias
Pink Jackson

for a hearing

DISTRICT OF COLUMBIA.   )

) to wit:

COUNTY OF WASHINGTON,)

To the Warden of the Jail in the District of Columbia:

WHEREAS Adams Hines alias Pink Jackson was committed to your Jail and custody on the 19th day of Decbr. 1866 upon a charge of robbery

(for a hearing)

by me, the subscriber, one of the Justices of the Peace in and for the said County. You are therefore hereby commanded to send me said A. Hines alias P.J

GIVEN under my hand and seal, this 22 day of December 1866.

                                   Chas. Walter   J.P.   SEAL

On verso: 1936

District of Columbia,

COUNTY OF WASHINGTON, } to wit:

To the Warden of the Jail in the District of Columbia;

WHEREAS *Charles Stives alias R.R. Ferdeson* was committed to your Jail and custody on the 19th day of *October* 186_6_ upon a charge of *Robbery*

for a hearing

by me, the subscriber, one of the Justices of the Peace in and for the said County, ~~both, before me, found sufficient surety for his personal appearance at our next Criminal Court, to be held on the~~ _____ day of _____ ~~next, then and there to answer such matter as shall be objected~~

~~against him for the offense aforesaid~~: You are therefore hereby commanded, ~~that if the said~~ *to send me David A. Hortzalso R.f.* _____ do remain in Jail for the said cause, and none ~~other, then you forbear to detain him any longer, but deliver him thence, and suffer him to go at large~~

GIVEN under my hand and seal, this *22* day of *December* 186 *6*

Chs Walter J.P. (SEAL)

DISTRICT OF COLUMBIA,

COUNTY OF WASHINGTON, to wit:

To the Warden of the Jail in the District of Columbia:

Whereas Edward Smith & John Allen was committed to your Jail and custody on the 19th day of December upon a charge of

having in their possession a pair of new boots (each) believed to be stolen property, for further examination by me, the subscriber, Metropolitan Police Magistrate and one of the Justices of the Peace in and for the said County, and no further evidence being produced before me, you are therefore

hereby commanded, that if the said Edward Smith & John Allen do remain in jail for the said cause, and none other, then you forbear to detain him any longer, but suffer him to go at large.

GIVEN under my hand and seal, this 3rd day of January in the year of Lord one thousand eight hundred and sixty-six.

_____D.K. Morsell_____   L.S.
Met'n Police Magistrate and J.P.

On verso:
1941-42
United States
viz. release
Edward Smith &
John Allen

District of Columbia,

COUNTY OF WASHINGTON, to wit:

To the Warden of the Jail in the District of Columbia :

Whereas *Edward Smith John Allen* was committed to your Jail and custody on the *19th* day of *December* upon a charge of *having in their possession a pair of New Boots (Each) believed to be Stolen property, for further examination :*

by me, the subscriber, Metropolitan Police Magistrate and one of the Justices of the Peace in and for the said County, ~~hath, before me, found sufficient surety for his personal appearance at our next Criminal Court to be held on the_____ day of_____~~ *And whereof the several and all so really and satisfactorily disposed of* ~~You are therefore hereby commanded, that if the said~~ *Edward Smith John Allen* ~~do remain in Jail for the said cause, and none other, then you forbear to detain him any longer,~~ but deliver him thence, and suffer him to go at large.

GIVEN under my hand and seal, this *3rd* day of *January* in the year of Lord one thousand eight hundred and sixty-*six*.

D. W. Howell [L.S.]

Met'n Police Magistrate and J. P.

U.S. MARSHAL'S OFFICE.

Washington City, D.C.,   Decr. 20th. 1866

Mr. T. B. Brown

    Warden U.S. Jail, D.C.,

    Receive into your custody the following=named Prisoner, for safe=keeping until released, viz:

        Joseph Bateman

                D.S. Gooding
                U.S. Marshal, D.C.

On verso:
1944
Com. of
Joseph Bateman

U.S. MARSHAL'S OFFICE,

Washington City, D.C.,   Decr. 22d, 1866

Mr. T.B. Brown

Warden U.S. Jail. D.C.

Release from Jail the following=named Prisoner, to be brought before the Judge now in session, viz:

Joseph Bateman

D.S. Gooding
U.S. Marshal, D.C.

On verso: 1944

U. S. Marshal's Office,

Washington City, D. C., Dec'r 22', 186[?].

Mr. T. B. Brown

Warden U. S. Jail, D. C.

Release from Jail the following-named Prisoner, to be brought before the Judge now in session, viz:

Joseph Bateman

[signature]
U. S. Marshal, D. C.

DISTRICT OF COLUMBIA,

COUNTY OF WASHINGTON, TO WIT:

To the Warden of the Jail in the District of Columbia:

RECEIVE into your custody the body of William Garner herewith sent by F. Straub, Metropolitan Police Officer of the said County, brought before me, the undersigned, a Metropolitan Police Magistrate and one of the Justices of the Peace in and for the said County, and charged before me upon the oath of F. Straub with having

been concerned in stealing and carrying away in the said County on the 22d Decr. 1866 a piece of iron machinery the property of some person at present unknown

him therefore safely keep in your said custody until he shall be further examined, and for so doing this shall be your sufficient Warrant.

GIVEN under my hand and seal, this 22d day of Decr. in the year of our Lord one thousand eight hundred and sixty-six.

_____W. Thompson_____L.S.
Metropolitan Police Magistrate and
a Justice of the Peace.

On verso:
1947.
Commitment of Wm. Garner for further
hearing

District of Columbia,

County of Washington, TO WIT:

To the Warden of the Jail in the District of Columbia:

RECEIVE into your custody the body of *William Garee*

herewith sent by *F. Straub*, Metropolitan Police Officer of the said County,

brought before me, *the undersigned*, a Metropolitan

Police Magistrate and one of the Justices of the Peace in and for the said County, and charged before me

upon the oath of *F. Straub* with having

been concerned in stealing and carrying away in the said county on the 22 Decr 1866 a pice of iron machinery the property of some person at present unknown

him therefore safely keep in your said custody until he shall be discharged by the course of law, and for

so doing this shall be your sufficient Warrant. *further examined*

GIVEN under my hand and seal, this *22* day of, *Dec*

in the year of our Lord one thousand eight hundred and sixty- *six*

W. Thompson

[L.S.]

Metropolitan Police Magistrate and a Justice of the Peace.

DISTRICT OF COLUMBIA,

COUNTY OF WASHINGTON, TO WIT:

To the Warden of the Jail in the District of Columbia:

Receive into your custody the body of F.T. Drew herewith sent by F. Straub, Metropolitan Police Officer of the said County, brought before me, the undersigned, a Metropolitan Police Magistrate and one of the Justices of the Peace in and for the said County, and charged before me upon the oath of F. Straub with having

stolen & carried away a piece of iron machinery on the 22d January 1866 in said County, the property of some person at present unknown

him therefore safely keep in your said custody until he shall be discharged by due course of law, and for so doing this shall be your sufficient Warrant.

GIVEN under my hand and seal, this 22d day of Decr. in the year of our Lord one thousand eight hundred and sixty-six.

_____W. Thompson_____ L.S.
Metropolitan Police Magistrate and
a Justice of the Peace.

On verso:
1948.
Commitment of F.T. Drew
for further hearing

County of Washington, TO WIT:

To the Warden of the Jail in the District of Columbia:

RECEIVE into your custody the body of H. Drew

herewith sent by Hestraub

brought before me, the undersigned , a Metropolitan

Police Magistrate and one of the Justices of the Peace in and for the said County, and charged before me.

upon the oath of Hestraub

, Metropolitan Police Officer of the said County,

with having

stolen strained away a few of iron machinery on the 22 January 1866 in said county, the property of some person at present unknown

him therefore safely keep in your said custody until he shall be discharged by due course of law, and for so doing this shall be your sufficient Warrant.

GIVEN under my hand and seal, this 22 day of Dec

in the year of our Lord one thousand eight hundred and sixty-six

[L.S.]

Y.H. Thompson

....
Metropolitan Police Magistrate and a Justice of the Peace.

DISTRICT OF COLUMBIA,

COUNTY OF WASHINGTON, To wit:

To the Warden of the Jail in the District of Columbia:

RECEIVE into your custody the bodys of Chas. Snyder, Danl. Donovan & John English herewith sent by J.W. Coomes Metropolitan Police Officer of the said County, brought before me, Charles Walter, one of the Justices of the Peace in and for the said County, and charged before me upon the information of J.W. Coomes with

the robbery of a store
(for a hearing)

them therefore safely keep in your said custody until they shall be discharged by due course of law, and for so doing this shall be your sufficient Warrant.

GIVEN under my hand and seal, this 23rd day of December in the year of our Lord one thousand eight hundred and sixty-six,

_____Chas. Walter_____   SEAL.
Justice of the Peace.

On verso:
1950, 1951, 1952.
Committment of
Chas. Snyder
Danl. Donovan
John English
for a hearing

DISTRICT OF COLUMBIA,

COUNTY OF WASHINGTON, To wit:

To the Warden of the Jail in the District of Columbia:

RECEIVE into your custody the body of *Chas. Ingular - Paul Jonathan & the English* ...., Metropolitan Police Officer of the said County,

herewith sent by *J. M. Earney* ...., brought before me, *Charles Walter* ...., Superintendent

of Metropolitan Police and ex officio one of the Justices of the Peace in and for the said County, and

charged before me upon the oath of *information off Mr. Earney* .... with ~~having~~ ....

the robbery of a Store

(for a hearing)

You therefore safely keep in your said custody until he shall be discharged by due course of law, and for so

doing this shall be your sufficient Warrant.

GIVEN under my hand and seal, this *23rd* day of *December*

in the year of our Lord one thousand eight hundred and sixty *six*

Chas Walter

Supt. Met. Police and ex officio Justice of the Peace.

U.S. MARSHAL'S OFFICE.
Washington City, D.C.,   Decr. 24, 1866.

Mr. T.B. Brown

Warden U.S. Jail, D.C.

Release from Jail the following=named Prisoner, to be brought before the Judge now in session, viz:

James Clark

D.S. Gooding
U.S. Marshal, D.C.

On verso:
1934.

U. S. Marshal's Office,

Washington City, _D. C._, _Dec 24_, _1866_.

Mr. _J. B. Brown,_

Warden U. S. Jail, D. C.

Release from Jail the following-named _Prisoner_, to be brought before the Judge now in session, viz:

James Colerik

[signature]
U. S. Marshal, D. C.

DISTRICT OF COLUMBIA,

COUNTY OF WASHINGTON, to wit:

To the Warden of Jail of the District of Columbia:

WHEREAS George E. Poulton was committed to your Jail and custody on the 22d day of Decr. 1866 upon a charge of threatening with personal violence Mary Sattell on the 22d day of December 1866

by me the subscriber, one of the Justices of the Peace in and for the said County, hath, before me, found sufficient surety to keep the peace towards the said Mary Sattell & other citizens: You are therefore hereby commanded, that if the said G.E. Poulton do remain in Jail for the said cause, and none other, then you forbear to detain him any longer, but deliver him thence, and suffer him to go at large.

Given under my hand and seal this 24th day of Decr. in the year of our Lord one thousand eight hundred and sixty-six.

W. Thompson   J.P.   SEAL

On verso: 1949.

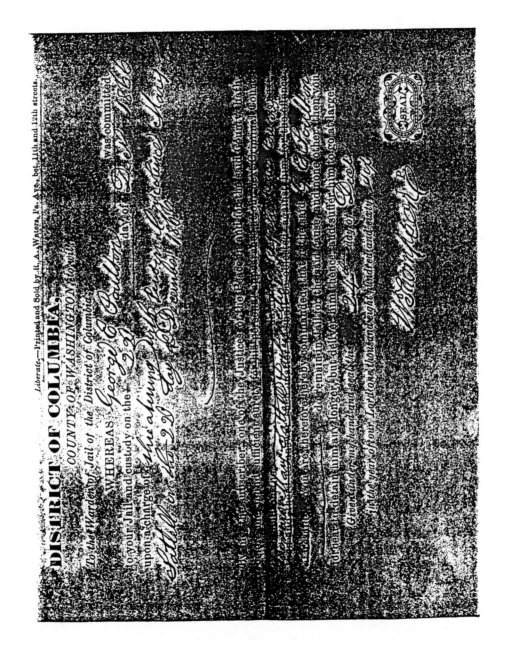

DISTRICT OF COLUMBIA,

COUNTY OF WASHINGTON, to wit:

To the Warden of Jail of the District of Columbia:

WHEREAS F.T. Drew was committed to your Jail and custody on the 22d day of December 1866 upon a charge of larceny and for a further hearing by me, the subscriber, one of the Justices of the Peace in and for the said County: You are hereby commanded, that if the said F.T. Drew do remain in Jail for the said cause and none other, then you forbear to detain him any longer. but deliver him to F. Straub Patrolman.

Given under my hand and seal this 26th day of Decr. in the year of our Lord one thousand eight hundred and sixty-six.

W. Thompson   J.P.

On verso:
1948.
Release of
F.T. Drew

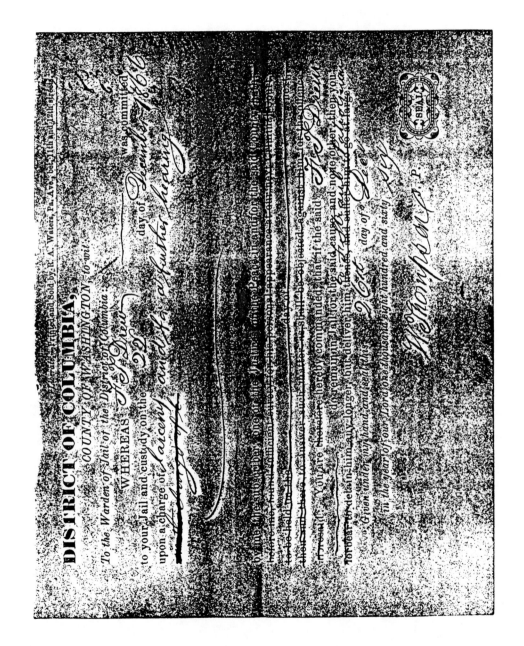

DISTRICT OF COLUMBIA,

COUNTY OF WASHINGTON, TO WIT:

To the Warden of the Jail in the District of Columbia:

RECEIVE into your custody the body of Isaac Washington herewith sent by G.C. Harris, Metropolitan Police Officer of the said County, brought before me the subscriber, a Metropolitan Police Magistrate and one of the Justices of the Peace in and for the said County, and charged before me upon the oath of W.C. King with having

received one bacon ham under false pretences from M.R. Roach for the use of Wm. Forsyth on the 2nd day of Jany. 1867 at the County of Washington

him therefore safely keep in your said custody until he shall be discharged by due course of law, and for so doing this shall be your sufficient Warrant.

GIVEN under my hand and seal, this 6th day of January in the year of our Lord one thousand eight hundred and sixty-seven.

_____Samuel Drury_____L.S.

Metropolitan Police Magistrate and
a Justice of the Peace.

On verso: 1999.
Isaac Washington
Commitment

Witnesses
Geo. C. Harris
W.C. King

District of Columbia,
County of Washington, TO WIT:

To the Warden of the Jail in the District of Columbia:

RECEIVE into your custody the body of *John Washington* herewith sent by *G E Harris*, Metropolitan Police Officer of the said County, brought before me, *H Interior* ————, a Metropolitan Police Magistrate and one of the Justices of the Peace in and for the said County, and charged before me upon the oath of *W C Stein* ———— with having

Received one broken under fake pretences from M. R. Royal for the use of Wm Forsyth on the 2nd day of Aug 1867 in the county of Washington —————

him therefore safely keep in your said custody until he shall be discharged by due course of law, and for so doing this shall be your sufficient Warrant.

GIVEN under my hand and seal, this *6th* ———— day of *January* in the year of our Lord one thousand eight hundred and sixty-*seven*

[L.S.]

James Drury
Metropolitan Police Magistrate and a Justice of the Peace.

DISTRICT OF COLUMBIA,

COUNTY OF WASHINGTON, TO WIT:

To the Warden of the Jail in the District of Columbia:

RECEIVE into your custody the body of George Smith herewith sent by W. H. Howes, Metropolitan Police Officer of the said County, brought before me, the undersigned, a Metropolitan Police Magistrate and one of the Justices of the Peace in and for the said County, and charged before me upon the oath of Wm. H. Brett with having

stolen & carried away on the 10th Jany. 1867 in said county a carpet bag, the property of said Wm. Brett (value $4.50)

him therefore safely keep in your said custody until he shall be discharged by due course of law, and for so doing this shall be your sufficient Warrant.

GIVEN under my hand and seal, this 11th day of Jany in the year of our Lord one thousand eight hundred and sixty-seven.

_____W Thompson_____L.S.
Metropolitan Police Magistrate and
a Justice of the Peace.

On verso: 2024.
Commitment of
George Smith for Criminal Court in Session
U.S. Witness
Wm. H. Brett   No. 313
F Street.

District of Columbia,

County of Washington, TO WIT:

To the Warden of the Jail in the District of Columbia:

RECEIVE into your custody the body of *George Smith* herewith sent by *M Morriss* , Metropolitan Police Officer of the said County, brought before me, *the undersigned* , a Metropolitan Police Magistrate and one of the Justices of the Peace in and for the said County, and charged before me upon the oath of *Wm Brett* with having

Stolen Carried away on the 10th Jany 1867 in Cash a purse of money containing in Gold & Silver a Wallet a pocket Book Notes &c the property of said Wm Brett

(value of $404.50)

him therefore safely keep in your said custody until he shall be discharged by due course of law, and for so doing this shall be your sufficient Warrant.

GIVEN under my hand and seal, this *11th* day of *Jany* in the year of our Lord one thousand eight hundred and sixty- *seven*

W Thompson

[L.S.]

Metropolitan Police Magistrate and a Justice of the Peace.

DISTRICT OF COLUMBIA,   )

) to wit:

COUNTY OF WASHINGTON,   )

To the Warden of the Jail in the District of Columbia:

RECEIVE into your custody the body of Edward Smith col. herewith sent by A. Eckloff, Metropolitan Police Officer of the said County, brought before me, Charles Walter, one of the Justices of the Peace in and for the said County, and charged before me upon the oath of George W. Whitington with having

stolen a piece of Opera Cloth valued $10—the property of said Whitington on the 11th January 1867 in said County

him therefore safely keep in your said custody until he shall be discharged by due course of law, and for so doing this shall be your sufficient warrant.

GIVEN under my hand and seal, this 11 day of Jany 1867.

                         C Walter   J.P.   SEAL

On verso:
2027.
Committment of Edward Smith col.
Witness
Geo. W. Whitington
Cor. 4 & Mass. Ave.

District of Columbia, } to wit:
COUNTY OF WASHINGTON, }

To the Warden of the Jail in the District of Columbia:

RECEIVE into your custody the body of *Edward Smith arl*

herewith sent by *A - Eggloff* Metropolitan Police Officer of the said County,

brought before me, *Charles Walter* one of the

Justices of the Peace in and for the said County, and charged before me upon the oath of *George* with having

Mr Whidington stolen a piece of Afora bloth valued $10 — the property of said Whidington on the 11th January 186 in said County

him therefore safely keep in your said custody until he shall be discharged by due course of law, and for so doing this shall be your sufficient warrant.

GIVEN under my hand and seal, this *11* day of *Jany* 186*7*

[signature] J. P. (SEAL)

DISTRICT OF COLUMBIA,

COUNTY OF WASHINGTON, TO WIT:

To the Warden of the Jail in the District of Columbia:

RECEIVE into your custody the body of Paul Wish herewith sent by any qualified, Metropolitan Police Officer of the said County, brought before me, the subscriber, a Metropolitan Police Magistrate and one of the Justices of the Peace in and for the said County, and charged before me upon the oath of Lucy Parker, with having

feloniously stolen, taken and carried away from her premises in the city of Washington, in said county, on the 10th day of January 1867, about fifteen dollars in United States Currency, and failing to give security for his appearance before me for further hearing,

him therefore safely keep in your said custody for further hearing, until he shall be discharged by due course of law, and for so doing this shall be your sufficient Warrant.

GIVEN under my hand and seal, this 11th day of January in the year of our Lord one thousand eight hundred and sixty-seven.

_____D.K. Morsell_____ L.S.
Metropolitan Police Magistrate and
a Justice of the Peace.

On verso:
2030.
United States viz. comt. for further hearing
Paul Wish
Grand Larceny

District of Columbia,
County of Washington, TO WIT:

To the Warden of the Jail in the District of Columbia:

RECEIVE into your custody the body of *Paul Noist* herewith sent by *Any qualified* , Metropolitan Police Officer of the said County, brought before me, *the subscriber*, ———— , a Metropolitan Police Magistrate and one of the Justices of the Peace in and for the said County, and charged before me upon the oath of *Lucy Parker* ———— with having *feloniously stolen, taken and carried away from her dwelling in the City of Washington, in said County on the 1st day of January 1867 about fifteen dollars in United States Currency, and failing to give security for his appearance before me for further examination & hearing for the further larceny;*

him therefore safely keep in your said custody until he shall be discharged by due course of law, and for so doing this shall be your sufficient Warrant.

GIVEN under my hand and seal, this 11th ———— day of *January* in the year of our Lord one thousand eight hundred and sixty-*seven*.

[signature]

Metropolitan Police Magistrate and a Justice of the Peace.

L.S.

DISTRICT OF COLUMBIA,

COUNTY OF WASHINGTON, TO WIT:

To the warden of the Jail in the District of Columbia:

RECEIVE into your custody the body of Osborn Woodruff herewith sent by any qualified, Metropolitan Police Officer of the said County, brought before me, the subscriber, a Metropolitan Police Magistrate and one of the Justices of the Peace in and for the said County, and charged before me upon the oath of Benedict Hutchins and Stephen Casey with having

on or about the 1st day of January 1867, feloniously stolen, taken and carried away from the premises of the said Hutchins, in said County, of the value of one dollar & fifty cents, of the Goods and chattels of the said Benedict Hutchins, and failing to give the security required by law,

him therefore safely keep in your said custody until he shall be discharged by due course of law, and for so doing this shall be your sufficient Warrant.

GIVEN under my hand and seal, this 15th day of January in the year of our Lord one thousand eight hundred and sixty-seven.

_____D.K. Morsell_____ L.S.
Metropolitan Police Magistrate and
a Justice of the Peace.

On verso:
No. 2039.
United States vz. comt.
Osborn Woodruff
Pettit Larceny
Witnesses for U. States
Benedict Hutchins No. 27 6, 8th bet. M & N Streets
Stephen Casey, 9th Bet. N & O Sts.

District of Columbia,

County of Washington, TO WIT:

To the Warden of the Jail in the District of Columbia:

RECEIVE into your custody the body of *Osborn Woodruff*

herewith sent by *Amy Grabfield* , Metropolitan Police Officer of the said County,

brought before me, *The Subscriber* , a Metropolitan

Police Magistrate and one of the Justices of the Peace in and for the said County, and charged before me

upon the oath of *Benjamin Hutchins and Stephen Casey*

with having

On or about the 1st day of January 1867, feloniously stole tables and carried away from the premises of the said Hutchins, in all County of the Sales of one dollar fifty cents of the Goods and Chattels of the said Benedict Ostry and taking to give the security required by law —

him therefore safely keep in your said custody until he shall be discharged by due course of law, and for
so doing this shall be your sufficient Warrant.

GIVEN under my hand and seal, this *15th* day of *January*

in the year of our Lord one thousand eight hundred and sixty *seven*,

J.M. Morsell

[L.S.]

Metropolitan Police Magistrate and a Justice of the Peace.

DISTRICT OF COLUMBIA,

COUNTY OF WASHINGTON, TO WIT:

To the Warden of the Jail in the District of Columbia:

RECEIVE into your custody the body of John Seybert herewith sent by T. Markwood, Metropolitan Police Officer of the said County, brought before me the undersigned, a Metropolitan Police Magistrate and one or the Justices or the Peace in and for the said County, and charged before me upon the oath of Ellen Seybert with having

threatened to take away her life in the county aforesaid on the 10th January 1867 and at other times and the said John Seybert, having failed to give security to keep the peace as required by law,

him therefore safely keep in your said custody until he shall be discharged by due course of law, and for so doing this shall be your sufficient Warrant.

GIVEN under my hand and seal, this 20th day of January in the year of our Lord one thousand eight hundred and sixty-seven.

_____W. Thompson_____ L.S.
Metropolitan Police Magistrate and
a Justice of the Peace.

On verso:
2051.
Commitment of John Seybert in
default of security to keep the Peace.

District of Columbia,
County of Washington, TO WIT:

To the Warden of the Jail in the District of Columbia:

RECEIVE into your custody the body of *John Seybert*
herewith sent by *J. Harwood* ———— Metropolitan Police Officer of the said County,
brought before me, *the undersigned* , a Metropolitan
Police Magistrate and one of the Justices of the Peace in and for the said County, and charged before me
upon the oath of *Ellen Seybert*
with having

threatened to take away her life in the events aforesaid with 18th January 1867 and at other times and the said John Seybert having failed to give security to keep the peace and to be
by law,

him therefore safely keep in your said custody until he shall be discharged by due course of law, and for
so doing this shall be your sufficient Warrant.

GIVEN under my hand and seal, this *20th* day of *January*
in the year of our Lord one thousand eight hundred and sixty- *seven*

L.S.

W. Thompson
Metropolitan Police Magistrate and a Justice of the Peace.

U.S. MARSHAL'S OFFICE,

WASHINGTON CITY, D.C.,   Feby. 18, 1867

Mr. T.B. Brown

     Warden U.S. Jail, D.C.

     Release from Jail the following=named Prisoner, to be brought before the Judge now in session, viz:

        3R Thomas H. Matthews, Feb. 15th
        1L Joseph Gorden, Jan. 25th
        Robt. Sales Debt   Dec. 18th

               D.S. Gooding
               U.S. Marshal, D.C.

On verso:
1933.
2070—2149

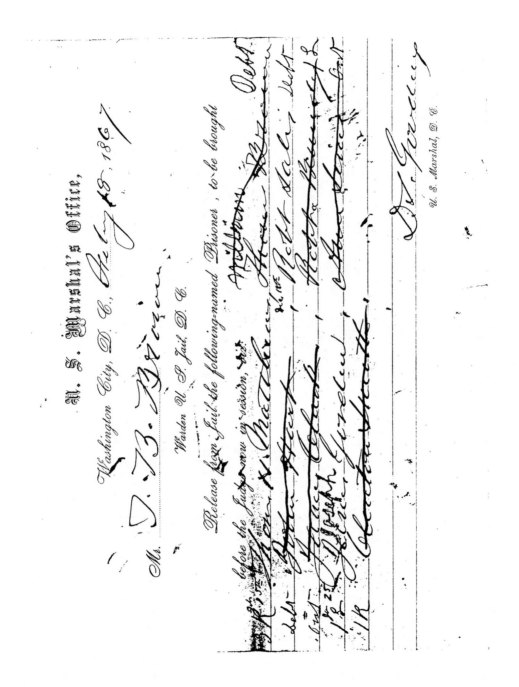

General Commitment.—Printed and Sold by R.A. Waters, Pa. Ave. bet.
11th and 12th Streets.

DISTRICT OF COLUMBIA,

COUNTY of WASHINGTON, To wit:

To the Warden of Jail of the District of Columbia:

RECEIVE into your custody the body of Amanda Mathews herewith sent by any qualified Met. Police Officer, Constable of the said County, brought before me, F.A. Boswell, one of the Justices of the Peace in and for the said County, and charged before me upon the oath of Chas. E. Goodnoe & Wm. H. Evans with having on or about the 14th day of March 1867, in the county aforesaid

received stolen property such as draws, shirts, calicos, & socks, knowing the same to be stolen property of William A. Sampson value $40.00.

him therefore safely keep in your said custody until he shall be discharged by due course of law; and for so doing, this shall be your sufficient warrant.

GIVEN under my hand and seal this 15th day of March in the year of our Lord one thousand eight hundred and sixty-seven.

F.A. Boswell   J.P.   SEAL.

On verso: 2229.
United States vs. Amanda Mathews
Summons for U. States
William A. Sampson
Charles E. Goodnoe
South 'A,' Bet. 2 & 3 St. East
Wm. H. Evans Met Police

F.A. Boswell   J.P.

DISTRICT OF COLUMBIA,
COUNTY OF WASHINGTON, *To wit :*

To the Warden of Jail of the District of Columbia :

RECEIVE into your custody the body of *[handwritten]* Constable of the said county, herewith sent by me, *[handwritten]* one of the brought before me, *[handwritten]* and charged before me upon the oath of Justices of the Peace in and for the said county, with having *[handwritten]*

him therefore safely keep in your said custody until he shall be discharged by due course of law; and for so doing, this shall be your sufficient warrant

GIVEN under my hand and seal this _____ day of _____

in the year of our Lord one thousand eight hundred and sixty *[handwritten]*

[SEAL]

2229.

United States
v.s.
Amanda Mathews

Summons for U. State
William A Sampson
Charles E. Godwin
Smith, A. Bn. 2 & 3 Lt.
Eqpt

W. H. Evans Witt Police

J. D. Connell D.C.

General Commitment.—Printed and Sold by R.A. Waters, Pa. Ave. bet. 11th and 12th Streets.

DISTRICT OF COLUMBIA,

COUNTY OF WASHINGTON, To wit:

To the Warden of Jail of the District of Columbia:

RECEIVE into your custody the body of Mary A.E. Hawkins herewith sent by any qualified Met. Police Officer, Constable of the said County, brought before me, F.A. Boswell, one of the Justices of the Peace in and for the said County, and charged before me upon the oath of Chas. E. Goodnoe & Wm. H. Evans with having

on or about the 14th day of March 1867 in the County aforesaid secured stolen goods, such as, draws, Socks, calicos, & shirts, property of William A. Sampson, knowing the same to be stolen. Value of $40.

him therefore safely keep in your said custody until he shall be discharged by due course of law; and for so doing this shall be your sufficient warrant.

GIVEN under my hand and seal this 15th day of March in the year of our Lord one thousand eight hundred and sixty-seven.

F. A. Boswell   J.P.   SEAL.

On verso:
2230.
<u>United States vs. Mary A.E. Hawkins</u>
Summons for U. States
William A. Sampson
Charles E. Goodnoe
South (A) St. bet.
2 & 3 St. East
Wm. H. Evans
Met. Police

F.A. Boswell J.P.

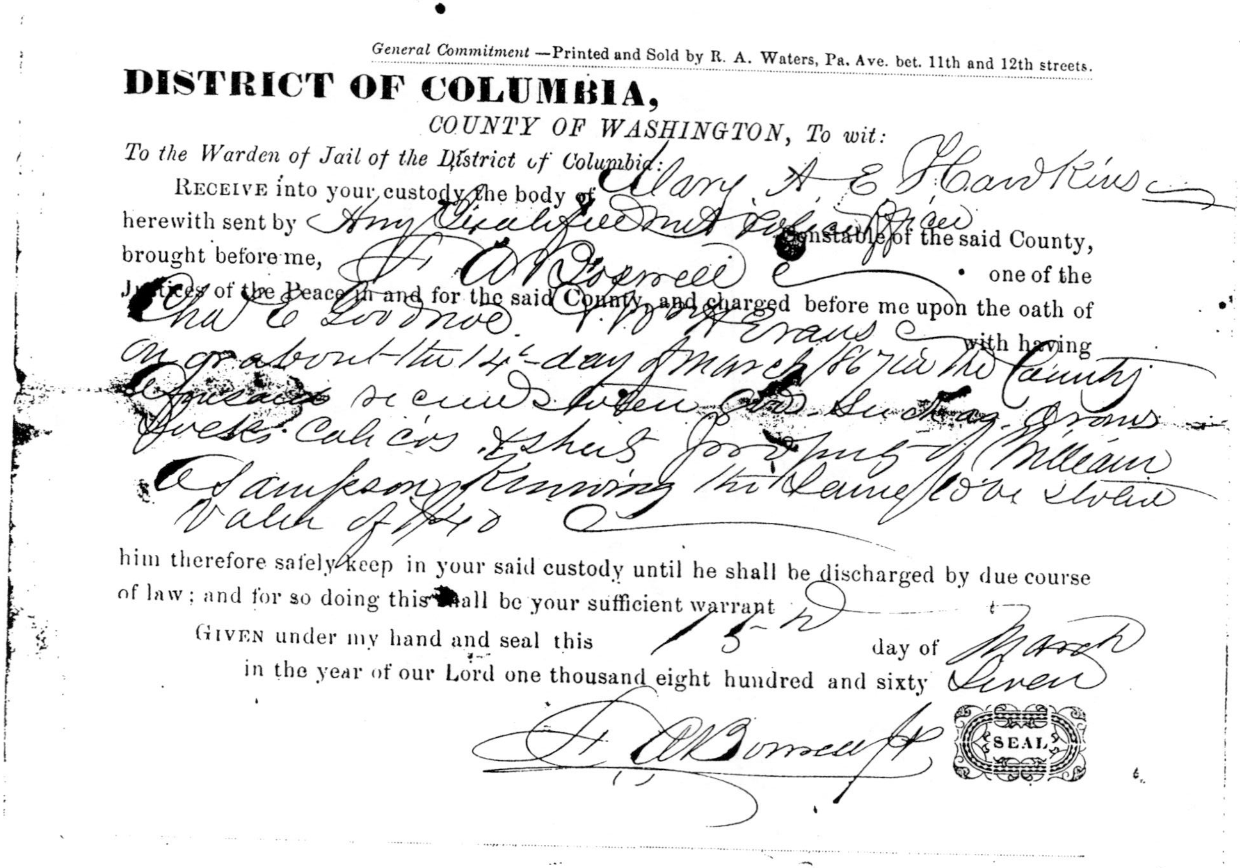

General Commitment — Printed and Sold by R. A. Waters, Pa. Ave. bet. 11th and 12th streets.

DISTRICT OF COLUMBIA,

COUNTY OF WASHINGTON, To wit:

To the Warden of Jail of the District of Columbia:

RECEIVE into your custody the body of *[illegible handwriting]*

herewith sent by *[illegible handwriting]* constable of the said County,

brought before me, *[illegible]*

J *[illegible]* of the peace in and for the said County, and charged before me upon the oath of

[illegible] one of the

[several lines of illegible handwriting] with having

[several lines of illegible handwriting]

him therefore safely keep in your said custody until he shall be discharged by due course

of law; and for so doing this shall be your sufficient warrant

GIVEN under my hand and seal this _____ day of _____

in the year of our Lord one thousand eight hundred and sixty _____

[SEAL]

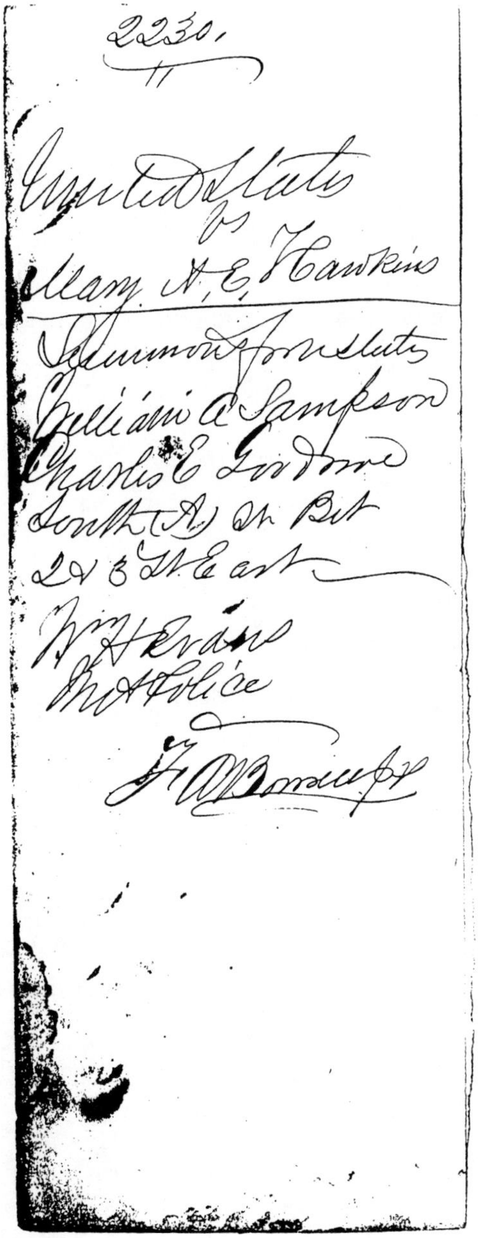
2230.
11

United States
vs
Mary A. E. Hawkins

Summons for U. States
William A. Sampson
Charles E. Gordon
South A. Dr Bet
2 & 3 St. East

W. H. Evans
Mt Police

F. A. Boswell

DISTRICT OF COLUMBIA

WASHINGTON COUNTY

To the Warden of the Jail Greeting:

Whereas Elijab B. Lee was committed to your Jail and Custody this day upon a charge of assaulting and beating John Chaney with intent to kill, for a further examination before me the subscriber a Justice of the Peace in and for said County, have found sufficient Bail for a further examination you are hereby commanded that if the said Elijah B. Lee, do remain in Jail for said cause and none other then you forbear to detain him no longer but deliver him thence and suffer him to go at large.

GIVEN under my hand and seal this 19th day of March A.D. 1867.

E.H. Bates   J.P.   SEAL
Justice of the Peace

On verso: 2242.
Release of
Elijah B. Lee

District of Columbia
Washington County } To wit;

To the Warden of the Jail Greeting;
Whereas Elijah B Lee was
Committed to your Jail and Custody
this day upon a Charge of assaulting
and beating John Chaney with intent
to Kill; for a Further Examination
before me the Subscriber a Justice of the
Peace in and for said County, have found
Sufficient Bail for a further Examination
You are hereby Commanded that if the
Said Elijah B Lee, do remain in Jail
for said Cause and none other then you
forbear to detain him no longer but
Deliver him thence and Suffer him
to go at large,
Given under My hand and Seal this
19th day of March AD 1867,

C H Bates J.P. (Seal)
Justice of the Peace

General Commitment.—Printed and Sold by R.A. Waters, Pa. Ave., bet. 11th and 12th streets.

DISTRICT OF COLUMBIA,

COUNTY OF WASHINGTON, To wit:

To the Warden of Jail of the District of Columbia:

RECEIVE into your custody the body of Elijah B. Lee herewith sent by any M.P. Officer, Constable of the said County, brought before me, E.A. Bates, one of the Justices of the Peace in and for the said County, and charged before me upon the oath of Charles Harrigan with having

committed an assault & Battery with intent to kill John Chaney on this day in the County and district aforesaid

He having failed to give security for a further examination him therefore safely keep in your said custody until he shall be discharged by due course of law; and for so doing, be your sufficient warrant.

GIVEN under my hand and seal this 19th day of March in the year of our Lord one thousand eight hundred and sixty-seven.

E.A. Bates   J.P.   SEAL.

On verso: 2242.
Commitment of
Elijah B. Lee
for
further examination

DISTRICT OF COLUMBIA,

COUNTY OF WASHINGTON, To wit :

To the Warden of Jail of the District of Columbia:

RECEIVE into your custody the body of *Elijah B. Lee*
herewith sent by *any* Constable of the said County,
brought before me, *Elijah* one of the
Justices of the Peace in and for the said County, and charged before me upon the oath of
with having

Charles Flanigan committed an assault & Battery with intent to Kill upon Chaney in this day in the before and to give to offence he having failed to give security for a fine and recognizance

him therefore safely keep in your said custody until he shall be discharged by due course
of law; and for so doing, this shall be your sufficient warrant.

GIVEN under my hand and seal this *19* day of *March*
in the year of our Lord one thousand eight hundred and sixty *seven*

[SEAL]

E. W. Bates Jr.

General Commitment.—Printed and sold by R.A. Waters, Pa. Av. bet.
11th and 12th streets.

DISTRICT OF COLUMBIA,

COUNTY OF WASHINGTON, to wit:

To the Warden of Jail of the District of Columbia:

RECEIVE into your custody the body of Edward O'Brien herewith sent by D. Felt M.P. Officer of the said County, brought before me, Charles Walter one of the Justices of the Peace in and for the said County, and charged before me upon the oath of Seth W. Kipp with having

stolen an overcoat of him on the 20th March 1867 in said County

him therefore safely keep in your said custody until he shall be discharged by due course of law; and for so doing this shall be your sufficient warrant.

GIVEN under my hand and seal this in the year of our Lord one thousand eight hundred and sixty-seven.

Chas. Walter   J.P.

On verso:
2244.
Committment of
Edward O'Brien
Witness—
Seth W. Kipp

DISTRICT OF COLUMBIA,

COUNTY OF WASHINGTON, to wit:

To the Warden of Jail of the District of Columbia;

RECEIVE into your custody the body of *Leonard P Brien*
herewith sent by *J. Felt M. Clolvier* ——————— of the said County,
brought before me, *Charles Walter* ——————— one of the
Justices of the Peace in and for the said County, and charged before me upon the oath of
with having

[handwritten text]

him therefore safely keep in your said custody until he shall be discharged by due course
of law; and for so doing this shall be your sufficient warrant.

GIVEN under my hand and seal this ——— day of *March*
in the year of our Lord one thousand eight hundred and sixty seven

[SEAL]

[signature]

General Commitment.—Printed and Sold by R.A. Waters, Pa. Ave., bet. 11th and 12th streets.

DISTRICT OF COLUMBIA,

COUNTY OF WASHINGTON, To wit:

To the warden of Jail of the District of Columbia:

RECEIVE into your custody the body of Kitty Swann herewith sent by any qualified officer of the said County, brought before me, F.A. Boswell, one of the Justices of the Peace in and for the said County, and charged before me upon the oath of J.W. Kelly with having

on the 19th day of March 1867 in the County aforesaid feloniously stolen taken and carried away one ten dollar bill, 1 (one) dollar bill & one fifty cents bill United States money property of the said Kitty Swann

him therefore safely keep in your said custody until he shall be discharged by due course of law; and for so doing, this shall be your sufficient warrant.

GIVEN under my hand and seal this 19th day of March in the year of our Lord one thousand eight hundred and sixty-seven.

F.A. Boswell   J.P.

On verso:
2245.
United States vs. Kitty Swann
Summons for U.S.
J.W. Kelley
Mrs. Kelly
Cor. Md. Ave. & 12th St.
W.H. White
Met. Police Officer

F.A. Boswell Jr.

General Commitment.—Printed and Sold by R. A. Waters, Pa. Ave. bet. 11th and 12th

DISTRICT OF COLUMBIA,

COUNTY OF WASHINGTON, To wit:

To the Warden of Jail of the District of Columbia:

RECEIVE into your custody the body of *[illegible handwriting]* herewith sent by *[illegible]* brought before me, *[illegible]* ———— one of the Justices of the Peace in and for the said County, and charged before me upon the oath of ———— with having *[illegible handwriting]*

him therefore safely keep in your said custody until he shall be discharged by due course of law; and for so doing, this shall be your sufficient warrant.

GIVEN under my hand and seal this *[illegible]* day of *[illegible]* in the year of our Lord one thousand eight hundred and sixty *[illegible]*

[SEAL]

2345

United States
vs
Kitty Simmons

Summons

J. W. Kelley
Thos Kelly

J. H. White
Mt. Police Officer

F. W. Barrett J.P.

DISTRICT OF COLUMBIA,

COUNTY OF WASHINGTON, TO WIT:

To the Warden of the Jail in the District of Columbia:

RECEIVE into your custody the body of William Johnson herewith sent by E.B. Caton , Metropolitan Police Officer of the said County, brought before me, John S. Hollingshead, a Metropolitan Police Magistrate and one of the Justices of the Peace in and for the said County, and charged before me upon the oath of William Ross with having

Committed an assault and battery on him with intent to kill him by throwing a whole brick at him while his back was turned and striking him on the head with the same on this day in the county aforesaid

him therefore safely keep in your said custody until he shall be discharged by due course of law, and for so doing this shall be your sufficient Warrant.

GIVEN under my hand and seal, this 20th day of March in the year of our Lord one thousand eight hundred and sixty-seven.

_____John S. Hollingshead_____ L.S.
Metropolitan Police Magistrate and
a Justice of the Peace.

On verso:
2247.
United States vs. Wm. Johnson
Witness
Wm. Ross
Wm. Taylor
at Eslen's Cor. N.
& New Jersey Ave.

District of Columbia,

County of Washington, TO WIT:

To the Warden of the Jail in the District of Columbia :

RECEIVE into your custody the body of *William Johnson* , Metropolitan Police Officer of the said County, herewith sent by *E. C. Eaton* , a Metropolitan brought before me, *John S. Hollingshead* Magistrate and one of the Justices of the Peace, in and for the said County, and charged before me upon the oath of *William Eng* with having committed an assault and battery on him with intent to kill him by throwing a whole brick at him while his back was turned and striking him on the head with the same on thursday in the county aforesaid

him therefore safely keep in your said custody until he shall be discharged by due course of law, and for so doing this shall be your sufficient Warrant.

GIVEN under my hand and seal, this *20th* day of *March*

in the year of our Lord one thousand eight hundred and sixty-*seven*

John Hollingshead

[L.S.]

Metropolitan Police Magistrate and a Justice of the Peace.

DISTRICT OF COLUMBIA,

COUNTY OF WASHINGTON, TO WIT:

To the Warden of the Jail in the District of Columbia:

RECEIVE into your custody the body of Arthur Chase herewith sent by A.D. Higton, Metropolitan Police Officer of the said County, brought before me, the undersigned, a Metropolitan Police Magistrate and one of the Justices of the Peace in and for the said County, and charged before me upon the oath of Peter Brasman with having

stolen and carried away on the 15th March 1867 in said County a piece of cloth of the value of eight dollars, the property of said Peter Brasman

him therefore safely keep in your said custody until he shall be discharged by due course of law, and for so doing this shall be your sufficient Warrant.

GIVEN under my hand and seal, this 22d day of March in the year of our Lord one thousand eight hundred and sixty-seven.

_____W. Thompson_____L.S.
Metropolitan Police Magistrate and
a Justice of the Peace.

On verso:
2250
Commitment of Arthur Chase for Criminal Court in Session
U.S. Witnesses
Kitty Brasman New York
Avenue between 17th & 18th St.
Townsend Turner
Wm. Smith Pawnbroker 9th St.
between Pe. Ave. & D St.

District of Columbia,

County of Washington, TO WIT:

To the Warden of the Jail in the District of Columbia:

Receive into your custody the body of *Peter Brennan*, herewith sent by _____ , the undersigned Police Magistrate and one of the Justices of the Peace in and for the said County, and charged before me upon the oath of *Peter Brennan*,

brought before me, _Hammond D. Arthur Chase_ , Metropolitan Police Officer of the said County, a Metropolitan

with having stolen and carried away on the 18th day of March 1867 .....

him therefore safely keep in your said custody until he shall be discharged by due course of law, and for so doing this shall be your sufficient Warrant.

GIVEN under my hand and seal, this _29th_ day of _March_ in the year of our Lord one thousand eight hundred and sixty-_seven_

_____
Metropolitan Police Magistrate and Justice of the Peace.

L.S.

2250.

Commitment of
Arthur Chase for
Criminal Court in session

U S witnesses
Kitty Brannan New York
Avenue between 17 th & 18 th st
Townsend Sumer —
Wm Smith Pawnbroker 9 th st
between P av & D st

U.S. MARSHAL'S OFFICE.
Washington City, D.C.,   March 25, 1867.

Mr. T.B. Brown

Warden U.S. Jail, D.C.

Release from Jail the following=named Prisoner, to be brought before the Judge now in session, viz:

Kitty Swann

D.S. Gooding
U.S. Marshal, D.C.

On verso:
2245.

U. S. Marshal's Office,

Washington City, D. C., March 25, 1867.

Mr. T. G. Brown

Warden U. S. Jail, D. C.

Release from Jail the following-named Prisoner, to be brought before the Judge now in session, viz:

Kitty Brown

A. G. Gooding
U. S. Marshal, D. C.

U.S. Marshal's Office,
Washington City, D.C., March 26, 1867.

Mr. T.B. Brown

Warden U.S. Jail, D.C.

Release from Jail the following=named Prisoner, to be brought before the Judge now in session, viz:

William Johnson

D.S. Gooding
U.S. Marshal, D.C.

On verso:
2247.

U. S. Marshal's Office,

Washington City, D. C., March 26, 1867.

Mr. D. B. Brown
Warden U. S. Jail, D. C.
Release from Jail the following=named Prisoner ; to be brought before the Judge now in session, viz:
William Johnson

D.S. Gooding
U. S. Marshal, D. C.

General Commitment.—Printed and Sold by R.A. Waters, Pa. Ave., bet.
11th and 12th streets.

DISTRICT OF COLUMBIA,

COUNTY OF WASHINGTON, To wit:

To the Warden of Jail of the District of Columbia:

RECEIVE into your custody the body of Samuel James herewith sent by Joseph Acton, Constable of the said County, brought before me, the undersigned, one of the Justices of the Peace in and for the said County, and charged before me upon the oath of Peter Nelson with having

stolen and carried away on the 6th June 1867 in said County a coat the property of said Peter Nelson

him therefore safely keep in your said custody until he shall be discharged by due course of law; and for so doing this shall be your sufficient warrant.

GIVEN under my hand and seal this 6th day of June in the year of our Lord one thousand eight hundred and sixty-seven.

W. Thompson
J.P.   SEAL

On verso:
192.
Commitment of Samuel James
for June term of Criminal Court.
U.S. Witnesses
Peter Nelson   Howard House corner 9th St. & Pa. Av.
James King   6th St. east between A & B Capitol
George Miller   6th St. betwn. A & B Capitol Hill

General Commitment —Printed and Sold by R. A. Waters, Pa. Ave. bet. 11th and 12th streets.

DISTRICT OF COLUMBIA,

COUNTY OF WASHINGTON, To wit:

To the Warden of Jail of the District of Columbia:

RECEIVE into your custody the body of *Samuel James*

herewith sent by *Joseph Peter,* ————— Constable of the said County,

brought before me, *the undersigned* ————— one of the

Justices of the Peace in and for the said County, and charged before me upon the oath of

Peter Nelson with having

stolen and carried away on the 6th Sun 187 in said county, a coat the property of said Peter Nelson

him therefore safely keep in your said custody until he shall be discharged by due course of law ; and for so doing this shall be your sufficient warrant

GIVEN under my hand and seal this *One* day of *June*

in the year of our Lord one thousand eight hundred and sixty *seven*

[SEAL]

192.

Commitment of
Samuel James for
June term of Criminal
Court

US witnesses

Peter Nelson Howard House
corner 9th st & Pa Av.
James King 6th st east, betwee
A & B Capitol Hill
George Miller 6th st. betwn A & B
Cap Hill

DISTRICT OF COLUMBIA,

COUNTY OF WASHINGTON, TO WIT:

To the Warden of the Jail in the District of Columbia:

RECEIVE into your custody the body of Frederick Buckner herewith sent by a, Metropolitan Police Officer of the said County, brought before me, William W. Tucker, a Metropolitan Police Magistrate and one of the Justices of the Peace in and for the said County, and charged before me upon the oath of Mary Mangon with having

feloniously stolen taken and carried away twelve chickens of the value of four dollars and fifty cents the property of said Mary Mangon on or about the sixth day of June 1867 in the district and county aforesaid

him therefore safely keep in your said custody until he shall be discharged by due course of law, and for so doing this shall be your sufficient Warrant.

GIVEN under my hand and seal, this eighth day of June in the year of our Lord one thousand eight hundred and sixty-seven.

___William W. Tucker___ L.S.
Metropolitan Police Magistrate and
a Justice of the Peace.

On verso:
193.
Commitment of Frederick Buckner
for larceny
Summon for U.S.
Mary Mangon) G Street south between
Mahaly Soniter) 3rd & 4 1/2 Street
James W. Gessford, Lt. M.P. 10th prect.

District of Columbia,

County of Washington, TO-WIT:

To the Warden of the Jail in the District of Columbia:

RECEIVE into your custody the body of _Forbes N. Shekner_

herewith sent by _____, Metropolitan Police Officer of the said County,

brought before me, _William B. Webb_ , a Metropolitan

Police Magistrate and one of the Justices of the Peace in and for the said County, and charged before me

upon the oath of _Mary Morgan_ with having

feloniously stolen, taken and carried away twelve chickens of the value of four dollars, said chickens being the property of said Mary Morgan on or about the 16th day of June 1867 in the county and County aforesaid

him therefore safely keep in your said custody until he shall be discharged by due course of law, and for

so doing this shall be your sufficient Warrant.

GIVEN under my hand and seal, this _Eighth_ day of _June_

in the year of our Lord one thousand eight hundred and sixty-Seven.

[L.S.]

William B. Webb

Metropolitan Police Magistrate and a Justice of the Peace.

DISTRICT OF COLUMBIA,   )
) to wit:

    COUNTY OF WASHINGTON,   )

To the Warden of the Jail in the District of Columbia:

RECEIVE into your custody the body of Ellen Lewis & Betty Brown (col) herewith sent by James McColgan, Metropolitan Police Officer of the said County, brought before me, Charles Walter, one of the Justices of the Peace in and for the said County, and charged before me upon the oath of H. Davis with having

stolen a gold ring & $10-cash
   (for a hearing)

them therefore safely keep in your said custody until they shall be discharged by due course of law, and for so doing this shall be your sufficient warrant.

GIVEN under my hand and seal, this 8th day of June 1867.

                           Charles Walter   J.P.   SEAL

On verso:
194-195
Committment of
Ellen Lewis &
Betty Brown (col)
for a hearing

CHAS. WALTER, 397 D street, opposite City Hall.

District of Columbia,

COUNTY OF WASHINGTON, } to wit:

To the Warden of the Jail in the District of Columbia:

RECEIVE into your custody the body of *Ellen Lewis & Betty Brown (col)*

herewith sent by *James McTogart* Metropolitan Police Officer of the said County,

brought before me, *Charles Walter* one of the

Justices of the Peace in and for the said County, and charged before me upon the oath of

Davis with having

Stolen a gold ring of $10 — each

(for a hearing)

Then therefore safely keep in your said custody until they shall be discharged by due course of law, and for so doing this shall be your sufficient warrant.

GIVEN under my hand and seal, this *8th* day of *June* 186*7*,

Charles Walter J. P. (SEAL)

194–195.

No Committment
of
Ellen Lewis
&
Betty Brown

for a hearing

<u>CHAS. WALTER, 397 D street, opposite City Hall.</u>

DISTRICT OF COLUMBIA,

    COUNTY OF WASHINGTON,)

To the Warden of the Jail in the District of Columbia:

    WHEREAS Ellen Lewis and Betty Brown (col). was committed to your Jail and custody on the 8th day of June 1867 upon a charge of

stealing a gold ring and $10 (for a hearing)

by me, the subscriber, one of the Justices of the Peace in and for the said County, before me, found sufficient surety for a hearing, you are therefore hereby commanded, that if the said Ellen Lewis & Betty Brown do remain in Jail for the said cause, and none other, then you forbear to detain them any longer, but deliver them thence, and suffer them to go at large.

    GIVEN under my hand and seal, this 12th day of June 1867.

                Charles Walter   J.P.   SEAL

On verso:
194-195
Release of
Ellen Lewis
Betty Brown

District of Columbia,

COUNTY OF WASHINGTON, ⟩ to wit:

To the Warden of the Jail in the District of Columbia:

WHEREAS *Ellen Lewis and Betty Brown (col)* was committed to your Jail and custody on the *8th* day of *June 1867* — upon a charge of *Stealing a gold ring and pin for a hearing)*

by me, the subscriber, one of the Justices of the Peace in and for the said County, hath, before me, found sufficient surety for ~~his personal appearance at our next Criminal Court, to be held on the ~~ day of ~~ next, then and there to answer such matter as shall be objected against him for the offence aforesaid.~~ *a hearing & Betty Brown* You are therefore hereby commanded, that if the said *Ellen Lewis* ——— do remain in Jail for the said cause, and none other, then you forbear to detain *them* any longer, but deliver *them* thence, and suffer *them* to go at large.

GIVEN under my hand and seal, this *12th* day of *June* 186*7*

Geo. Walter J. P. (SEAL)

DISTRICT OF COLUMBIA,

COUNTY OF WASHINGTON, to wit:

To the Warden of the Jail in the District of Columbia:

WHEREAS Neely Gladmon was committed to your Jail and custody on the 11 day of June 1867 upon a charge of assaulting with intent to kill E.L. Dawson, and for a further hearing on the 13th instant at 6 1/2 oclock P.M.

by me, the subscriber, Metropolitan Police Magistrate and one of the Justices of the Peace in and for the said County, You are hereby commanded, that if the said, Neely Gladmon do remain in Jail for the said cause, and none other, then you forbear to detain him any longer, but deliver him thence to Thos. Price N.P. for further hearing.

GIVEN under my hand and seal, this 13th day of June in the year of Lord one thousand eight hundred and sixty-seven.

_____W. Thompson_____ L.S.
Met'n Police Magistrate and J.P.

On verso:
204
Release of Neely Gladmon

District of Columbia,

COUNTY OF WASHINGTON, to wit:

To the Warden of the Jail in the District of Columbia :

Whereas Neely Gladman   was committed to your

Jail and custody on the ___ day of June 1867 upon a charge of Stealing

a silk velvet hat of I Dauson and for a further hearing

on the 13 instant at O'clock P.M.

by me, the subscriber, Metropolitan Police Magistrate and one of the Justices of the Peace in

and for the said County, ~~hath before me, found sufficient surety for his personal appearance at~~

~~our next Criminal Court, to be held on the~~ ___ day of ___

~~next, then and there to answer such matter as shall be objected against him for the offense afore~~

~~said~~. You are therefore hereby commanded, that if the said Neely Gladman

do remain in Jail for the said cause, and none other, then you forbear to detain him any longer,

but deliver him thence, ~~and suffer him to go at large,~~ to allow free N.P. for

further hearing.

GIVEN under my hand and seal, this 13th day of June

in the year of Lord one thousand eight hundred and sixty. seven

_____

Met'n Police Magistrate and J. P.

[L.S.]

DISTRICT OF COLUMBIA,   )

) to wit:

COUNTY OF WASHINGTON,   )

To the Warden of the Jail in the District of Columbia:

RECEIVE into your custody the body of John H. Francis (col). herewith sent by D. Felt Metropolitan Police Officer of the said County, brought before me, Charles Walter, one of the Justices of the Peace in and for the said County, and charged before me upon the oath of Wm. Philips & George Price with having

stolen $20 in cash & 1 watch of them on the 10 June 1867 in said County

him therefore safely keep in your said custody until he shall be discharged by due course of law, and for so doing this shall be your sufficient warrant.

GIVEN under my hand and seal, this 12 day of June 1867

                           Charles Walter   J.P.   SEAL

On verso:
205
Committment of
John H. Francis (col).
Witnesses
Wm. Philips (col).
George Price (col).
Va. Ave. betw. 2 & 3rd Sts. Islande

District of Columbia,

COUNTY OF WASHINGTON, } to wit:

To the Warden of the Jail in the District of Columbia:

RECEIVE into your custody the body of *John H. Francis (col.)*

herewith sent by *J. Fell Walter* Metropolitan Police Officer of the said County,

brought before me, *Charles Walter* one of the

Justices of the Peace in and for the said County, and charged before me upon the oath of *Wm* with having

Philips & George Price

Stolen $20 in cash & watch & chain

on the premises of the said County

him therefore safely keep in your said custody until he shall be discharged by due course of law, and for so doing this shall be your sufficient warrant.

GIVEN under my hand and seal, this *12* day of *June* 186*7*

Charles Walter J.P. (SEAL)

205.

Commitment
of

John H. Francis (col.)

Witness

Wm Philips (col)

Geo ye Price col —
Ja Ave. betw: 2 & 3rd Sts
Island

To the Warden of the Washington County, Greeting

Receive into your custody Charles Offellow who stands charged before me with stealing a shoulder of Bacon value of $1.25 the property of Nathan Blum on the 14th day of June 1867 in the City of Washington D.C.

You will him safekeep in your said custody for his personal appearance to answer at the next Grand Jury to be held for the County of Washington unless he is discharged by a due course of law and this shall he your sufficient warrant and authority for so doing.

Given under my hand & Seal this 14th day of June

Jas. Cull, J.P.   Seal

To Wm. H. Lusby
Metropolitan Officer

On verso: 201
I summon for U. States
Nathan Blum
Richard Griffin

Jas. Cull J. P.

To the Warden of the Washington County
Greeting,
Receive into your custody
Charles Offellow who stands charged
before me with stealing a shoulder of
Bacon valued $1.25 the property of
Nathan Blum on the 14th day of June
1867 in the City of Washington DC

You will him safe keep in your safe
custody for his personal appearance to
answer at the next Grand Jury to be held
for the County of Washington
unless he is discharged by a
due course of Law And this shall be
your sufficient warrant and authority
for so doing

Given under my hand & seal this
14th day of June

J. A. Hall J.P.

To Officer H. Lusby
Metropolitan Officer

District of Columbia.   )

) to wit:

County of Washington,   )

To the warden of the Jail in the District of Columbia:

RECEIVE into your custody the body of John H. Brooks (col) alias Gant herewith sent by Saml. P. Crown, Metropolitan Police Officer of the said County, brought before me, Charles Walter, one of the Justices of the Peace in and for the said county, and charged before me upon the oath of Anne H. Gant (col.) with having

committed assault & battery on her with intent to kill on the 12 June 1867 in said County

him therefore safely keep in your said custody until he shall be discharged by due course of law, and for so doing this shall be your sufficient warrant.

GIVEN under my hand and seal, this 13th day of June 1867.

                                   Chas. Walter   J.P.   SEAL

On verso:
206
Committment of John H. Brooks (col)
alias Gant
Witnesses Anne H. Gant (col.)
Campbell Hospital

District of Columbia, }
COUNTY OF WASHINGTON, } to wit:

To the Warden of the Jail in the District of Columbia:

RECEIVE into your custody the body of *John H. Brooks (alias Jutergard)* herewith sent by *Abiel S. Crown* Metropolitan Police Officer of the said County, brought before me, *Chas. Walter* one of the Justices of the Peace in and for the said County, and charged before me upon the oath of *Anne* with having

committed assault & battery on her with intent to ride on the regular fare in said County

him therefore safely keep in your said custody until he shall be discharged by due course of law, and for so doing this shall be your sufficient warrant.

GIVEN under my hand and seal, this *19th* day of *June* 186*7*

Chas. Walter J. P. (SEAL)

206

Committment
of
John H Brooks or
alias Gant

Mr Anefer
Anne H Gant col.
        Campbell Hospital

DISTRICT OF COLUMBIA,

COUNTY OF WASHINGTON, To wit:

To the warden of the Jail in the District of Columbia:

RECEIVE into your custody the body of James Alston herewith sent by J.W. Pool, Metropolitan Police Officer of the said County, brought before me, William W. Tucker, one of the Justices of the Peace in and for the said County, and charged before me upon the oath of James Selden with having

feloniously stolen taken and carried away a mule of the value of seventy five dollars the property of said James Selden on or about the fifth day of December 1866 in the District and County aforesaid

him therefore safely keep in your said custody until he shall be discharged by due course of law, and for so doing this shall be your sufficient Warrant.

GIVEN under my hand and seal, this thirteenth day of June in the year of our Lord one thousand eight hundred and sixty-seven.

____William W. Tucker____   SEAL.
Justice of the Peace

On verso: 207
Commitment of
James Alston
for Larceny

Summon for U.S.
James Selden 7th Street between M & North
J.W. Pool M.P. 2nd Prct.
Augustus Selden as Jas. Seldens

DISTRICT OF COLUMBIA,

COUNTY OF WASHINGTON, *To wit:*

To the Warden of the Jail in the District of Columbia:

RECEIVE into your custody the body of *John Doe*

herewith sent by *William H. Tucker*, Metropolitan Police Officer of the said County,

brought before me, *William H. Tucker*, Superintendent
of Metropolitan Police and ex-officio one of the Justices of the Peace in and for the said County, and
charged before me upon the oath of *James Allen* with having

feloniously stolen taken and carried away a Bale of blankets of Seventy five dollars the property of Eric Phillips on or about the fifth of December 1866 in the District of Columbia apprising

him therefore safely keep in your said custody until he shall be discharged by due course of law, and for so
doing this shall be your sufficient Warrant.

GIVEN under my hand and seal, this *thirteenth* day of *June*
in the year of our Lord one thousand eight hundred and sixty *seven*

William H. Tucker
⟨⟨⟨ SEAL. ⟩⟩⟩
Supt. Met'n Police and ex-officio a Justice of the Peace.

General Commitment.—Printed and Sold by R.A. Waters, Pa. Ave. bet.
11th and 12th streets.

DISTRICT OF COLUMBIA,

WASHINGTON COUNTY to wit:

To the warden of the Jail of the District of Columbia:

RECEIVE into your custody the body of John G. Anthony herewith sent by S.W. Koontz, Constable of the said County, brought before me, the undersigned, one of the Justices of the Peace in and for the said County, and charged before me upon the oath of Maria Anthony with having

committed and assault and battery upon her in the county aforesaid, on the 12th day of June, 1867.

him therefore safely keep in your said custody until he shall find security for his appearance at the present Criminal Court, or be discharged by due course of law, and for so doing this shall be your sufficient warrant.

GIVEN under my hand and seal this 13th day of June, in the year of our Lord one thousand eight hundred and sixty-seven.

John T.C. Clark,   J.P.

On verso: 208.
United States vs.
John G. Anthony

General Commitment.—Printed and Sold by R. A. Waters, Pa. Ave. bet. 11th and 12th streets.

DISTRICT OF COLUMBIA.

WASHINGTON COUNTY to wit:

To the Warden of the Jail of the District of Columbia;

RECEIVE into your custody the body of *John S. Anthony*

herewith sent by *C. W. Harry* _____ Constable of the said County,

brought before me, *the undersigned* _____ one of the

Justices of the Peace in and for the said County, and charged before me upon the oath of

Bara Anthony _____ with having

committed and brought here before me at his own request in

County appeared in this 12th day of June, 1867

_____

_____

And securing for his absence at the hour, transient about

him therefore safely keep in your said custody until he shall be discharged by due course

of law, and for so doing this shall be your sufficient warrant

GIVEN under my hand and seal this *13th* _____ day of *June,*

in the year of our Lord one thousand eight hundred and sixty-*seven,*

John C. W. Harry, JP.

[SEAL]

U.S. MARSHAL'S OFFICE,
WASHINGTON CITY, D.C., June 14, 1867

Mr. T.B. Brown

    Warden U.S. Jail. D.C.

    Receive into your custody the following=named Prisoner, for safe=keeping until released, viz:

       J. W. Edmondson

                D.S. Gooding
                U.S. Marshal, D.C.

On verso: 212.

U. S. Marshal's Office,

Washington City, D. C., May 14, 1867.

Mr. T. B. Brown

Warden U. S. Jail, D. C.

Receive into your custody the following-named Prisoner, for safe-keeping until released, viz:

D. M. Henderson

D. S. Gooding
U. S. Marshal, D. C.

U.S. MARSHAL'S OFFICE,
Washington City, D.C.,   June 22, 1867

Mr. T.B. Brown

Warden U.S. Jail, D.C.

Release from your custody the following=named Prisoner, for Bail:

John H. Brooks

D.S. Gooding
U.S. Marshal, D.C.

On verso: 206

Mr. J. B. Brown,

Warden U. S. Jail, D. C.

Release from your custody the following-named Prisoners, for

safe keeping, ____ viz.

____ U. S. Marshal, D. C.

U.S. MARSHAL'S OFFICE,
WASHINGTON CITY. D.C.,   June 15. 1867

Mr. T.B. Brown

    Warden U.S. Jail, D.C.

    Release from custody the following=named Prisoner:

    John G. Anthony for Bail

              David S. Gooding
              U.S. Marshal, D.C.

On verso: 208

Washington City, D. C., June 15, 1878

Mr. J. B. Brown

Warden U. S. Jail, D. C.

Receive into your custody the following-named Prisoner, ~

~

John A. Sarrell

for father, E. Anthony for Bail

David S. ~

U. S. Marshal, D. C.

U.S. Marshal's Office,
Washington City, D.C.,   July 16th, 1867.

Mr. T.B. Brown

Warden U. S. Jail. D.C.

Release from your custody the following=named Prisoner,

Leroy Wallace

D.S. Gooding
U.S. Marshal. D.C.

On verso: 224

𝕌. 𝕊. 𝕄arshal's 𝕆ffice,

Washington City, D. C., July 16th, 186

Mr. J. B. Blades

Warden U. S. Jail, D. C.

Dear Sir,

Receive into your custody the following=named Prisoner; for
safe keeping until delivered, viz:

Lorey Wallace

J. Perri
U. S. Marshal, D. C.

U.S. MARSHAL's OFFICE
WASHINGTON CITY, D.C. Decr. 3d, 1867

W.H. Heustis

      I have this day rec'd the President of the U.S. warrant of pardon for Arthur Chase now confined in Jail.

      You will release said Chase from further imprisonment upon the receipt of this letter.

                                 I am & c.
                                 D.S. Gooding
                                 U.S. Marshal

On verso:
Release of Arthur Chase

U.S. Marshals Office
Washington City, D.C.
Dec. __ 1867

W H Hu____

_____ the _____ ____ the _____ of the _____ of said ___ for ____ ____ ____ now confined in Jail. You will release said ____ from _____ ___ prisoners _____ the receipt of this letter

_____

D____ Gooding
U.S. Marshal

CRIMINAL COURT, DEC. TERM, 1867.

Samuel James
Convicted of Larceny
sentenced to suffer imprisonment and
labor in the Penitentiary for the District
of Columbia for the period of twenty days

Test:

R.J. Meigs Clerk.
Dec. 11, 1867

On verso: June 192

CRIMINAL COURT, *Dec* TERM, 186 *7*.

Samuel James

Convicted of *Larceny*

sentenced to suffer imprisonment and labor in the

Penitentiary for the District of Columbia for the

period of *Twenty days*

Test:

R. J. Meigs Clerk.

Dec 11. 1867

Washington City, D.C.,   Jany. 6. 1868.

Mr W.H. Heustes

Warden U.S. Jail, D.C.

Release from your custody:

James Alston, this day pardoned by the President of the United States.

D.S. Gooding
U.S. Marshal, D.C.

On verso:
207
June

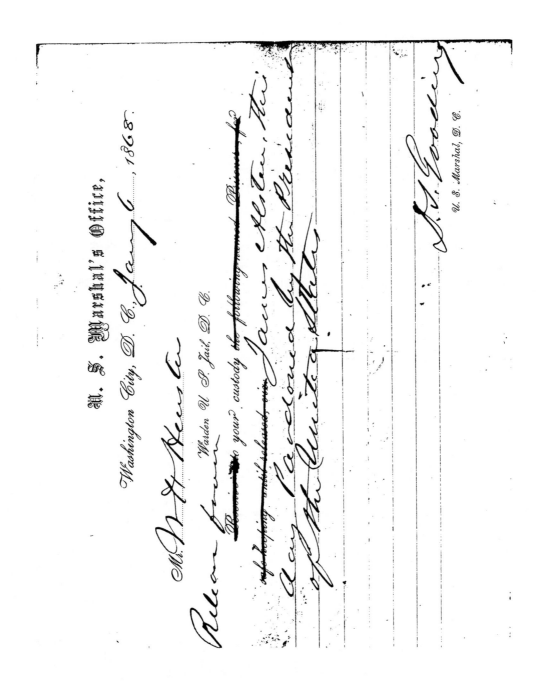

U. S. Marshal's Office,

Washington City, D. C., Jan'y 6......, 1868.

Mr. N. H. Rees Co

Warden U. S. Jail, D. C.

Release from your custody the following named Prisoner to

wit: having been released over Jacob Allen, the

day paroled by the President

of the United States.

J. S. Gooding

U. S. Marshal, D. C.

General Commitment.—Printed and Sold by R.A. Waters, Pa. Ave. bet. 11th and 12th streets.

DISTRICT OF COLUMBIA,

COUNTY OF WASHINGTON, To wit:

To the Warden of Jail of the District of Columbia:

RECEIVE into your custody the body of John Johnson & Jesse Gibson herewith sent by Benj. Leach M.P. of the said County, brought before me, O.E. P. Hazard, one of the Justices of the Peace in and for the said County, and charged before me upon the oath of John Dillard with having

made threats of personal violence towards him on the 7th day of Jany. 1868

them therefore safely keep in your said custody until he shall be discharged by due course of law; and for so doing this shall be your sufficient warrant.

GIVEN under my hand and seal this 7th day of Jany. in the year of our Lord one thousand eight hundred and sixty-eight.

<u>   O.E. P. Hazard   </u>   SEAL.

On verso: 802-803
Commitment for
John Johnson & Jesse Gibson

Annotated on obverse:
 18
  6
108

General Commitment.—Printed and Sold by R. A. Waters, Pa. Ave. bet. 11th and 12th streets.

DISTRICT OF COLUMBIA,

COUNTY OF WASHINGTON, *To wit:*

To the Warden of Jail of the District of Columbia:

RECEIVE into your custody the body of *John Thomas & Jane Gibson*

herewith sent by *_____* Constable of the said County,

brought before me, *O. E. Hazard* one of the

Justices of the Peace in and for the said County, and charged before me upon the oath of

_____ with having

_____

_____

_____

_____ him therefore safely keep in your said custody until he shall be discharged by due course

of law; and for so doing this shall be your sufficient warrant.

GIVEN under my hand and seal this *7th* day of *____*

in the year of our Lord one thousand eight hundred and sixty *eight*

O. E. Hazard

[SEAL]

DISTRICT OF COLUMBIA,   )
) to wit:
COUNTY OF WASHINGTON,   )

To the Warden of the Jail in the District of Columbia:

RECEIVE into your custody the body of John Bowen herewith sent by L.H. Hollinberger, Metropolitan Police Officer of the said County, brought before me, Charles Walter, one of the Justices of the Peace in and for the said County, and charged before me upon the oath of L.H. Hollinberger with having

        stolen a matting
        (for a hearing)

him therefore safely keep in your said custody until he shall be discharged by due course of law, and for so doing this shall be your sufficient warrant.

GIVEN under my hand and seal, this 9th day of January 1868.

                        Chas. Walter   J.P.   SEAL.

On verso:
807
Committment of John Bowen
for a hearing

District of Columbia,
County of Washington, } to wit:

To the Warden of the Jail in the District of Columbia:

RECEIVE into your custody the body of *John Bowen*

herewith sent by *L. H. Shellenberger* Metropolitan Police Officer of the said County,

brought before me, *Charles Walter* one of the

Justices of the Peace in and for the said County, and charged before me upon the oath of *L. H.* with having

Shellenberger

Stolen a Mattress

(for a hearing)

him therefore safely keep in your said custody until he shall be discharged by due course of law, and for so doing this shall be your sufficient warrant.

GIVEN under my hand and seal, this *9* day of *Jany* 186*8*

Chas Walter J.P. (SEAL)

5548. 437 Jail

CRIMINAL COURT, December Term, 1867.
William Johnson
Convicted of assault & Battery
sentenced to be imprisoned in the common
jail for the county of Washington for the
period of Sixty Days

Test:

                    R.J. Meigs   Clerk.
                    Feby 7, 1868

1548. 437 Jail

CRIMINAL COURT, December Term, 186 7

William Johnson

Convicted of Assault & Battery

sentenced to be imprisoned in the common jail

for the county of Washington for the period

of Sixty days

Test :

R. J. Meigs Clerk.
Feby 7, 1868

Mr. W.H. Heustes

Warden U.S. Jail, D.C.

Release from your custody the following=named Prisoner:

John Johnson
Jesse Gibson

D.S. Gooding
U.S. Marshal, D.C.

On verso: 802-803
Jury

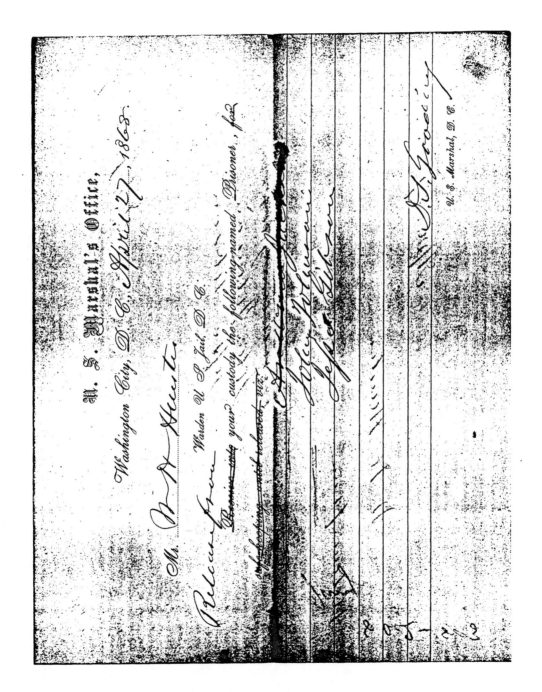

DISTRICT OF COLUMBIA,

COUNTY OF WASHINGTON, TO WIT:

To the Warden of the Jail in the District of Columbia:

Receive into your custody the body of William Cole herewith sent by Off. D. Noble, Metropolitan Police Officer of the said County, brought before me, M.V. Buckey, a Metropolitan Police Magistrate and one of the Justices of the Peace in and for the said County, and charged before me upon the oath of John M. White with having

feloniously, stealing, taking and carrying away, one shoulder of Bacon, the property of J.M. White on the 5th day of August 1868 in the County aforesaid valued at $2.87.

him therefore safely keep in your said custody until he shall be discharged by due course of law, and for so doing this shall be your sufficient Warrant.

GIVEN under my hand and seal, this 5th day of August in the year of our Lord one thousand eight hundred and sixty-eight.

_____M.V. Buckey_____L.S.
Metropolitan Police Magistrate and
a Justice of the Peace.

On verso: No. 1387
United States v.s. William Cole

Summons for U. States
John M. White
William H. Sullivan
Grafton Harper
Thos. White

District of Columbia,

County of Washington, TO WIT:

To the Warden of the Jail in the District of Columbia;,

RECEIVE into your custody the body of *William Cole* _____, Metropolitan Police Officer of the said County, herewith sent by *A D Cole* _____ , a Metropolitan brought before me, *Wm Twekley* _____

Police Magistrate and one of the Justices of the Peace in and for the said County, and charged before me

upon the oath of *John M White* _____ with having

Feloniously, Stealing taking and carrying away one Shoulder of Bacon, the property of Mr White on the 3rd day of August 1868 in the County aforesaid. Valued at $2.87

him therefore safely keep in your said custody until he shall be discharged by due course of law, and for

so doing this shall be your sufficient Warrant.

GIVEN under my hand and seal, this *5th* day of *August*

in the year of our Lord one thousand eight hundred and sixty- *eight*.

[L.S.]

Wm Twekley

Metropolitan Police Magistrate and a Justice of the Peace.

DISTRICT OF COLUMBIA,

COUNTY OF WASHINGTON, TO WIT:

To the Warden of the Jail in the District of Columbia:

RECEIVE into your custody the body of Patrick Murphey herewith sent by J.F. Guy, or any qualified, Metropolitan Police Officer of the said County, brought before me, the Subscriber, a Metropolitan Police Magistrate and one of the Justices of the Peace in and for the said County, and charged before me upon the oath of Sarah Murphey, Mary Smithey and Mrs. Fagan, & Mrs. Cook, with having

assaulted and threatened to take the life of his wife, the said Sarah Murphey, on the 11th day of August 1868, in said County, and being a drinking man, and violent and uncontrolable temper, she has abundant cause to fear the Patrick will put his threats into execution, and being required by me to give Security in sum of Five Hundred dollars, to keep the peace for one year, and failing give Security,

him therefore safely keep in your said custody until he shall find sureties or be discharged by due course of law, and for so doing this shall be your sufficient Warrant.

GIVEN under my hand and seal, this 12th day of August, in the year of our Lord one thousand eight hundred and sixty-eight.

_____D.K. Morsell_____L.S.
Metropolitan Police Magistrate and
a Justice of the Peace.

On verso: 1408
United States viz. comt. Patrick Murphy
Threats
Cepi In Jail

District of Columbia,
County of Washington, TO WIT:

To the Warden of the Jail in the District of Columbia:

RECEIVE into your custody the body of *Patrick Murphey* herewith sent by *J. F. Guy, or any qualified* Metropolitan Police Officer of the said County, brought before me, *subscriber*, a Metropolitan Police Magistrate and one of the Justices of the Peace in and for the said County, and charged before me upon the oath of *Sarah Murphey, Mary Smithey and* *Mrs. Fagan's hired cook* with having *assaulted and threatened to take the life of his wife. The said Sarah Murphey on the 1st day of August 1868 in said County and being so drinking than, and violent and incorrigible temper, she had abundant cause to fear the Patrick will did threats into execution, and being required me, I give security in sum of Five hundred dollars, to keep the peace for one year, and failing in such security* on...

him therefore safely keep in your said custody until he shall be discharged by due course of law, and for so doing this shall be your sufficient Warrant.

GIVEN under my hand and seal, this *10th* day of *August* in the year of our Lord one thousand eight hundred and sixty-*eight*.

[signature]

——————————————
Metropolitan Police Magistrate and a Justice of the Peace.

L.S.

DISTRICT OF COLUMBIA,

COUNTY OF WASHINGTON, to wit:

To the Warden of the Jail in the District of Columbia:

WHEREAS Patrick Murphy was committed to your Jail and custody on the 12th day of August 1868 upon a charge of assaulting and threatening Sarah Murphy his wife, on the oath of the said Sarah Murphy and others, in default of Security to keep the peace for one year,

by me, the subscriber, Metropolitan Police Magistrate and one of the Justices of the Peace in and for the said County, hash, before me, found sufficient surety to keep the peace as aforesaid,

You are therefore hereby commanded, that if the said Murphy do remain in Jail for the said cause, and none other, then you forbear to detain him any longer, but deliver him thence, and suffer him to go at large.

GIVEN under my hand and seal, this 14th day of August, in the year of Lord one thousand eight hundred and sixty-eight.

　　　　　　　　　　　___D.K. Morsell___ L.S.
　　　　　　　　　　　Met'n Police Magistrate and J.P.

On verso: 1408
United States viz. Release
Patrick Murphy

District of Columbia,

COUNTY OF WASHINGTON, *to wit:*

To the Warden of the Jail in the District of Columbia :

Whereas *Patrick Murphy* was committed to your Jail and custody on the *19th* day of *August 1868* upon a charge of *Assaulting on* ~~Bernard Murphy~~ *Murphy history? On the oats of Bernard* ~~Murphy and others, in default of security to keep~~ *the peace for one year,*

by me, the subscriber, Metropolitan Police Magistrate and one of the Justices of the Peace in and for the said County, hath, before me, found sufficient surety ~~for his personal appearance at our next Criminal Court, to be held on the~~ —— day of *Keep the peace as aforesaid* ~~next, then and there to answer such matter as shall be objected against him for the offense aforesaid:~~ You are therefore hereby commanded, that if the said *Patrick Murphy* do remain in Jail for the said cause, and none other, then you forbear to detain him any longer, but deliver him thence, and suffer him to go at large.

GIVEN under my hand and seal, this *14th* day of *August* in the year of Lord one thousand eight hundred and sixty-*eight.*

L.S.

Met'n Police Magistrate and J. P.

DISTRICT OF COLUMBIA,

COUNTY OF WASHINGTON, To wit:

To the Warden of the Jail in the District of Columbia:

RECEIVE into your custody the body of Isaac Landic herewith sent by James E. Beall, Metropolitan Police Officer of the said County, brought before me, Arthur Shepherd, one of the Justices of the Peace in and for the said County, and charged before me upon the oath of Eliza Davis with having

stolen from her a silver watch of the value of seven dollars, and who is committed to await and answer the charge of petit larceny before the next term of the Criminal Court

him therefore safely keep in your said custody until he shall be discharged by due course of law, and for so doing this shall be your sufficient Warrant.

GIVEN under my hand and seal, this 21st day of August in the year of our Lord one thousand eight hundred and sixty-eight.

_____Arthur Shepherd_____ SEAL.
Justice of the Peace.

On verso:
1426
Commitment of Isaac Landic
Witnesses
Eliza Davis
Wilhelmina King
Wm. B. Bell
All residing at Brightwood, D.C.

DISTRICT OF COLUMBIA,

COUNTY OF WASHINGTON, To wit:

To the Warden of the Jail in the District of Columbia:

RECEIVE into your custody the body of *Grace Landis*

herewith sent by *James E. Bell*, Metropolitan Police Officer of the said County,

brought before me, *Arthur Shipherd*, Superintendent

of Metropolitan Police and ex officio one of the Justices of the Peace in and for the said County, and

charged before me upon the oath of; *Eliza Davis*

with having

stolen from her a string watch of the
valued by seven dollars and fifty cents committee
to avail and deliver the charge of petit
larceny before the next term of the Criminal
Court

him therefore safely keep in your said custody until he shall be discharged by due course of law, and for so

doing this shall be your sufficient Warrant.

GIVEN under my hand and seal, this *21st* day of *August*

in the year of our Lord one thousand eight hundred and sixty *eight*

Arthur Shipherd

⬚ SEAL. ⬚

Supt. Metro Police and ex officio a Justice of the Peace.

DISTRICT OF COLUMBIA,

COUNTY OF WASHINGTON, TO WIT:

To the Warden of the Jail in the District of Columbia:

RECEIVE into your custody the body of Henry Wheeler herewith sent by James E. Beall, Metropolitan Police Officer of the said County, brought before me, Arthur Shepherd, one of the Justices of the Peace in and for th e said County, and charged before me upon the oath of Bernhard Dasenbrock with having

stolen from him a drawer containing money in cents and currency amounting to a sum over three dollars and not over two dollars, and who is to be committed to await and answer the charge of petit larceny before its next term of the Criminal Court of the District of Columbia

him therefore safely keep in your said custody until he shall be discharged by due course of law, and for so doing this shall be your sufficient Warrant.

GIVEN under my hand and seal, this 21st day of August in the year of our Lord one thousand eight hundred and sixty-eight.

_____Arthur Shepherd_____ SEAL.
a Justice of the Peace.

On verso:
1427
Commitment of Henry Wheeler
Witnesses
B. Dasenbrick 12th St. bet. T & U
Emanuel Wilkins 12 St. bet. T & U
Laura Wilkins 12th St. bet. T & U
Jas. Boyle Madison St. bet. M & N.
Peter Folge 11th St. Bet. U & V.

DISTRICT OF COLUMBIA,

COUNTY OF WASHINGTON, To wit:

To the Warden of the Jail in the District of Columbia:

RECEIVE into your custody the body of _Henry Wheeler_ herewith sent by _James L. Beall_, Metropolitan Police Officer of the said County, brought before me, _Arthur Shepherd_, Superintendent of Metropolitan Police and ex-officio one of the Justices of the Peace in and for the said County, and charged before me upon the oath of _Burkhart Reinbrock_ _____ with having

stolen from him a drawer containing money in chloroform and currency amounty to a certain debt Three dollars and fifty one, two dollars and who is to be committed to carrying through through the Charge of felth larceny to make him by the criminal Court the District of

him therefore safely keep in your said custody, until he shall be discharged by due course of law, and for so doing this shall be your sufficient Warrant.

GIVEN under my hand and seal, this _21st_ day of _August_ in the year of our Lord one thousand eight hundred and sixty _eight._

Arthur Shepherd

[SEAL]

Supt. Met'n Police and ex-officio a Justice of the Peace.

DISTRICT OF COLUMBIA,

COUNTY OF WASHINGTON, TO WIT:

To the Warden of the Jail in the District of Columbia:

RECEIVE into your custody the bodies of Thomas Meekins and Richard Carter herewith sent by a, Metropolitan Police Officer of the said County, brought before me, William W. Tucker, a Metropolitan Police Magistrate and one of the Justices of the Peace in and for the said County, and charged before me upon the oath of Nathan Blum with having

feloniously stolen, taken and carried away one piece of canvass (sic) of the value of six dollars and forty cents the property of said Nathan Blum on the twentieth day of August 1868 in the District and County aforesaid

them therefore safely keep in your said custody until they shall be discharged by due course of law, and for so doing this shall be your sufficient Warrant.

GIVEN under my hand and seal, this twenty-first day of August in the year of our Lord one thousand eight hundred and sixty-eight.

_____William W. Tucker_____L.S.
Metropolitan Police Magistrate and
a Justice of the Peace.

On verso:
1428
Commitment of
Thomas Meekins & Richard Carter
Summon for the United States
Nathan Blum) corner of 4th street
Jane Blum) east and D street south
Wm. H. Lusby M.P.
　　　　Sanitary office Hd. quarters

District of Columbia,

County of Washington, TO WIT:

To the Warden of the Jail in the District of Columbia:

RECEIVE into your custody the body of *Thomas Meekins and Richard Carter*
herewith sent by _____, a Metropolitan Police Officer of the said County,
brought before me, *William B. Webb*, a Metropolitan
Police Magistrate and one of the Justices of the 'Peace in and for the said County, and charged before me
upon the oath of *Nathan Blum*

with having

*feloniously stolen, taken and carrying away a piece of Canvas
of the Value of six dollars and forty cents the property of said
Nathan Blum and the twentieth day of August 1868 in
the District and County of said*

I therefore safely keep in your said custody until he shall be discharged by due course of law, and for
so doing this shall be your sufficient Warrant.

GIVEN under my hand and seal, this *twenty first* day of *August*
in the year of our Lord one thousand eight hundred and sixty-eight.

William B. Webb   L.S.

Metropolitan Police Magistrate and a Justice of the Peace.

DISTRICT OF COLUMBIA,

COUNTY OF WASHINGTON, to wit:

To the Warden of the Jail in the District of Columbia

WHEREAS Charles C. Blanchard was committed to your Jail and custody on the 21st day of August, 1868, upon a charge of

Threatening the life of Robert McCemranty in said county, on the 19th day of August 1868, in default of Security to keep the peace,

by me, the subscriber, Metropolitan Police Magistrate and one of the Justices of the Peace in and for the said County, hath before me, found sufficient surety to keep the peace for one year: You are therefore hereby commanded, that if the said Charles C. Blanchard, do remain in Jail for the said cause, and none other, then you forbear to detain him any longer, but deliver him thence, and suffer him to go at large.

GIVEN under my hand and seal, this 21st day of August in the year of Lord one thousand eight hundred and sixty-eight.

_____D.K. Morsell_____ L.S.
Met'n Police Magistrate and J.P.

On verso: 1430
United States viz. Release
Charles C. Blanchard

District of Columbia,

COUNTY OF WASHINGTON, to wit:

To the Warden of the Jail in the District of Columbia:

Whereas *Charles B. Blanchard* was committed to your Jail and custody on the *21st* day of *August 1868* upon a charge of *Threatening the life of Robert McGennany in Fairfax County* by me, the subscriber, Metropolitan Police Magistrate and one of the Justices of the Peace in and for the said County, hath, before me, found sufficient surety ~~for his personal appearance at our next Criminal Court, to be held on the~~ _____ day of _____, ~~then and there to answer such matter as shall be objected against him for the offense afore said:~~ You are therefore hereby commanded, that if the said *Charles B. Blanchard* do remain in Jail for the said cause, and none other, then you forbear to detain him any longer, but deliver him thence, and suffer him to go at large.

On the 19th day of August 1868, in default of security to keep the peace, to

to keep the peace for one year

GIVEN under my hand and seal, this *21st* day of *August* in the year of Lord one thousand eight hundred and sixty-*eight.*

W.B. Wall

L.S.

Met'n Police Magistrate and J. P.

DISTRICT OF COLUMBIA,

COUNTY OF WASHINGTON, TO WIT:

To the Warden of the Jail in the District of Columbia:

RECEIVE into your custody the body of Charles C. Blanchard herewith sent by any qualified, Metropolitan Police Officer of the said County, brought before me, the subscriber, a Metropolitan Police Magistrate and one of the Justices of the Peace in and for the said County, and charged before me upon the oath of Robert McCemrents and Elizabeth McClemrants with having

Made threats that he will take the life of the Roberts, so as to put him in bodily fear, that he will carry his threats into execution, and being required by me, to give
Security in the sum of two hundred and fifty dollars, to keep the peace for one year, and failing to give such security

him therefore safely keep in your said custody until he shall find sureties or be discharged by due course of law, and for so doing this shall be your sufficient Warrant.

GIVEN under my hand and seal, this 21st day of August, in the year of our Lord one thousand eight hundred and sixty-eight.

_____D.K. Morsell_____L.S.
Metropolitan Police Magistrate and
a Justice of the Peace.

On verso: 1431
United States viz. Comt.
Charles C. Blanchard
Threats
In default of security for Peace

District of Columbia,

County of Washington, TO WIT:

To the Warden of the Jail in the District of Columbia:

RECEIVE into your custody the body of

herewith sent by _My graphic_ _____
the subscriber _____

, Metropolitan Police Officer of the said County,

brought before me, _Charles C. Blanchard_ _____ , a Metropolitan

Police Magistrate and one of the Justices of the Peace in and for the said County, and charged before me

upon the oath of _Robert Mc.... and Elizabeth_ _____

Coleman, to _____ _____ with having

.... that he will take this life of this
parties so as to put him in bodily fear, that he
will carry his threat into execution, and being requi-
red to give security within the sum of two hundred
and fifty dollars, to keep the peace for one year, and
failing to give such security — _____

him therefore safely keep in your said custody until he shall _Give security_ be discharged by due course of law, and for

so doing this shall be your sufficient Warrant.

GIVEN under my hand and seal, this _27th_ _____ day of _August_,
in the year of our Lord one thousand eight hundred and sixty-_eight_.

_O.W....._

_____

[L.S.]

Metropolitan Police Magistrate and a Justice of the Peace.

1481

United States

vs. Court

Charles C. Blanchard

Threats —

In default of
Security for Peace

DISTRICT OF COLUMBIA,

COUNTY OF WASHINGTON, TO WIT:

To the Warden of the Jail in the District of Columbia:

RECEIVE into your custody the body of Annie Price and Arney Jones herewith sent by C.C. Langley, or any, Metropolitan Police Officer of the said County, brought before me, the undersigned, a Metropolitan Police Magistrate and one of the Justices of the Peace in and for the said County, and charged before me upon the oath of Michael Conner, Emily Brown, Thomas Biggins, Alice Brannagin, Ellenora Brannigin, Hattie Brannigin, with having

on or about the 22nd day of August 1868, feloniously stolen, taken, and carried away from the residence of the said Michael Conner , at the City of Washington, in said County, about thirty eight dollars, in silver coins, the monies, goods and chattels of the said Michael Conner, and failing to give the security required by law,

them therefore safely keep in your said custody until they shall be discharged by due course of law, and for so doing this shall be your sufficient Warrant.

GIVEN under my hand and seal, this 23rd day of August in the year of our Lord one thousand eight hundred and sixty-eight.

_____D.K. Morsell_____ L.S.
Metropolitan Police Magistrate and
a Justice of the Peace.

On verso: 1436
United States viz: Comt.
Annie Price and Arney Jones
Grand Larceny
Cepi in Jail

Witnesses for U. States,
Michael Conner, 22nd & H Sts.
Emily Brown 23rd & Va. Av.
& Theodorias Mudd
Thos. Biggins, 22nd & F Sts.

Elenora Brannigin   )
Allice Brannigin   ) 22nd & G Sts.
& Hattie Brannigan   )
Chas. C. Langley   M.P.   O. 4th Precinct
W. Wordling
        No. 109 Bridge St. Geo. Town

District of Columbia,
County of Washington, TO WIT:

To the Warden of the Jail in the District of Columbia:

RECEIVE into your custody the body of *Annie Richards Amey Frey*
herewith sent by *E. E. Earley, or Amy*, Metropolitan Police Officer of the said County,
brought before me, *The Undersigned*, a Metropolitan
Police Magistrate and one of the Justices of the Peace in and for the said County, and charged before me
upon the oath of *Michael Downer Craig Brown Thomas Biggins,*

Alice Branagan Ellen Branagin Ellin Branagin
on about the 28 day of August last, feloniously did
[illegible] away from the park of [illegible] Michael come into
[illegible] feloniously did Washington County, [illegible] Thirty eighty [illegible] did
[illegible] the Harris back and charge of the said Michael
[illegible] Washington the sum of twenty required by law

Then therefore safely keep in your said custody until *They* shall be discharged by due course of law, and for
so doing this shall be your sufficient Warrant.

GIVEN under my hand and seal, this *27 ado*   day of *August*
in the year of our Lord one thousand eight hundred and sixty-*eight*.

J. M. Bussell   [L.S.]

Metropolitan Police Magistrate and a Justice of the Peace.

1436

United States
vs Court,—

Annie Price and
Amey Jones

Grand Larceny

Cepi in Jail —

Witnesses for U. States,
Michael Conner 22nd H. Sts —
Emily Brown 23d & A Av,
& Theodocia Mudd —
Thos Riggins, 22nd & F. Sts,

Elenora Brannigan,
Allice Brannigan,
& Hattie Brannigan

22nd H. Sts

Chas C. Langley — M. P. O, H Av Pa

W. Nordling
No 109 Bridge
St G. Town

U.S. MARSHAL'S OFFICE,
Washington City, D.C.,   Sept. 10, 1868

Mr. W.H. Heustes

    Warden U.S. Jail, D.C.

    Release from Jail the following=named Prisoner, to be brought before the Judge now in session, viz:

    Richd. Carter

               D.S. Gooding
               U.S. Marshal, D.C.

On verso: 1428

U. S. Marshal's Office,

Washington City, D. C., Sepr. 10 1868

Mr. B. F. Auets

Warden U. S. Jail, D. C.

Release from Jail the following-named Prisoner, to be

~~brought before the Judge now in session for~~ Pres. Carter

B. J. Earueg

U. S. Marshal, D. C.

DISTRICT OF COLUMBIA,

COUNTY OF WASHINGTON, TO WIT:

To the Warden of the Jail in the District of Columbia:

Receive into your custody the body of Thomas Angel herewith sent by any , Metropolitan Police Officer of the said County, brought before me, the subscriber, a Metropolitan Police Magistrate and one of the Justices of the Peace in and for the said County, and charged before me upon the oath of Mary C. Angel his wife,

with abusing and turning her out of doors in the night, in the rain, and threatening her life, on the 14th day of September 1868, in said County, and being required by me to give security in the sum two hundred dollars, to keep the peace for year, and failing to give such security,

him therefore safely keep in your said custody until he shall find security for the peace, or be discharged by due course of law, and for so doing this shall be your sufficient Warrant.

GIVEN under my hand and seal, this 15th day of September in the year of our Lord one thousand eight hundred and sixty-eight.

_____D.K. Morsell_____ L.S.
Metropolitan Police Magistrate and
a Justice of the Peace.

On verso:
1515
United States viz. Comt.
Thomas Angel
In default of security for peace
Cepi in Jail

District of Columbia,

County of Washington, TO WIT:

To the Warden of the Jail in the District of Columbia:

RECEIVE into your custody the body of *Thomas Angel*

herewith sent by *Ang,* ————————, Metropolitan Police Officer of the said County,

brought before me, *the subscriber,* ———————— a Metropolitan

Police Magistrate and one of the Justices of the Peace in and for the said County, and charged before me

upon the oath of *Mary G. Angel his wife,*

with abusing and turning her out of doors in the night in the rain, and threatening her life on the 14th day of September 1865 in said County. And being required by me to give security to the sum two hundred Dollars to keep the peace for year, and failing to give such security,

him therefore safely keep in your said custody until he shall be discharged by due course of law, and for

so doing this shall be your sufficient Warrant.

GIVEN under my hand and seal, this *18th* day of *September*

in the year of our Lord one thousand eight hundred and sixty-*eight*

[L.S.]

Metropolitan Police Magistrate and a Justice of the Peace.

DISTRICT OF COLUMBIA,

COUNTY OF WASHINGTON, To wit:

To the warden of the Jail in the District of Columbia:

RECEIVE into your custody the body of Suker *alias* William Bell herewith sent by, Metropolitan Police Officer of the said County, brought before me, William C. Harper, one of the Justices of the Peace in and for the said County, and charged before me upon the oath of M. Morton Peake with having

on the 16th day of September 1868, in the County and District aforesaid, feloniously stolen, taken and carried away one woolen bed comforter of the value of Three dollars the property of L. J. Joyce

him therefore safely keep in your said custody until he shall find surety in the sum of one hundred dollars, and for so doing this shall be your sufficient Warrant.

GIVEN under my hand and seal, this 18th day of September in the year of our Lord one thousand eight hundred and sixty-eight.

_____Wm. C. Harper___J.P.____ SEAL.
a Justice of the Peace.

On verso:
1527
Jail Committment
United States vs. Suker *alias* Wm. Bell
Petit Larceny

M. Morton Peake) cor. 15th & D sts. at the
L. J. Joyce)Photograph Car
Jane Randall) Ohio Avenue
Rosana Thompson) near Raub's
Louisa Thompson) Soap Factory

DISTRICT OF COLUMBIA,

COUNTY OF WASHINGTON, To wit:

To the Warden of the Jail in the District of Columbia:

RECEIVE into your custody the body of *Luther alias William Bell*

herewith sent by _____, Metropolitan Police Officer of the said County,

brought before me, *William C. Barker* , ~~Superintendent~~

~~of Metropolitan Police and ex officio~~ one of the Justices of the Peace in and for the said County, and

charged before me upon the oath of *M. Morton Peake* _____

_____ with having

on the 16th day of September 1868 in the County and
District aforesaid feloniously stolen, taken and
carried away one wooden till, ~~of the~~ daughter of the
value of Three dollars the property of L. A. Boyce

him therefore safely keep in your said custody until he shall *feloniously in the sum of One hundred*
dollars ~~be discharged by due course of law,~~ and for so
doing this shall be your sufficient Warrant.

GIVEN under my hand and seal, this _____ *18th* _____ day of *September*

in the year of our Lord one thousand eight hundred and sixty *eighth*.

Wm. C. Barker J. P.

15 2 7

Jail Committment

United States

vs.

Suker alias Wm. Bell

Petit Larceny

M. Morton Peake cor 15th & D sts.
L. S. Joyce   at the
                    Photograph Car

Jane Randall   Ohio Avenue
Rosana Thompson   near Raubs
Louisa Thompson   Soap Factory

U. S. MARSHAL'S OFFICE,
WASHINGTON CITY, D.C.   Oct. 31st. 1868

Mr. W.H. Heustes

      Warden U.S. Jail, D.C.

      Release from Jail the following=named Prisoner, to be brought before the Judge now in session, viz:

      Frank Jones

                  D.S. Gooding
                  U.S. Marshal, D.C.

On verso: No. 1392

U. S. Marshal's Office,

Washington City, D. C., Oct 31st 1865

Mr. _____ Hewitt,

Warden U. S. Jail, D. C.

Please from Jail the following-named Prisoner, to be
brought before the Judge now in session, viz:

_____ _____

_____ _____
U. S. Marshal, D. C.

No. 6427   CRIMINAL COURT, Decmr. Term, 1868.

Wm. Cole
Convicted of Larceny
sentenced to be imprisoned in the common
jail for the county of Washington for
the period of one day.

Test:

         R.J. Meigs Clerk.
         Dec. 24', 1868

No. 6432

George Warren
Convicted of Larceny
sentenced to be imprisoned in the
common jail for the county of
Washington for the period of one day

Test:

R.J. Meigs Clerk
Dec. 24,th 1868

No 6432.

CRIMINAL COURT Dec' Term, 186 8

George Warren

Convicted of Larceny

sentenced to be imprisoned in the common jail

for the county of Washington for the period

of One day

Test:

R. J. Meigs. Clerk.

Dec 24,th 1868

No. 6427　　CRIMINAL COURT, Decmr. Term, 1868.

Wm. Cole
Convicted of Larceny
sentenced to be imprisoned in the common
jail for the county of Washington for
the period of one day.

Test:

R.J. Meigs Clerk.
Dec. 24', 1868

No. 6432

George Warren
Convicted of Larceny
sentenced to be imprisoned in the
common jail for the county of
Washington for the period of one day

Test:

R.J. Meigs Clerk
Dec. 24,th 1868

No 6432.

CRIMINAL COURT Dec. Term, 186 8.

George Warren

Convicted of Larceny

sentenced to be imprisoned in the common jail

for the county of Washington for the period

of One day

Test:

R.J. Meigs. Clerk.
Dec 24,th 1868

CRIMINAL COURT, Decr. Term, 1868.

No. 6445

Isaac Landic
Convicted of Larceny
sentenced to be imprisoned in the
common jail for the county of Washington
for the period of one day

Test:

R.J. Meigs   Clerk
Dec. 24,th 1868

No 6445.

CRIMINAL COURT, Decem^r *Term, 186 8.*

Isaac Landic

Convicted of Larceny

sentenced to be imprisoned in the common jail

for the county of Washington for the period

of one day

Test :

R.J. Meigs   *Clerk.*

Dec 24, '68

U.S. MARSHAL'S OFFICE,
WASHINGTON CITY, D.C., Jany. 20th 1869

Mr. W.H. Heustes

Warden U.S. Jail, D.C.

Release from Jail the following=named Prisoner, to be brought before the Judge now in session, viz:

Sucker alias Wm. Bell

D.S. Gooding
U.S. Marshal, D.C.

On verso: 1527

U. S. Marshal's Office,

Washington City, D. C., *January* 10th 1865

Mr. _____ Warden

Warden U. S. Jail, D. C.

Release from Jail the following-named Prisoner, to be brought before the Judge now in session, viz: _Shelton alias _____

_____
U. S. Marshal, D. C.